# SAVAGE WOLVERINE

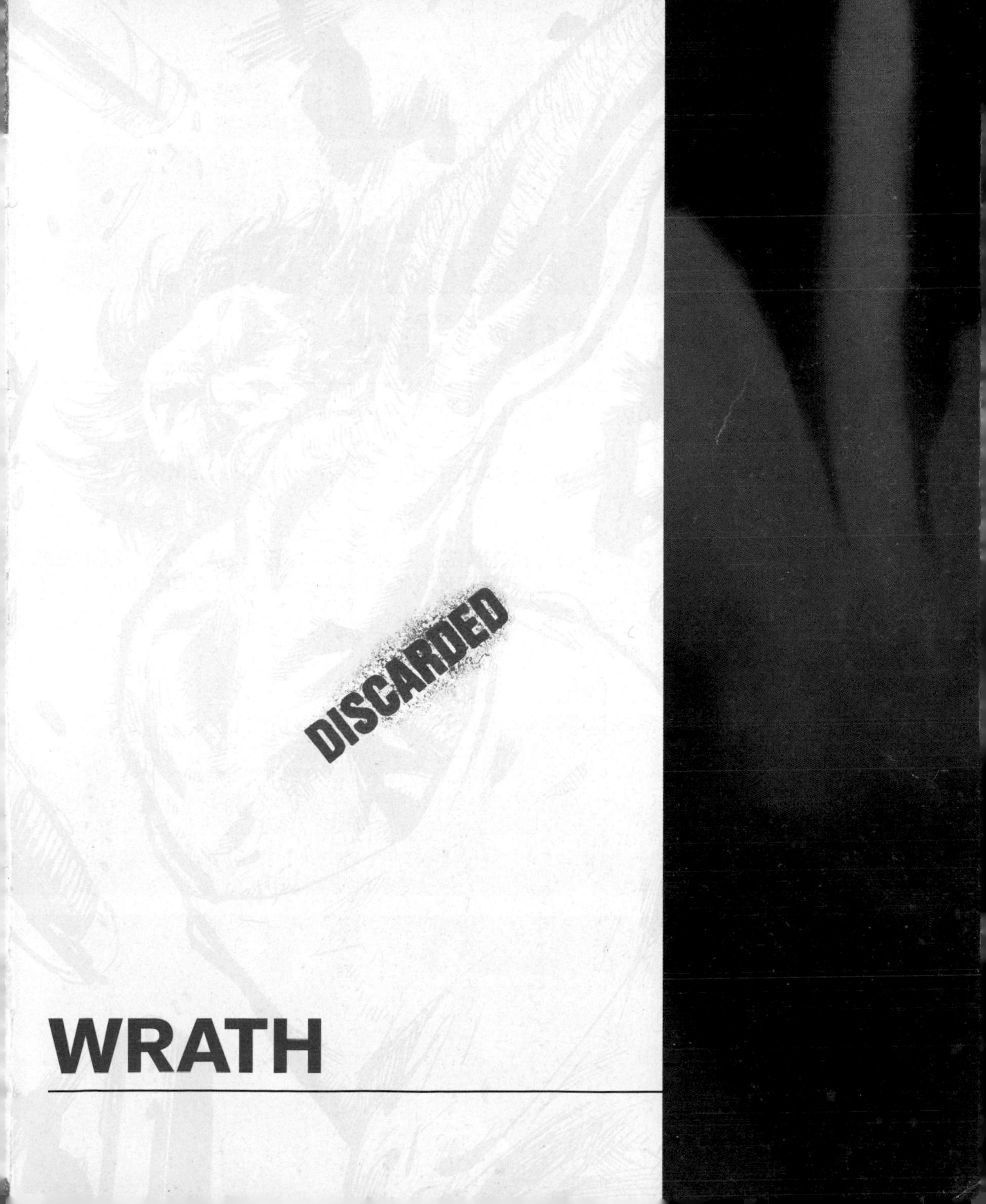



## WRATH

# SAVAGE WOLVERINE
## WRATH

### SAVAGE WOLVERINE #12-13

| WRITERS | ARTIST, #12 | BREAKDOWNS, #13 |
|---|---|---|
| **PHIL JIMENEZ &** | **PHIL JIMENEZ** | **PHIL JIMENEZ** |
| **SCOTT LOPE** | | |

| COLORIST | FINISHED ART, #13 |
|---|---|
| **RACHELLE ROSENBERG** | **PHIL JIMENEZ, TOM PALMER, SANDU FLOREA,** |
| | **PATRICK OLLIFFE & DAN GREEN** |

### SAVAGE WOLVERINE #14-17

STORY & ART
**RICHARD ISANOVE**

COVER ARTISTS
**PHIL JIMENEZ & FRANK D'ARMATA** (#12)**, PHIL JIMENEZ &**
**RACHELLE ROSENBERG** (#13) **AND RICHARD ISANOVE** (#14-17)

| LETTERER | ASSISTANT EDITOR | EDITORS | GROUP EDITOR |
|---|---|---|---|
| **VC'S CORY PETIT** | **FRANKIE JOHNSON** | **JEANINE SCHAEFER &** | **NICK LOWE** |
| | | **TOM BRENNAN** | |

COLLECTION EDITOR **ALEX STARBUCK**
ASSISTANT EDITOR **SARAH BRUNSTAD**
EDITORS, SPECIAL PROJECTS **JENNIFER GRÜNWALD & MARK D. BEAZLEY**
SENIOR EDITOR, SPECIAL PROJECTS **JEFF YOUNGQUIST**
SVP PRINT, SALES & MARKETING **DAVID GABRIEL**
BOOK DESIGN **JEFF POWELL & IRENE LEE**

EDITOR IN CHIEF **AXEL ALONSO**
CHIEF CREATIVE OFFICER **JOE QUESADA**
PUBLISHER **DAN BUCKLEY**
EXECUTIVE PRODUCER **ALAN FINE**

Many years ago, a secret government organization abducted the man called Logan, a mutant possessing razor-sharp bone claws and the ability to heal from any wound. In their attempt to create the perfect living weapon, the organization bonded the unbreakable metal Adamantium to his skeleton. The process was excruciating, and by the end there was little left of the man known as Logan. He had become…

# SAVAGE WOLVERINE

**SAVAGE WOLVERINE VOL. 3: WRATH.** Contains material originally published in magazine form as SAVAGE WOLVERINE #12-17. First printing 2015. ISBN# 978-0-7851-8964-0. Published by MARVEL WORLDWIDE, INC., a subsidiary of MARVEL ENTERTAINMENT, LLC. OFFICE OF PUBLICATION: 135 West 50th Street, New York, NY 10020. Copyright © 2013, 2014 and 2015 Marvel Characters, Inc. All rights reserved. All characters featured in this issue and the distinctive names and likenesses thereof, and all related indicia are trademarks of Marvel Characters, Inc. No similarity between any of the names, characters, persons, and/or institutions in this magazine with those of any living or dead person or institution is intended, and any such similarity which may exist is purely coincidental. **Printed in the U.S.A.** ALAN FINE, EVP - Office of the President, Marvel Worldwide, Inc. and EVP & CMO Marvel Characters B.V.; DAN BUCKLEY, Publisher & President - Print, Animation & Digital Divisions; JOE QUESADA, Chief Creative Officer; TOM BREVOORT, SVP of Publishing; DAVID BOGART, SVP of Operations & Procurement, Publishing; C.B. CEBULSKI, SVP of Creator & Content Development; DAVID GABRIEL, SVP Print, Sales & Marketing; JIM O'KEEFE, VP of Operations & Logistics; DAN CARR, Executive Director of Publishing Technology; SUSAN CRESPI, Editorial Operations Manager; ALEX MORALES, Publishing Operations Manager; STAN LEE, Chairman Emeritus. For information regarding advertising in Marvel Comics or on Marvel.com, please contact Niza Disla, Director of Marvel Partnerships, at ndisla@marvel.com. For Marvel subscription inquiries, please call 800-217-9158. Manufactured between 12/26/2014 and 2/2/2015 by R.R. DONNELLEY, INC., SALEM, VA, USA.

10 9 8 7 6 5 4 3 2 1

# 12 COME CONQUER THE BEASTS PART 1: CLAWS & TEETH

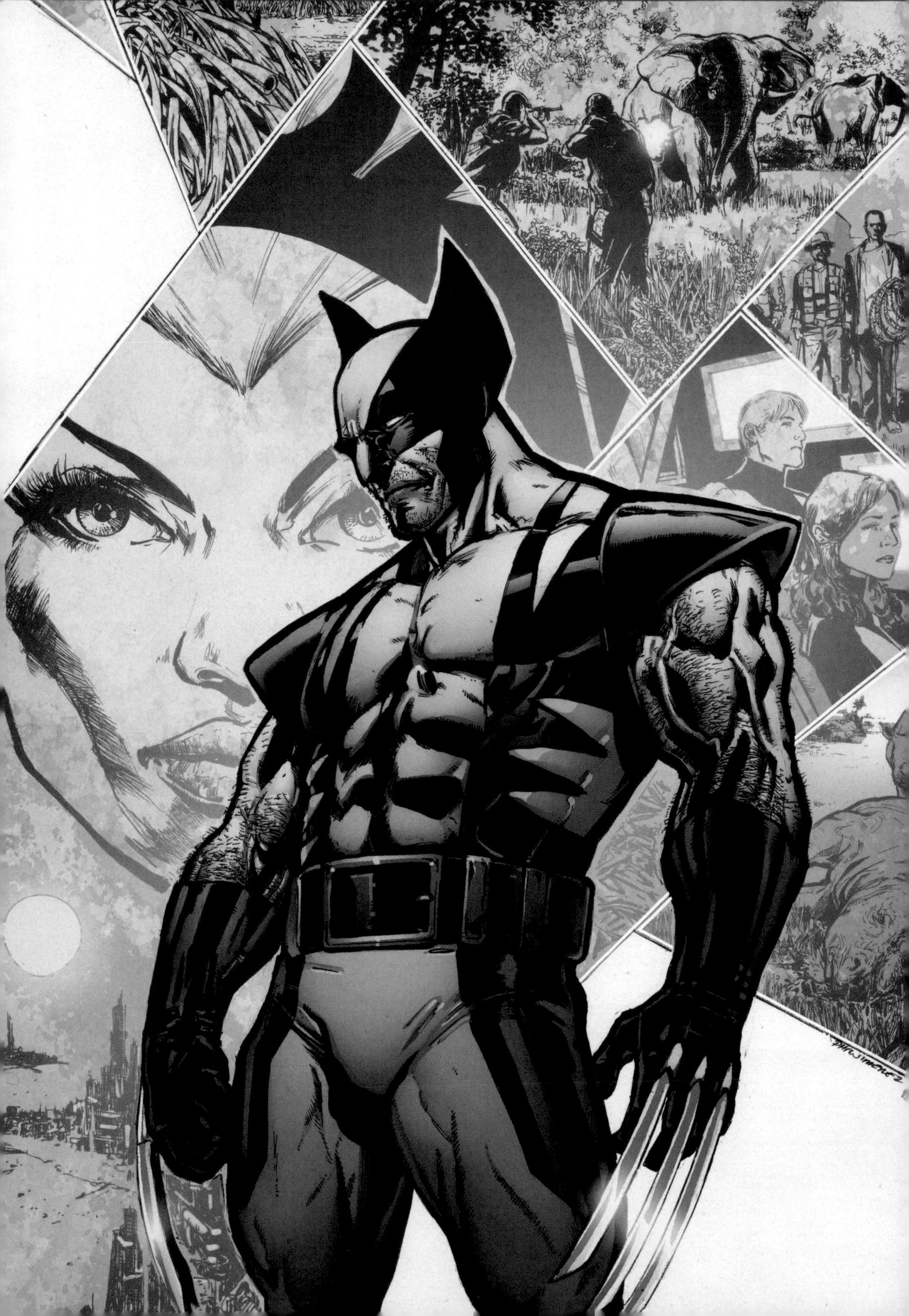

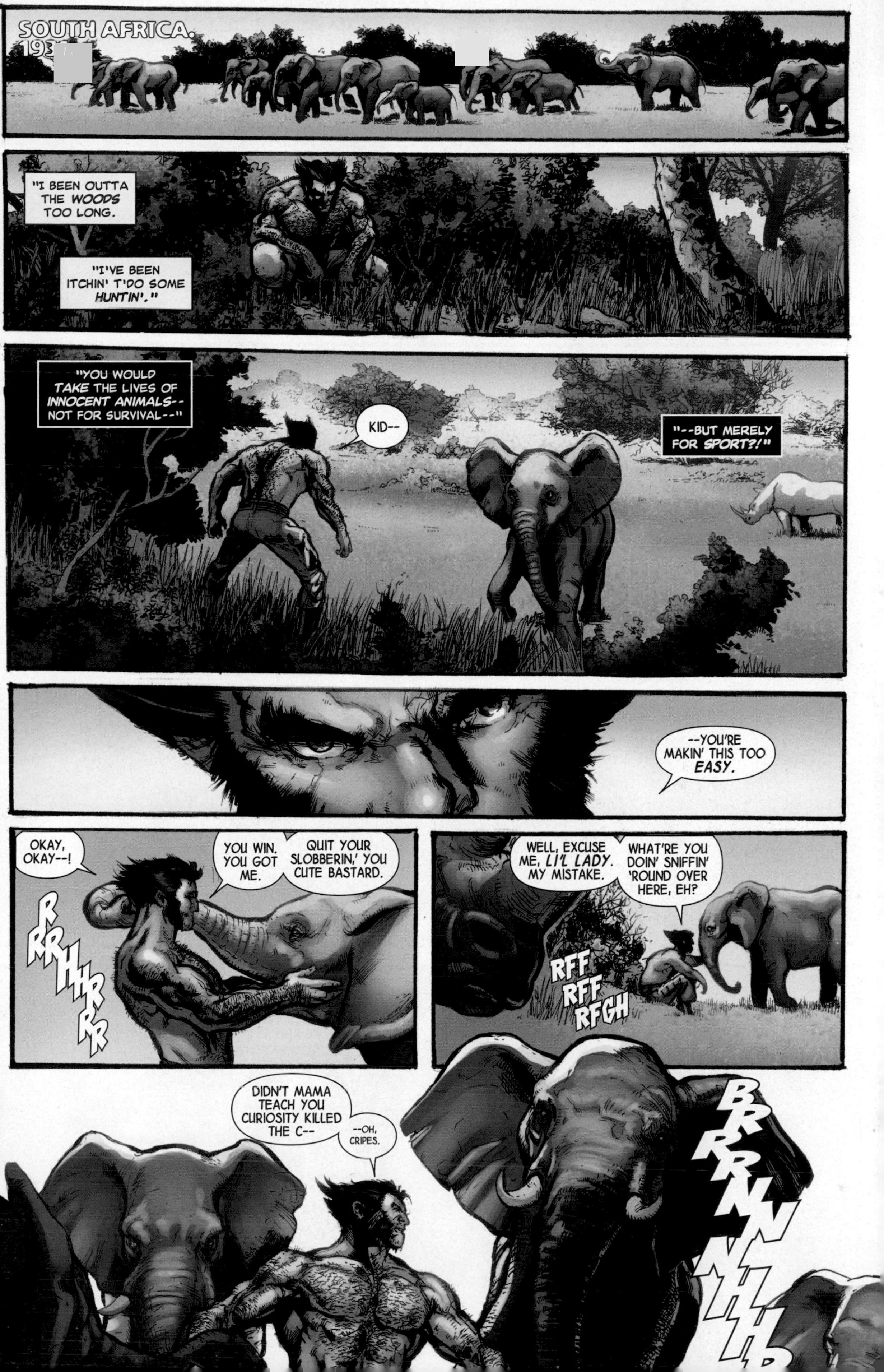
SOUTH AFRICA. 193
"I BEEN OUTTA THE WOODS TOO LONG.
"I'VE BEEN ITCHIN' T'DO SOME HUNTIN'."
"YOU WOULD TAKE THE LIVES OF INNOCENT ANIMALS--NOT FOR SURVIVAL--"
KID--
"--BUT MERELY FOR SPORT?!"
--YOU'RE MAKIN' THIS TOO EASY.
OKAY, OKAY--!
RRRHHRRR
YOU WIN. YOU GOT ME.
QUIT YOUR SLOBBERIN,' YOU CUTE BASTARD.
WELL, EXCUSE ME, LI'L LADY. MY MISTAKE.
WHAT'RE YOU DOIN' SNIFFIN' 'ROUND OVER HERE, EH?
RFF RFF RFGH
DIDN'T MAMA TEACH YOU CURIOSITY KILLED THE C--
--OH, CRIPES.
BRRRNNHHP

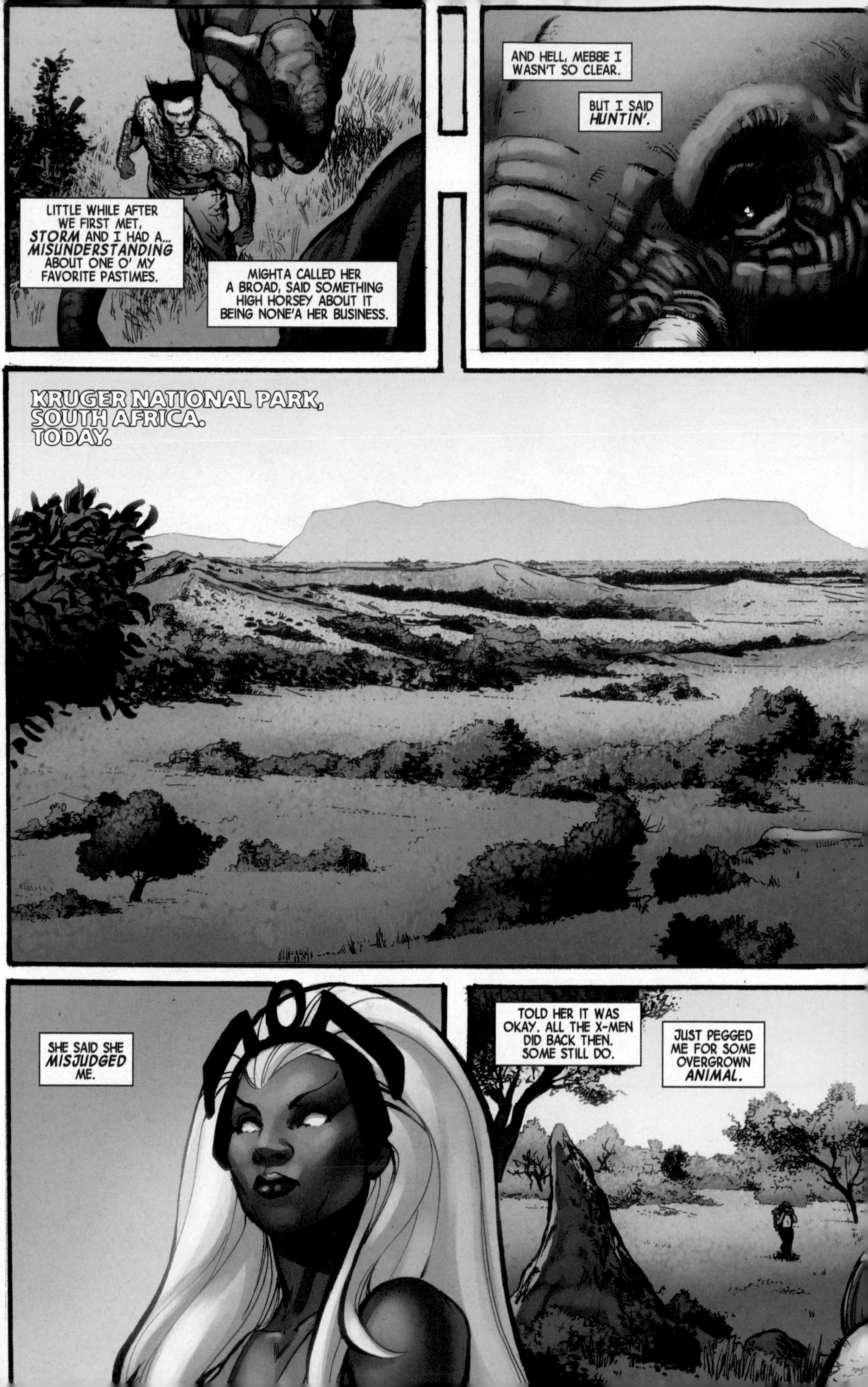
LITTLE WHILE AFTER WE FIRST MET, STORM AND I HAD A... MISUNDERSTANDING ABOUT ONE O' MY FAVORITE PASTIMES.
MIGHTA CALLED HER A BROAD, SAID SOMETHING HIGH HORSEY ABOUT IT BEING NONE'A HER BUSINESS.
AND HELL, MEBBE I WASN'T SO CLEAR.
BUT I SAID HUNTIN'.
KRUGER NATIONAL PARK, SOUTH AFRICA. TODAY.
SHE SAID SHE MISJUDGED ME.
TOLD HER IT WAS OKAY. ALL THE X-MEN DID BACK THEN. SOME STILL DO.
JUST PEGGED ME FOR SOME OVERGROWN ANIMAL.

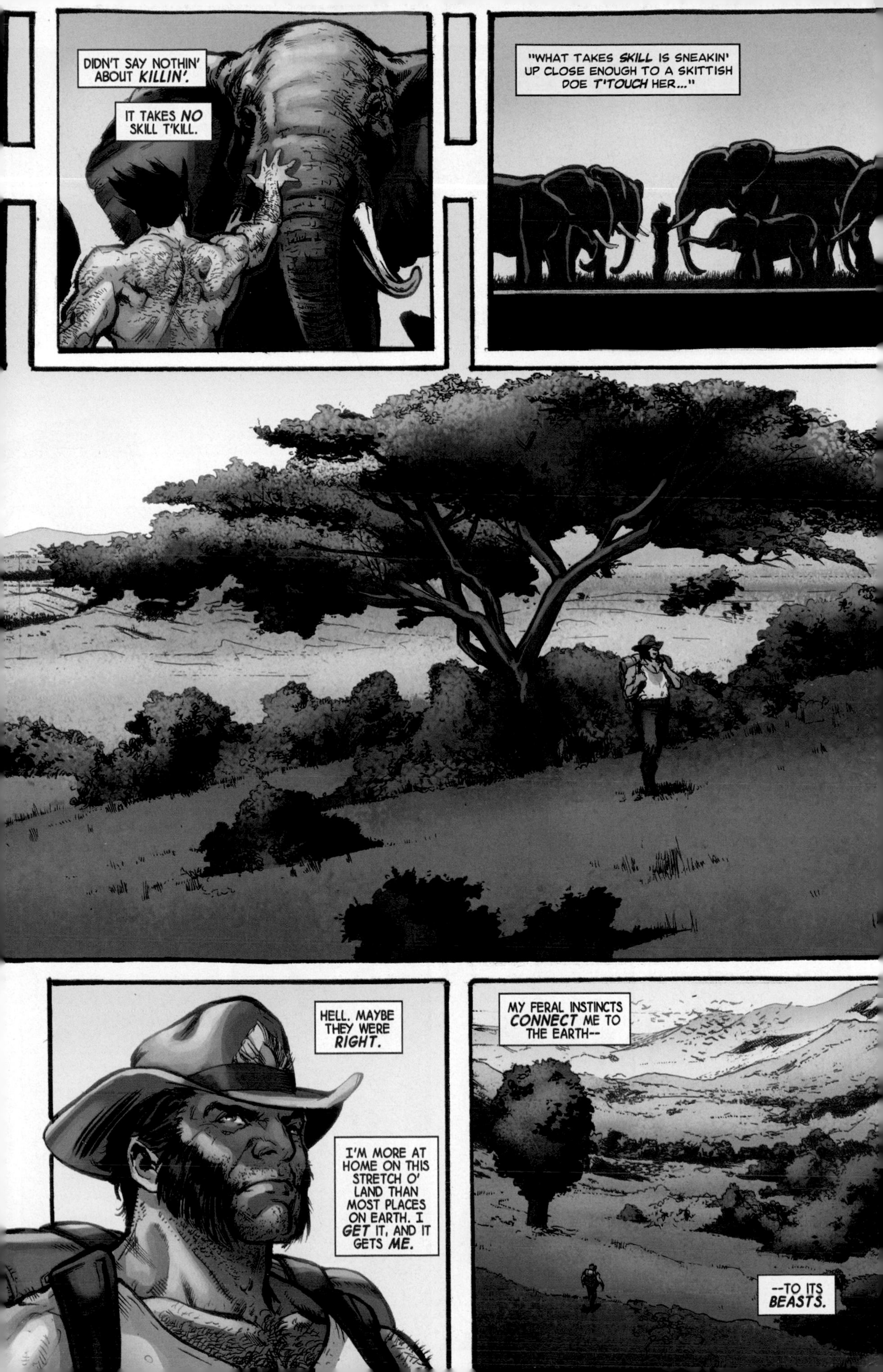
DIDN'T SAY NOTHIN' ABOUT KILLIN'.
IT TAKES NO SKILL T'KILL.
"WHAT TAKES SKILL IS SNEAKIN' UP CLOSE ENOUGH TO A SKITTISH DOE T'TOUCH HER..."
HELL. MAYBE THEY WERE RIGHT.
I'M MORE AT HOME ON THIS STRETCH O' LAND THAN MOST PLACES ON EARTH. I GET IT, AND IT GETS ME.
MY FERAL INSTINCTS CONNECT ME TO THE EARTH--
--TO ITS BEASTS.

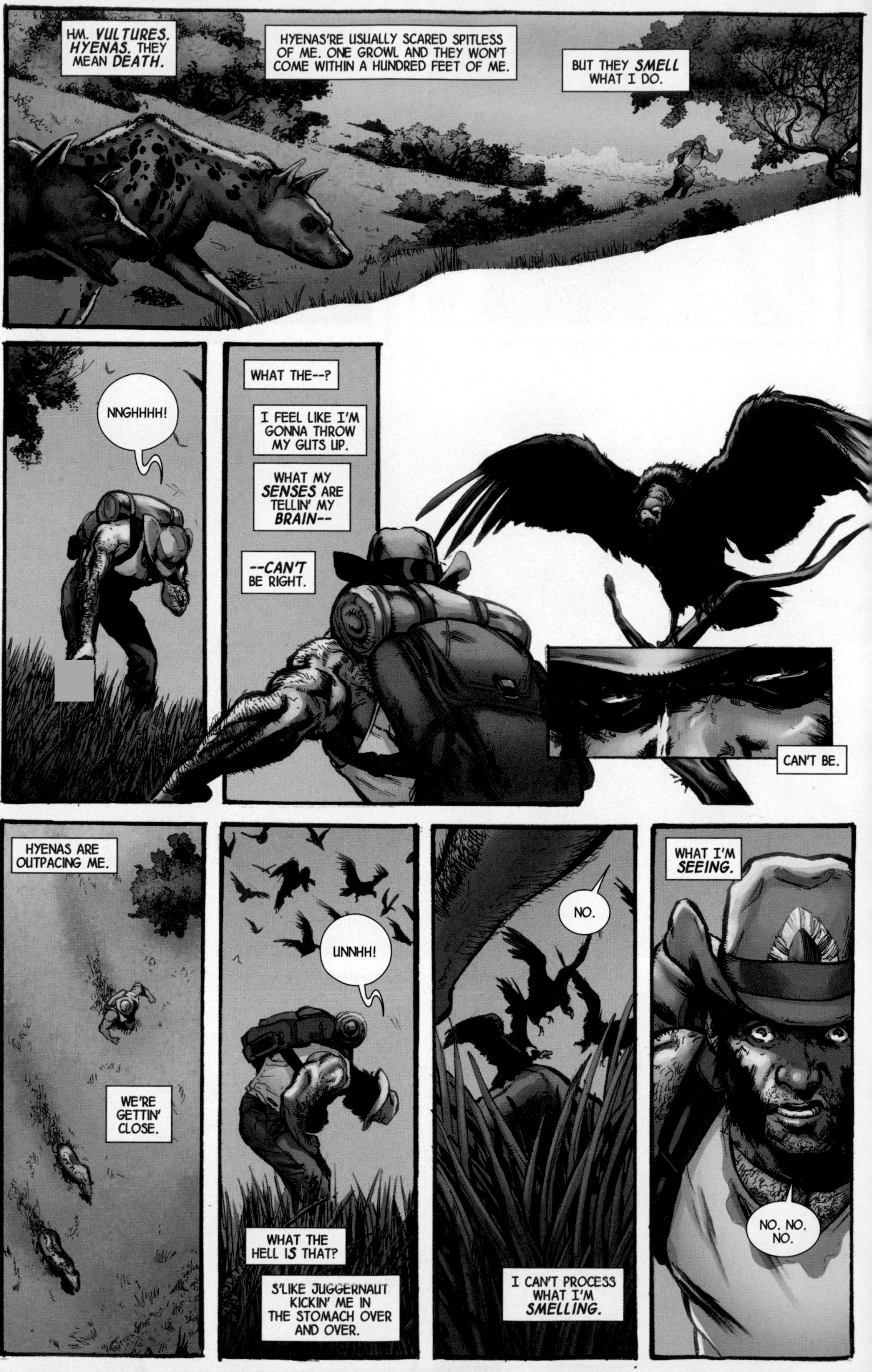
HM. VULTURES. HYENAS. THEY MEAN DEATH.
HYENAS'RE USUALLY SCARED SPITLESS OF ME. ONE GROWL AND THEY WON'T COME WITHIN A HUNDRED FEET OF ME.
BUT THEY SMELL WHAT I DO.
NNGHHHH!
WHAT THE--?
I FEEL LIKE I'M GONNA THROW MY GUTS UP.
WHAT MY SENSES ARE TELLIN' MY BRAIN--
--CAN'T BE RIGHT.
CAN'T BE.
HYENAS ARE OUTPACING ME.
WE'RE GETTIN' CLOSE.
UNNHH!
WHAT THE HELL IS THAT?
S'LIKE JUGGERNAUT KICKIN' ME IN THE STOMACH OVER AND OVER.
NO.
I CAN'T PROCESS WHAT I'M SMELLING.
WHAT I'M SEEING.
NO. NO. NO.

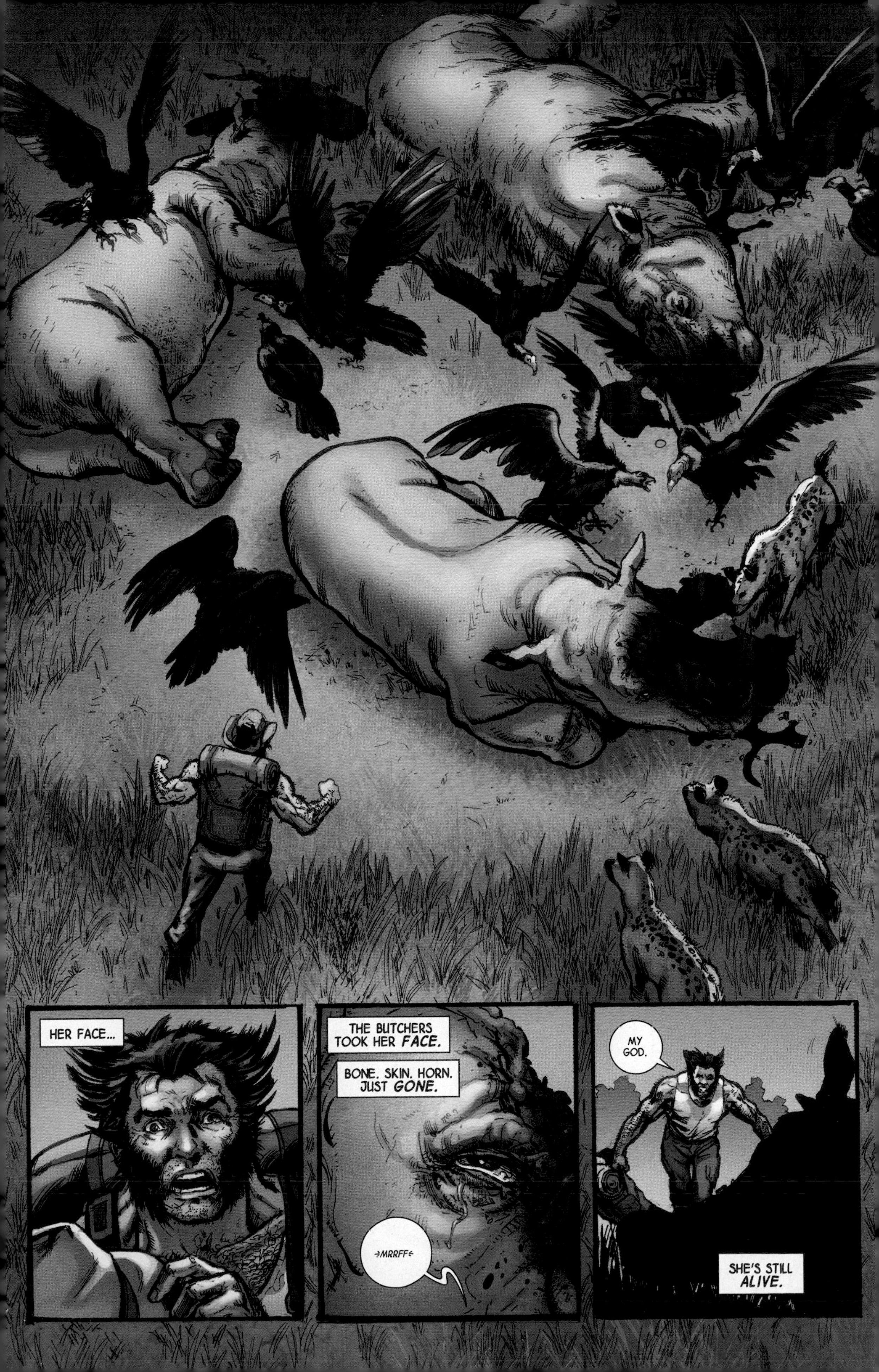
HER FACE...
THE BUTCHERS TOOK HER FACE.
BONE. SKIN. HORN. JUST GONE.
MRRFF
MY GOD.
SHE'S STILL ALIVE.

MARVEL ENTERTAINMENT PRESENTS

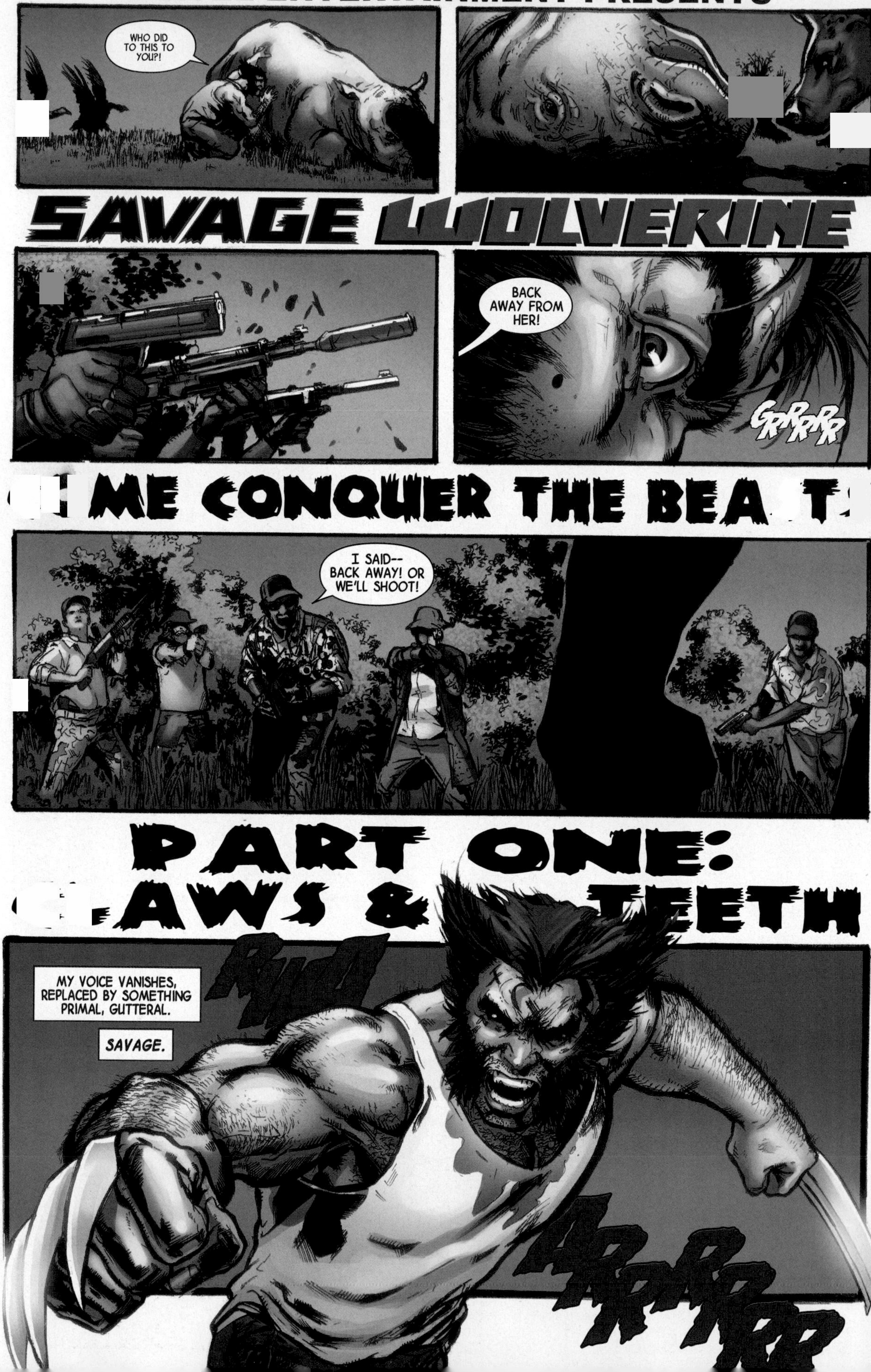
WHO DID TO THIS TO YOU?!
SAVAGE WOLVERINE
BACK AWAY FROM HER!
GRRRRR
CONQUER THE
I SAID-- BACK AWAY! OR WE'LL SHOOT!
PART ONE:
&
MY VOICE VANISHES, REPLACED BY SOMETHING PRIMAL, GUTTERAL.
SAVAGE.

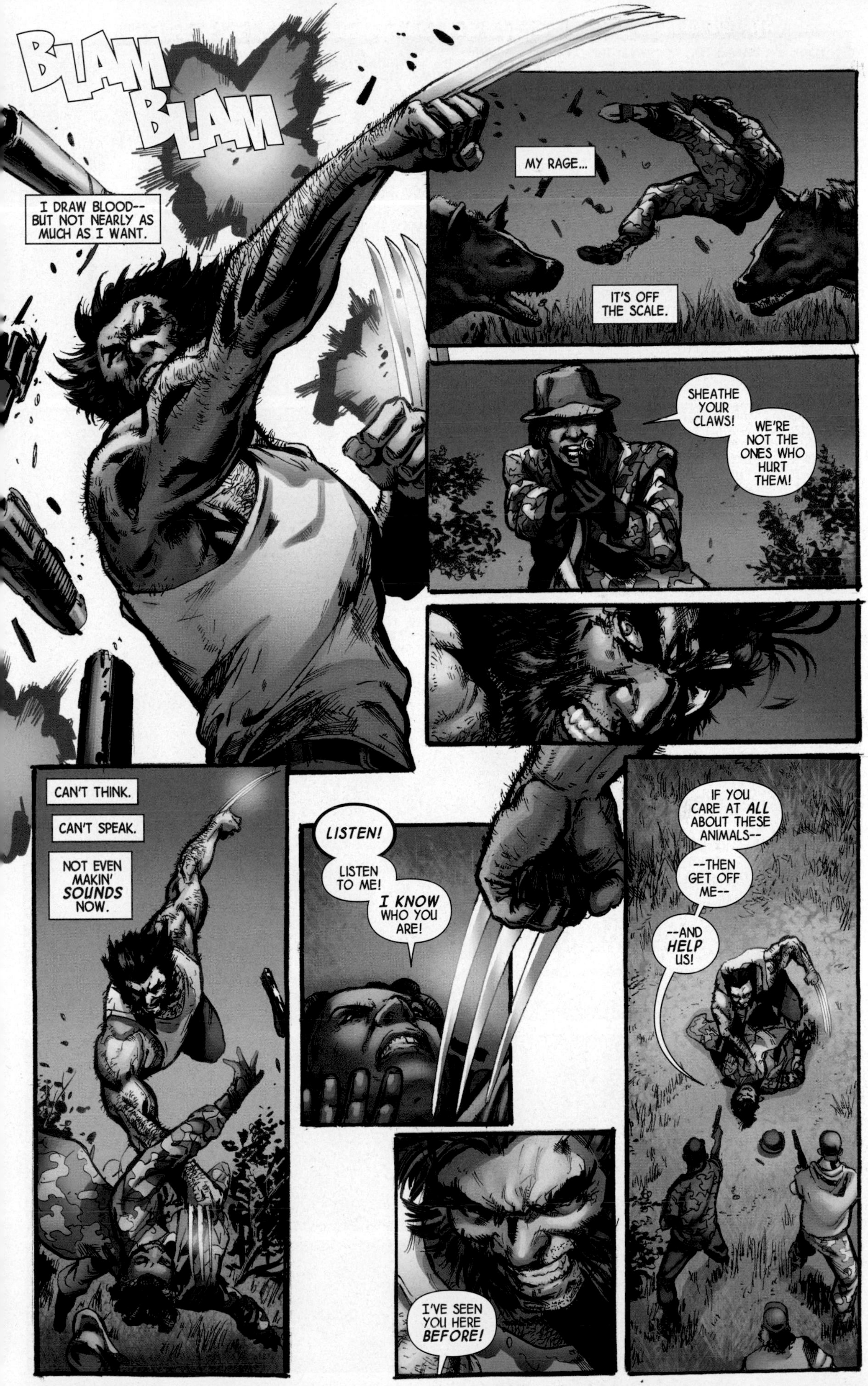
BLAM BLAM
I DRAW BLOOD-- BUT NOT NEARLY AS MUCH AS I WANT.
MY RAGE...
IT'S OFF THE SCALE.
SHEATHE YOUR CLAWS!
WE'RE NOT THE ONES WHO HURT THEM!
CAN'T THINK.
CAN'T SPEAK.
NOT EVEN MAKIN' SOUNDS NOW.
LISTEN!
LISTEN TO ME!
I KNOW WHO YOU ARE!
I'VE SEEN YOU HERE BEFORE!
IF YOU CARE AT ALL ABOUT THESE ANIMALS--
--THEN GET OFF ME--
--AND HELP US!

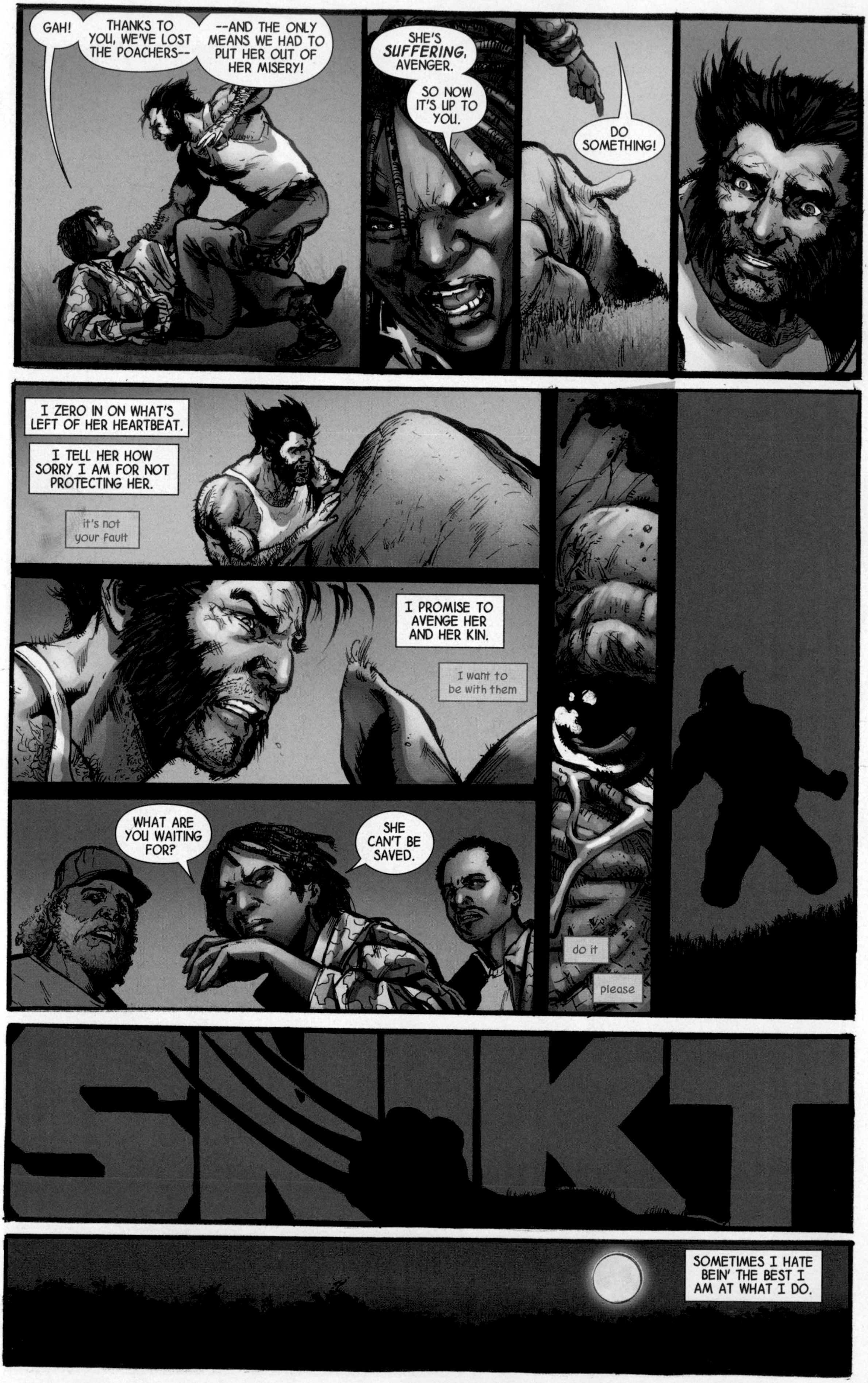
GAH!
THANKS TO YOU, WE'VE LOST THE POACHERS--
--AND THE ONLY MEANS WE HAD TO PUT HER OUT OF HER MISERY!
SHE'S *SUFFERING*, AVENGER.
SO NOW IT'S UP TO YOU.
DO SOMETHING!
I ZERO IN ON WHAT'S LEFT OF HER HEARTBEAT.
I TELL HER HOW SORRY I AM FOR NOT PROTECTING HER.
it's not your fault
I PROMISE TO AVENGE HER AND HER KIN.
I want to be with them
WHAT ARE YOU WAITING FOR?
SHE CAN'T BE SAVED.
do it
please
SNIKT
SOMETIMES I HATE BEIN' THE BEST I AM AT WHAT I DO.

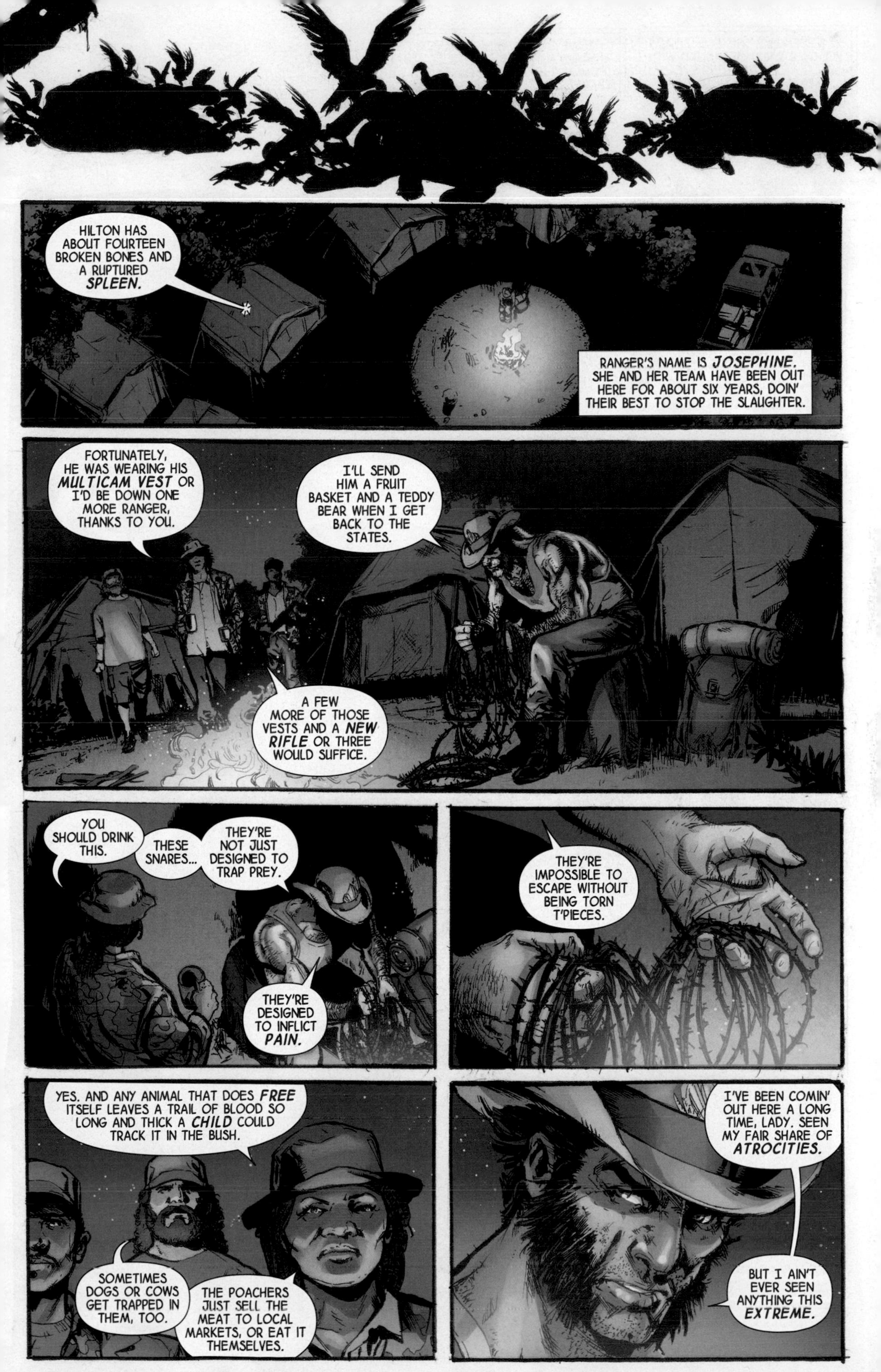
HILTON HAS ABOUT FOURTEEN BROKEN BONES AND A RUPTURED SPLEEN.
RANGER'S NAME IS JOSEPHINE. SHE AND HER TEAM HAVE BEEN OUT HERE FOR ABOUT SIX YEARS, DOIN' THEIR BEST TO STOP THE SLAUGHTER.
FORTUNATELY, HE WAS WEARING HIS MULTICAM VEST OR I'D BE DOWN ONE MORE RANGER, THANKS TO YOU.
I'LL SEND HIM A FRUIT BASKET AND A TEDDY BEAR WHEN I GET BACK TO THE STATES.
A FEW MORE OF THOSE VESTS AND A NEW RIFLE OR THREE WOULD SUFFICE.
YOU SHOULD DRINK THIS.
THESE SNARES...
THEY'RE NOT JUST DESIGNED TO TRAP PREY.
THEY'RE DESIGNED TO INFLICT PAIN.
THEY'RE IMPOSSIBLE TO ESCAPE WITHOUT BEING TORN T'PIECES.
YES. AND ANY ANIMAL THAT DOES FREE ITSELF LEAVES A TRAIL OF BLOOD SO LONG AND THICK A CHILD COULD TRACK IT IN THE BUSH.
SOMETIMES DOGS OR COWS GET TRAPPED IN THEM, TOO.
THE POACHERS JUST SELL THE MEAT TO LOCAL MARKETS, OR EAT IT THEMSELVES.
I'VE BEEN COMIN' OUT HERE A LONG TIME, LADY. SEEN MY FAIR SHARE OF ATROCITIES.
BUT I AIN'T EVER SEEN ANYTHING THIS EXTREME.

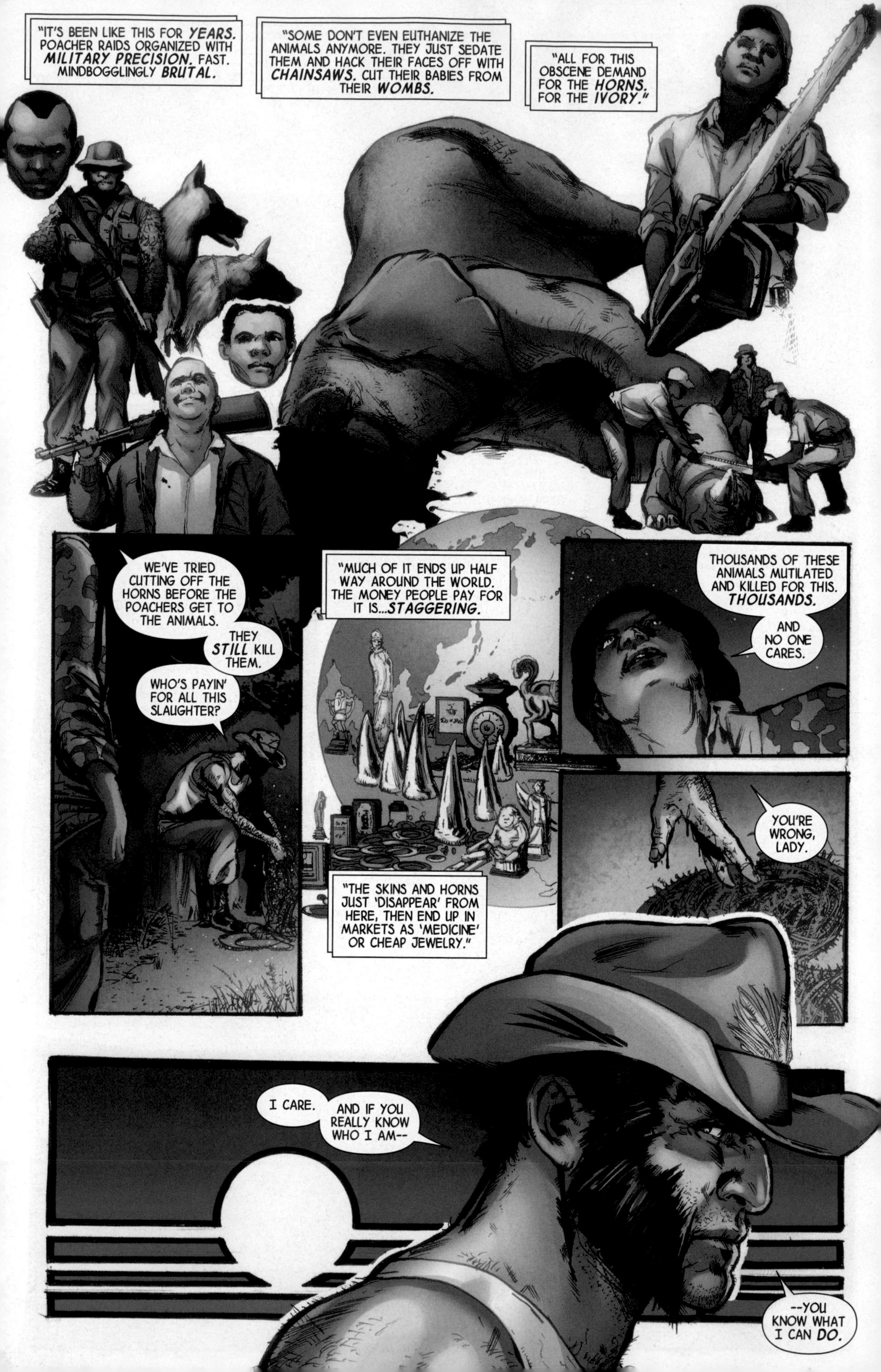
"IT'S BEEN LIKE THIS FOR YEARS. POACHER RAIDS ORGANIZED WITH MILITARY PRECISION. FAST. MINDBOGGLINGLY BRUTAL.
"SOME DON'T EVEN EUTHANIZE THE ANIMALS ANYMORE. THEY JUST SEDATE THEM AND HACK THEIR FACES OFF WITH CHAINSAWS. CUT THEIR BABIES FROM THEIR WOMBS.
"ALL FOR THIS OBSCENE DEMAND FOR THE HORNS. FOR THE IVORY."
WE'VE TRIED CUTTING OFF THE HORNS BEFORE THE POACHERS GET TO THE ANIMALS.
THEY STILL KILL THEM.
WHO'S PAYIN' FOR ALL THIS SLAUGHTER?
"MUCH OF IT ENDS UP HALF WAY AROUND THE WORLD. THE MONEY PEOPLE PAY FOR IT IS...STAGGERING.
"THE SKINS AND HORNS JUST 'DISAPPEAR' FROM HERE, THEN END UP IN MARKETS AS 'MEDICINE' OR CHEAP JEWELRY."
THOUSANDS OF THESE ANIMALS MUTILATED AND KILLED FOR THIS. THOUSANDS.
AND NO ONE CARES.
YOU'RE WRONG, LADY.
I CARE.
AND IF YOU REALLY KNOW WHO I AM--
--YOU KNOW WHAT I CAN DO.

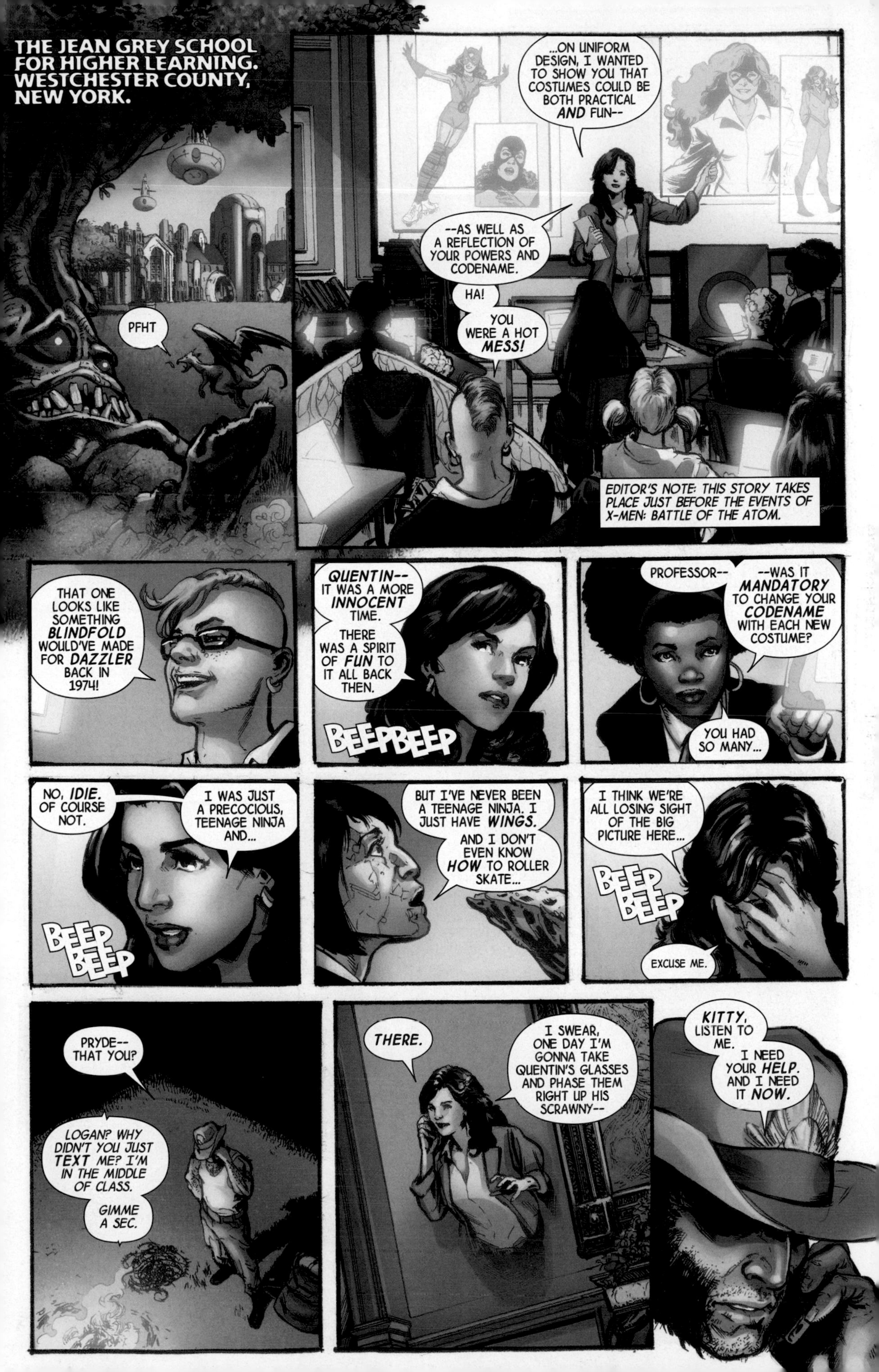
THE JEAN GREY SCHOOL FOR HIGHER LEARNING. WESTCHESTER COUNTY, NEW YORK.
...ON UNIFORM DESIGN, I WANTED TO SHOW YOU THAT COSTUMES COULD BE BOTH PRACTICAL AND FUN--
--AS WELL AS A REFLECTION OF YOUR POWERS AND CODENAME.
HA!
YOU WERE A HOT MESS!
PFHT
EDITOR'S NOTE: THIS STORY TAKES PLACE JUST BEFORE THE EVENTS OF X-MEN: BATTLE OF THE ATOM.
THAT ONE LOOKS LIKE SOMETHING BLINDFOLD WOULD'VE MADE FOR DAZZLER BACK IN 1974!
QUENTIN-- IT WAS A MORE INNOCENT TIME.
THERE WAS A SPIRIT OF FUN TO IT ALL BACK THEN.
BEEPBEEP
PROFESSOR--
--WAS IT MANDATORY TO CHANGE YOUR CODENAME WITH EACH NEW COSTUME?
YOU HAD SO MANY...
NO, IDIE. OF COURSE NOT.
I WAS JUST A PRECOCIOUS, TEENAGE NINJA AND...
BEEP BEEP
BUT I'VE NEVER BEEN A TEENAGE NINJA. I JUST HAVE WINGS.
AND I DON'T EVEN KNOW HOW TO ROLLER SKATE...
I THINK WE'RE ALL LOSING SIGHT OF THE BIG PICTURE HERE...
BEEP BEEP
EXCUSE ME.
PRYDE-- THAT YOU?
LOGAN? WHY DIDN'T YOU JUST TEXT ME? I'M IN THE MIDDLE OF CLASS.
GIMME A SEC.
THERE.
I SWEAR, ONE DAY I'M GONNA TAKE QUENTIN'S GLASSES AND PHASE THEM RIGHT UP HIS SCRAWNY--
KITTY, LISTEN TO ME.
I NEED YOUR HELP. AND I NEED IT NOW.

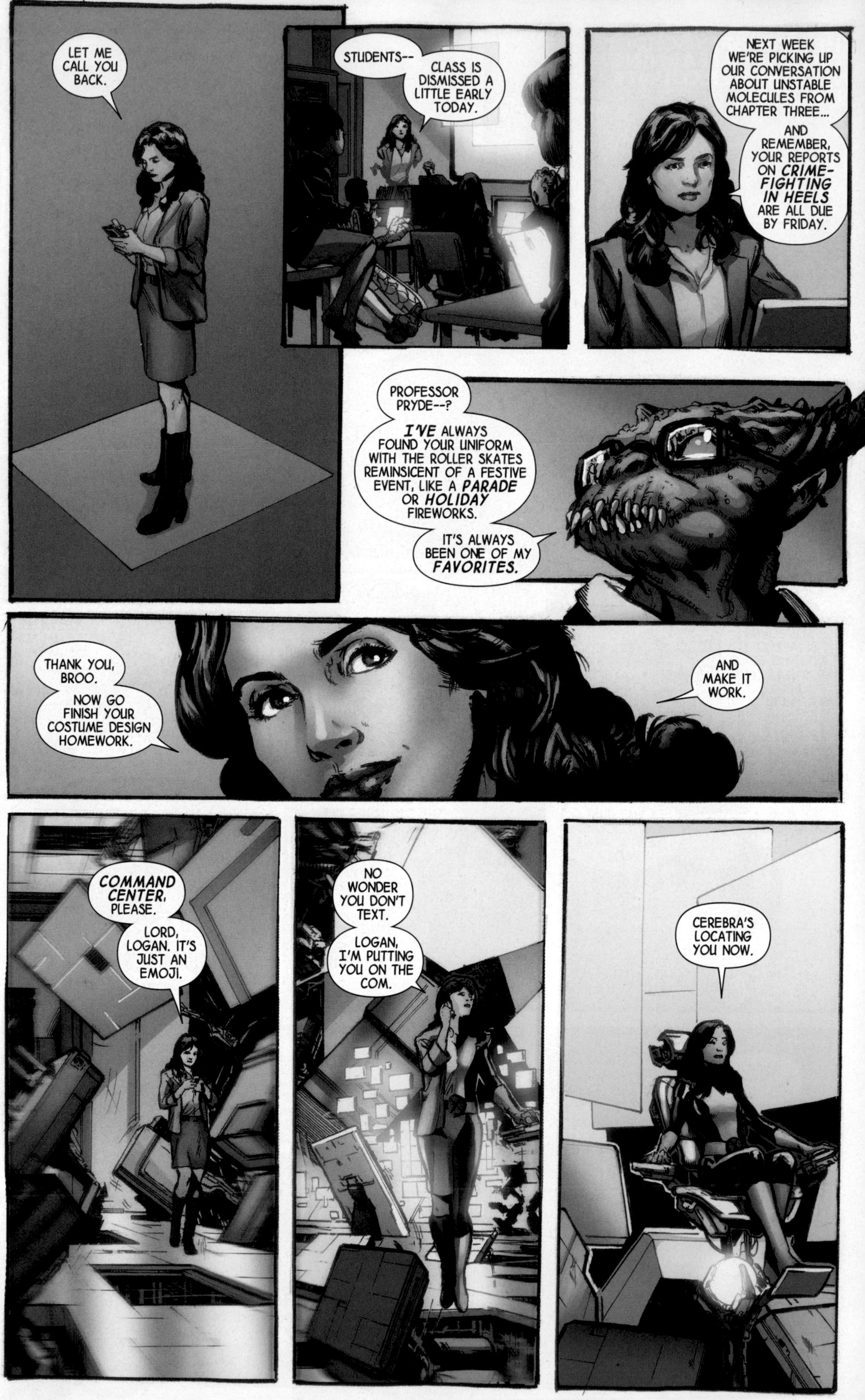

LET ME CALL YOU BACK.
STUDENTS--
CLASS IS DISMISSED A LITTLE EARLY TODAY.
NEXT WEEK WE'RE PICKING UP OUR CONVERSATION ABOUT UNSTABLE MOLECULES FROM CHAPTER THREE...
AND REMEMBER, YOUR REPORTS ON CRIME-FIGHTING IN HEELS ARE ALL DUE BY FRIDAY.
PROFESSOR PRYDE--?
I'VE ALWAYS FOUND YOUR UNIFORM WITH THE ROLLER SKATES REMINISCENT OF A FESTIVE EVENT, LIKE A PARADE OR HOLIDAY FIREWORKS.
IT'S ALWAYS BEEN ONE OF MY FAVORITES.
THANK YOU, BROO.
NOW GO FINISH YOUR COSTUME DESIGN HOMEWORK.
AND MAKE IT WORK.
COMMAND CENTER, PLEASE.
LORD, LOGAN. IT'S JUST AN EMOJI.
NO WONDER YOU DON'T TEXT.
LOGAN, I'M PUTTING YOU ON THE COM.
CEREBRA'S LOCATING YOU NOW.

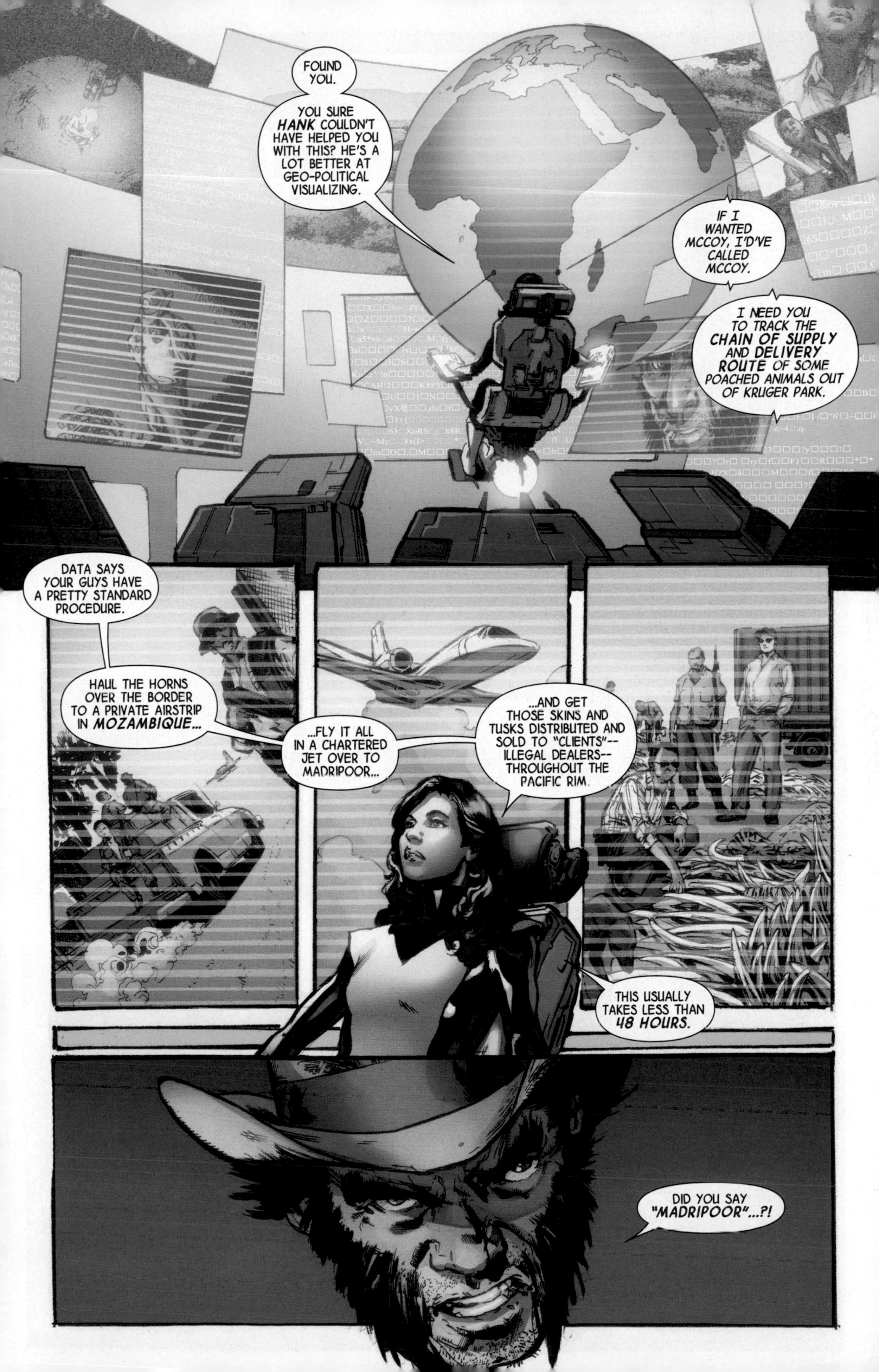
FOUND YOU.
YOU SURE HANK COULDN'T HAVE HELPED YOU WITH THIS? HE'S A LOT BETTER AT GEO-POLITICAL VISUALIZING.
IF I WANTED MCCOY, I'D'VE CALLED MCCOY.
I NEED YOU TO TRACK THE CHAIN OF SUPPLY AND DELIVERY ROUTE OF SOME POACHED ANIMALS OUT OF KRUGER PARK.
DATA SAYS YOUR GUYS HAVE A PRETTY STANDARD PROCEDURE.
HAUL THE HORNS OVER THE BORDER TO A PRIVATE AIRSTRIP IN MOZAMBIQUE...
...FLY IT ALL IN A CHARTERED JET OVER TO MADRIPOOR...
...AND GET THOSE SKINS AND TUSKS DISTRIBUTED AND SOLD TO "CLIENTS"-- ILLEGAL DEALERS-- THROUGHOUT THE PACIFIC RIM.
THIS USUALLY TAKES LESS THAN 48 HOURS.
DID YOU SAY "MADRIPOOR"...?!

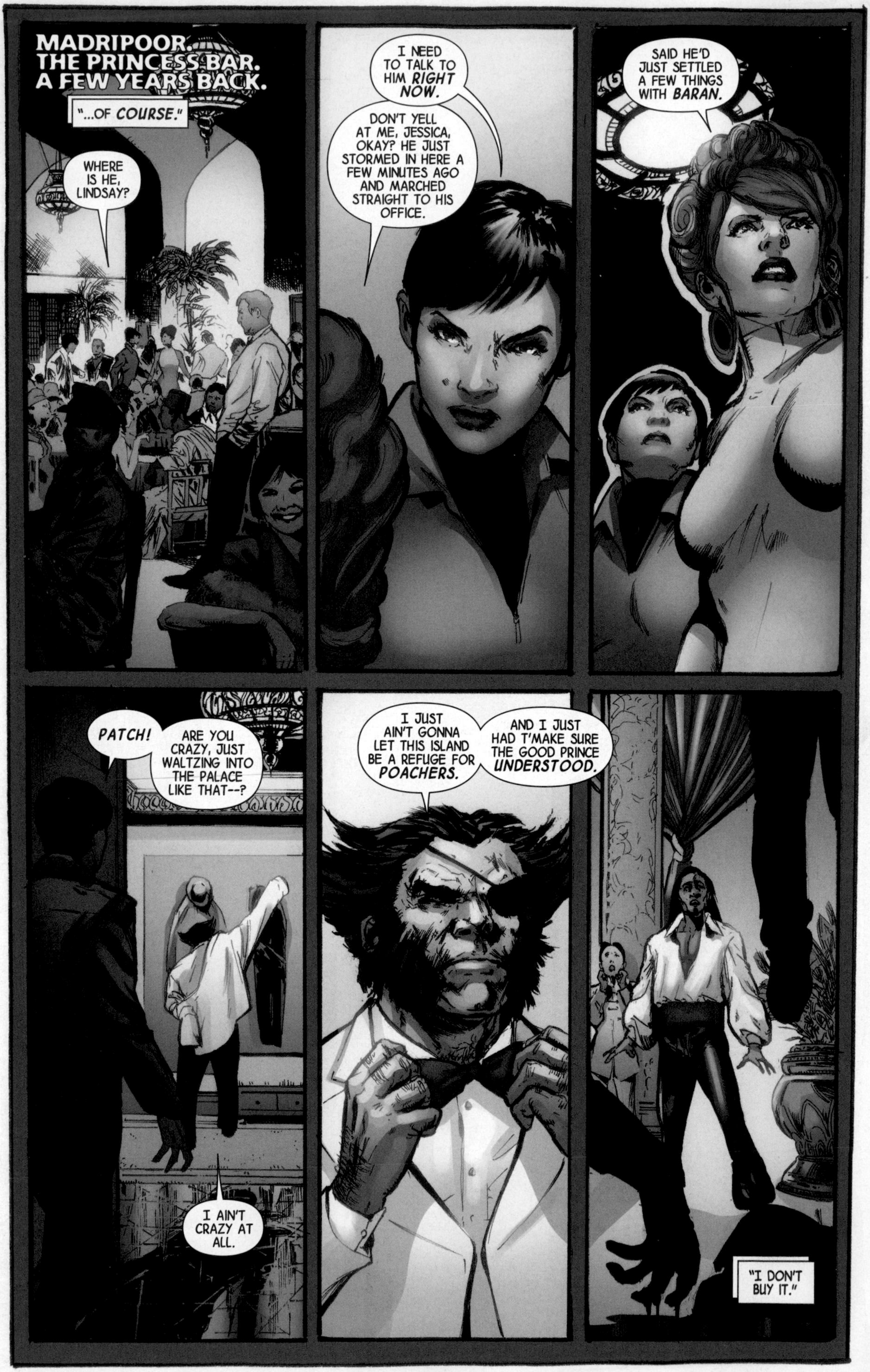
MADRIPOOR. THE PRINCESS BAR. A FEW YEARS BACK.
"...OF COURSE."
WHERE IS HE, LINDSAY?
I NEED TO TALK TO HIM RIGHT NOW.
DON'T YELL AT ME, JESSICA, OKAY? HE JUST STORMED IN HERE A FEW MINUTES AGO AND MARCHED STRAIGHT TO HIS OFFICE.
SAID HE'D JUST SETTLED A FEW THINGS WITH BARAN.
PATCH!
ARE YOU CRAZY, JUST WALTZING INTO THE PALACE LIKE THAT--?
I AIN'T CRAZY AT ALL.
I JUST AIN'T GONNA LET THIS ISLAND BE A REFUGE FOR POACHERS.
AND I JUST HAD T'MAKE SURE THE GOOD PRINCE UNDERSTOOD.
"I DON'T BUY IT."

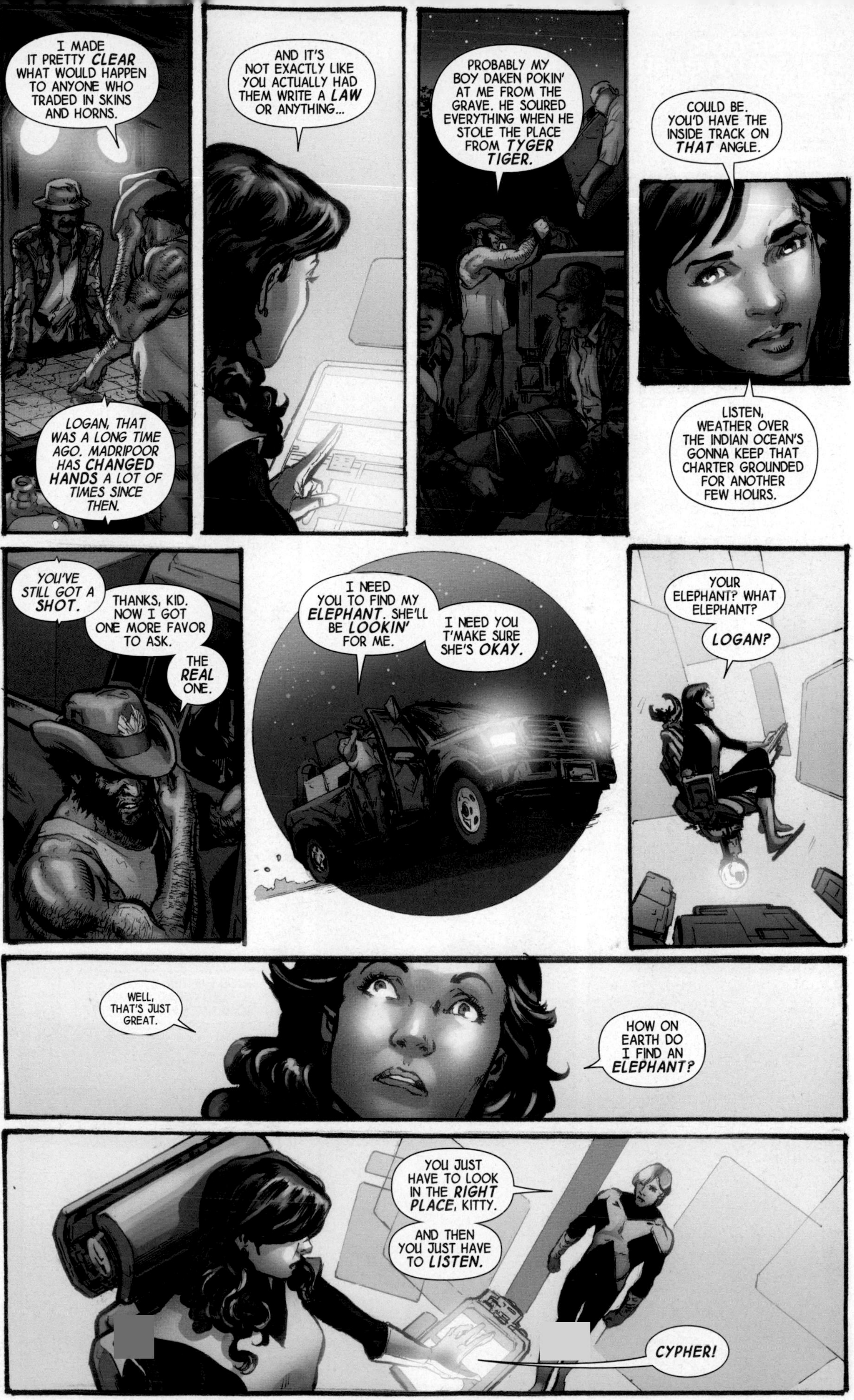

I MADE IT PRETTY CLEAR WHAT WOULD HAPPEN TO ANYONE WHO TRADED IN SKINS AND HORNS.
LOGAN, THAT WAS A LONG TIME AGO. MADRIPOOR HAS CHANGED HANDS A LOT OF TIMES SINCE THEN.
AND IT'S NOT EXACTLY LIKE YOU ACTUALLY HAD THEM WRITE A LAW OR ANYTHING...
PROBABLY MY BOY DAKEN POKIN' AT ME FROM THE GRAVE. HE SOURED EVERYTHING WHEN HE STOLE THE PLACE FROM TYGER TIGER.
COULD BE. YOU'D HAVE THE INSIDE TRACK ON THAT ANGLE.
LISTEN, WEATHER OVER THE INDIAN OCEAN'S GONNA KEEP THAT CHARTER GROUNDED FOR ANOTHER FEW HOURS.
YOU'VE STILL GOT A SHOT.
THANKS, KID. NOW I GOT ONE MORE FAVOR TO ASK.
THE REAL ONE.
I NEED YOU TO FIND MY ELEPHANT. SHE'LL BE LOOKIN' FOR ME.
I NEED YOU T'MAKE SURE SHE'S OKAY.
YOUR ELEPHANT? WHAT ELEPHANT?
LOGAN?
WELL, THAT'S JUST GREAT.
HOW ON EARTH DO I FIND AN ELEPHANT?
YOU JUST HAVE TO LOOK IN THE RIGHT PLACE, KITTY.
AND THEN YOU JUST HAVE TO LISTEN.
CYPHER!

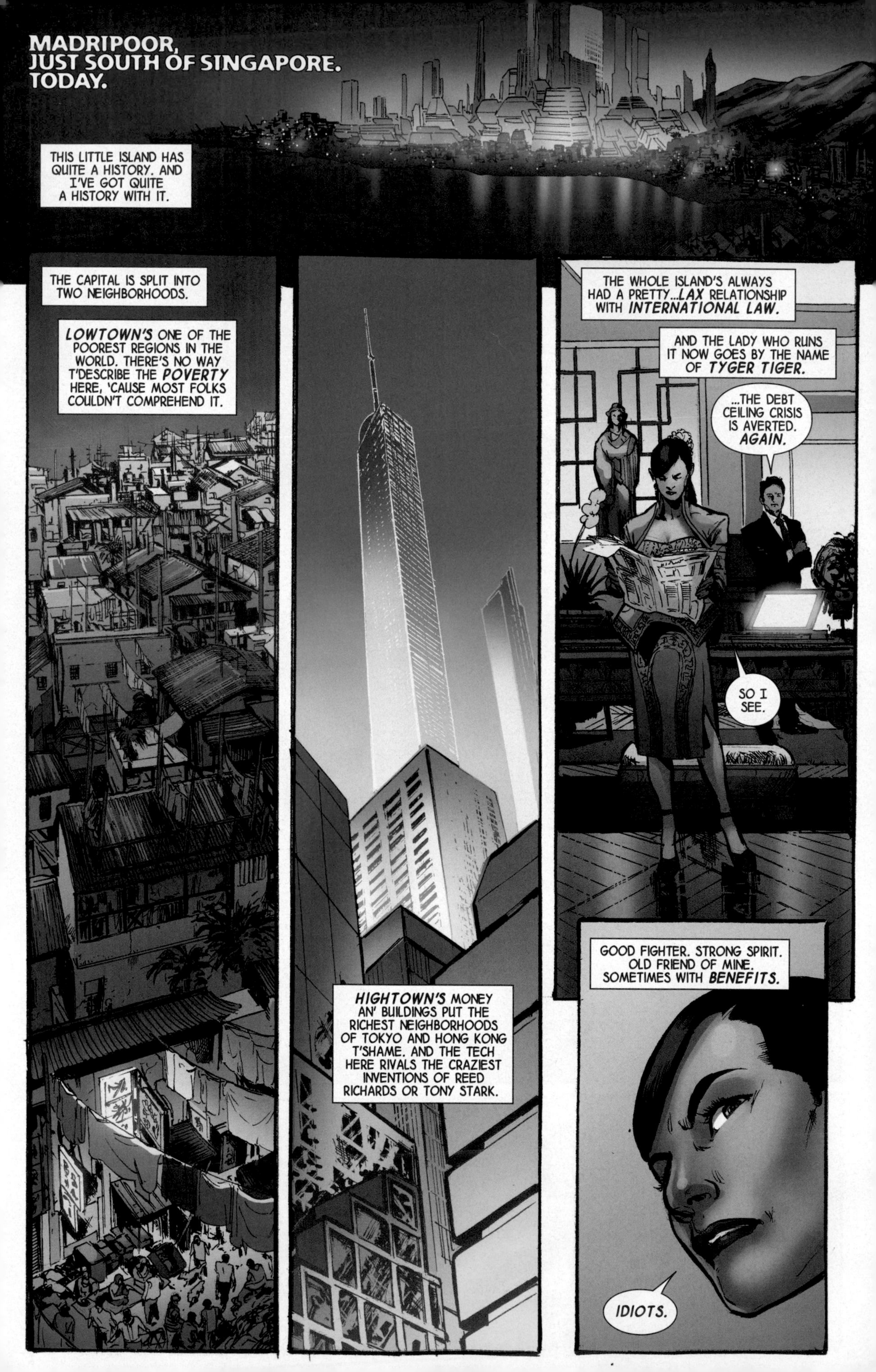
MADRIPOOR, JUST SOUTH OF SINGAPORE. TODAY.
THIS LITTLE ISLAND HAS QUITE A HISTORY. AND I'VE GOT QUITE A HISTORY WITH IT.
THE CAPITAL IS SPLIT INTO TWO NEIGHBORHOODS.
LOWTOWN'S ONE OF THE POOREST REGIONS IN THE WORLD. THERE'S NO WAY T'DESCRIBE THE POVERTY HERE, 'CAUSE MOST FOLKS COULDN'T COMPREHEND IT.
HIGHTOWN'S MONEY AN' BUILDINGS PUT THE RICHEST NEIGHBORHOODS OF TOKYO AND HONG KONG T'SHAME. AND THE TECH HERE RIVALS THE CRAZIEST INVENTIONS OF REED RICHARDS OR TONY STARK.
THE WHOLE ISLAND'S ALWAYS HAD A PRETTY...LAX RELATIONSHIP WITH INTERNATIONAL LAW.
AND THE LADY WHO RUNS IT NOW GOES BY THE NAME OF TYGER TIGER.
...THE DEBT CEILING CRISIS IS AVERTED. AGAIN.
SO I SEE.
GOOD FIGHTER. STRONG SPIRIT. OLD FRIEND OF MINE. SOMETIMES WITH BENEFITS.
IDIOTS.

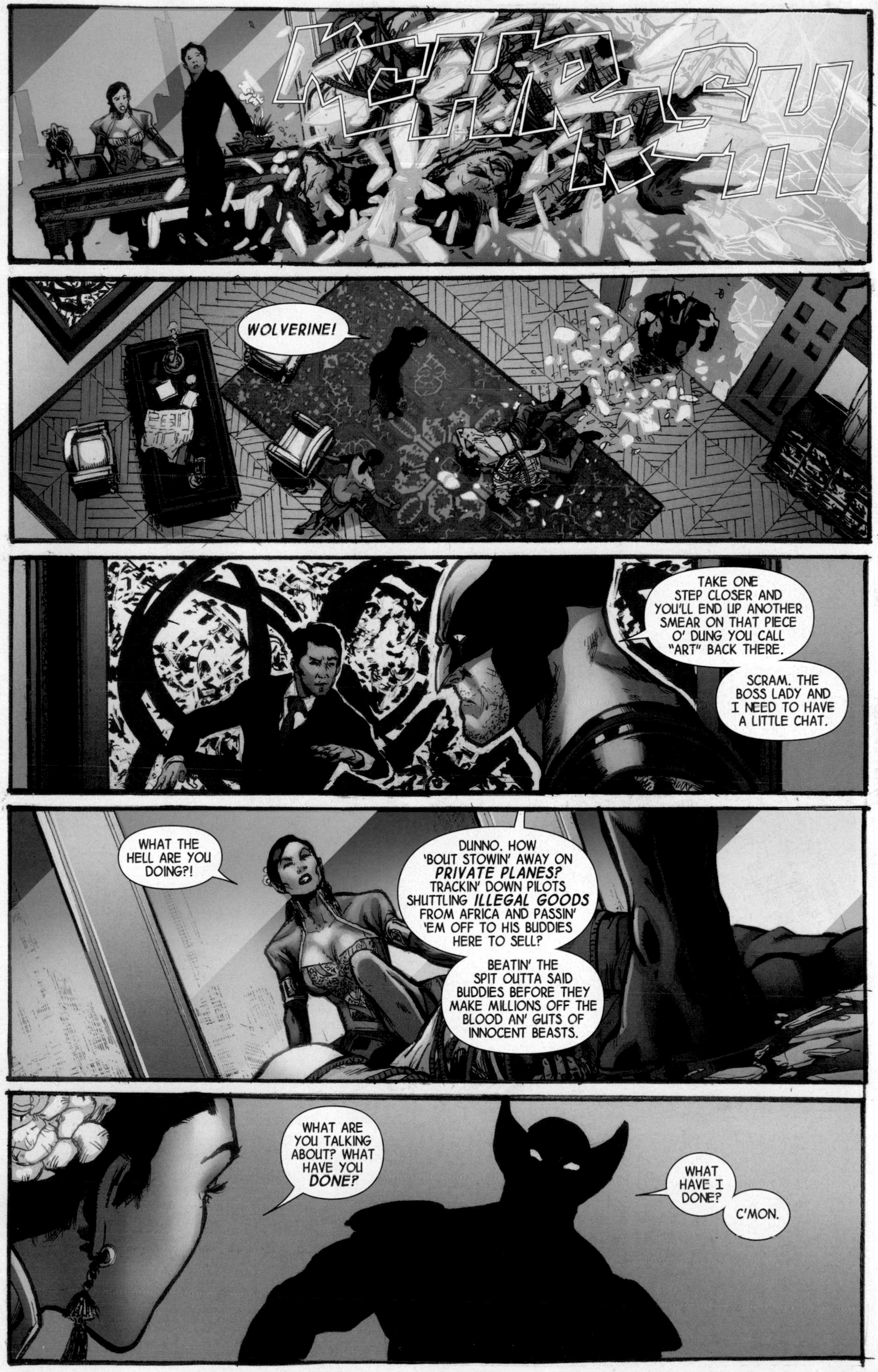
KRAASH
WOLVERINE!
TAKE ONE STEP CLOSER AND YOU'LL END UP ANOTHER SMEAR ON THAT PIECE O' DUNG YOU CALL "ART" BACK THERE.
SCRAM. THE BOSS LADY AND I NEED TO HAVE A LITTLE CHAT.
WHAT THE HELL ARE YOU DOING?!
DUNNO. HOW 'BOUT STOWIN' AWAY ON PRIVATE PLANES? TRACKIN' DOWN PILOTS SHUTTLING ILLEGAL GOODS FROM AFRICA AND PASSIN' 'EM OFF TO HIS BUDDIES HERE TO SELL?
BEATIN' THE SPIT OUTTA SAID BUDDIES BEFORE THEY MAKE MILLIONS OFF THE BLOOD AN' GUTS OF INNOCENT BEASTS.
WHAT ARE YOU TALKING ABOUT? WHAT HAVE YOU DONE?
WHAT HAVE I DONE?
C'MON.

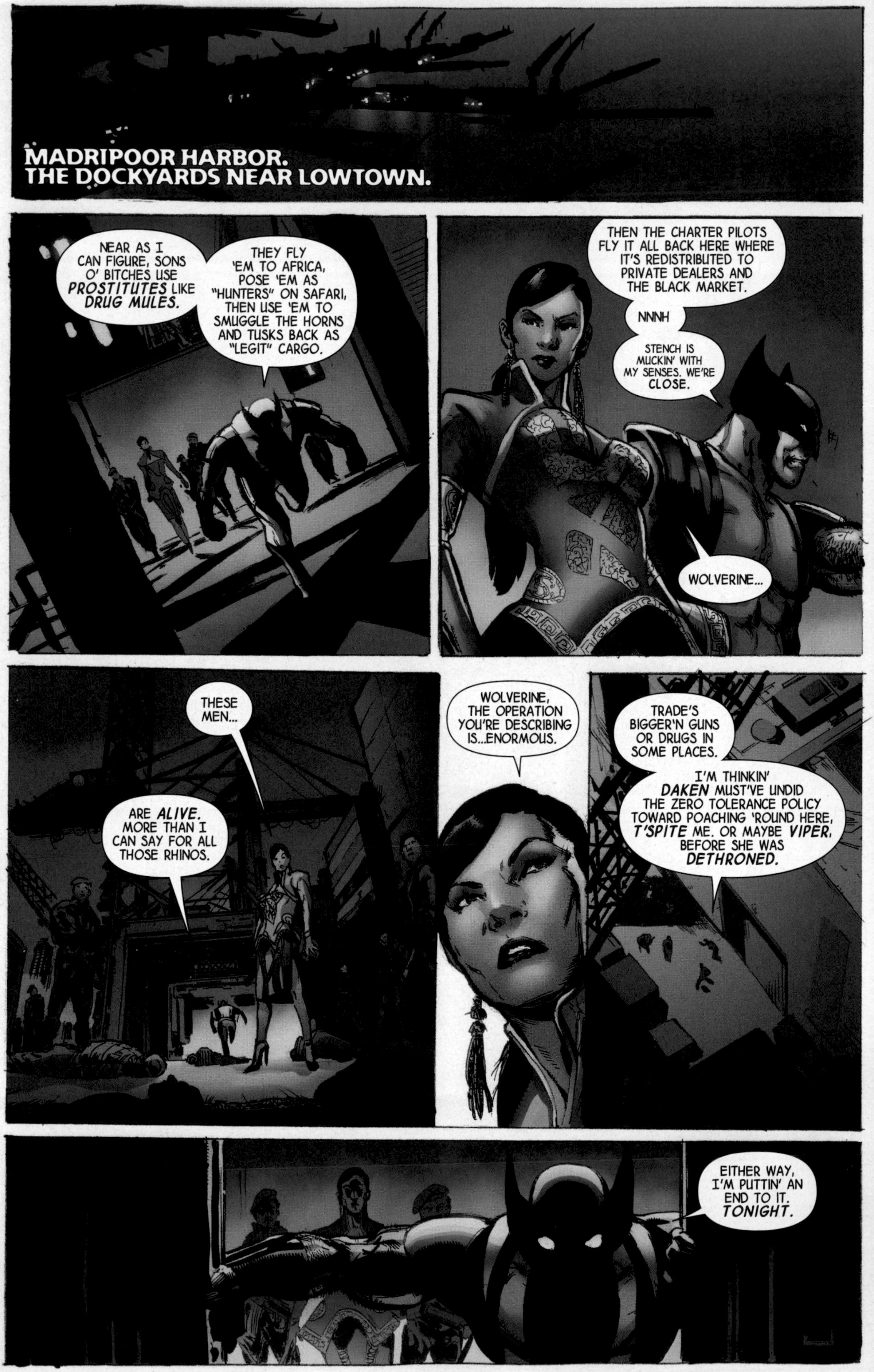
MADRIPOOR HARBOR. THE DOCKYARDS NEAR LOWTOWN.
NEAR AS I CAN FIGURE, SONS O' BITCHES USE PROSTITUTES LIKE DRUG MULES.
THEY FLY 'EM TO AFRICA, POSE 'EM AS "HUNTERS" ON SAFARI, THEN USE 'EM TO SMUGGLE THE HORNS AND TUSKS BACK AS "LEGIT" CARGO.
THEN THE CHARTER PILOTS FLY IT ALL BACK HERE WHERE IT'S REDISTRIBUTED TO PRIVATE DEALERS AND THE BLACK MARKET.
NNNH
STENCH IS MUCKIN' WITH MY SENSES. WE'RE CLOSE.
WOLVERINE...
THESE MEN...
ARE ALIVE. MORE THAN I CAN SAY FOR ALL THOSE RHINOS.
WOLVERINE, THE OPERATION YOU'RE DESCRIBING IS...ENORMOUS.
TRADE'S BIGGER'N GUNS OR DRUGS IN SOME PLACES.
I'M THINKIN' DAKEN MUST'VE UNDID THE ZERO TOLERANCE POLICY TOWARD POACHING 'ROUND HERE, T'SPITE ME. OR MAYBE VIPER, BEFORE SHE WAS DETHRONED.
EITHER WAY, I'M PUTTIN' AN END TO IT. TONIGHT.

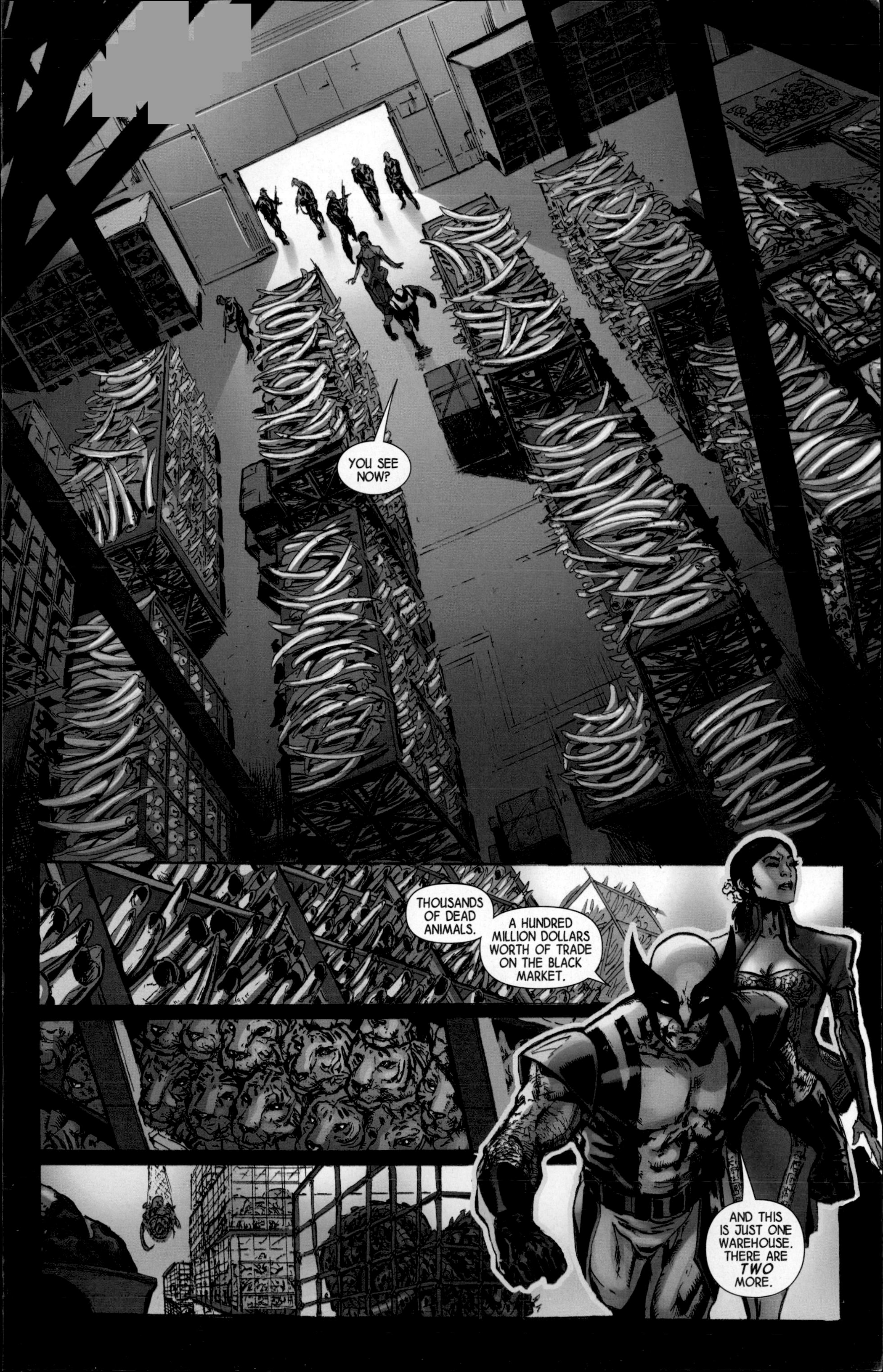
YOU SEE NOW?
THOUSANDS OF DEAD ANIMALS.
A HUNDRED MILLION DOLLARS WORTH OF TRADE ON THE BLACK MARKET.
AND THIS IS JUST ONE WAREHOUSE. THERE ARE TWO MORE.

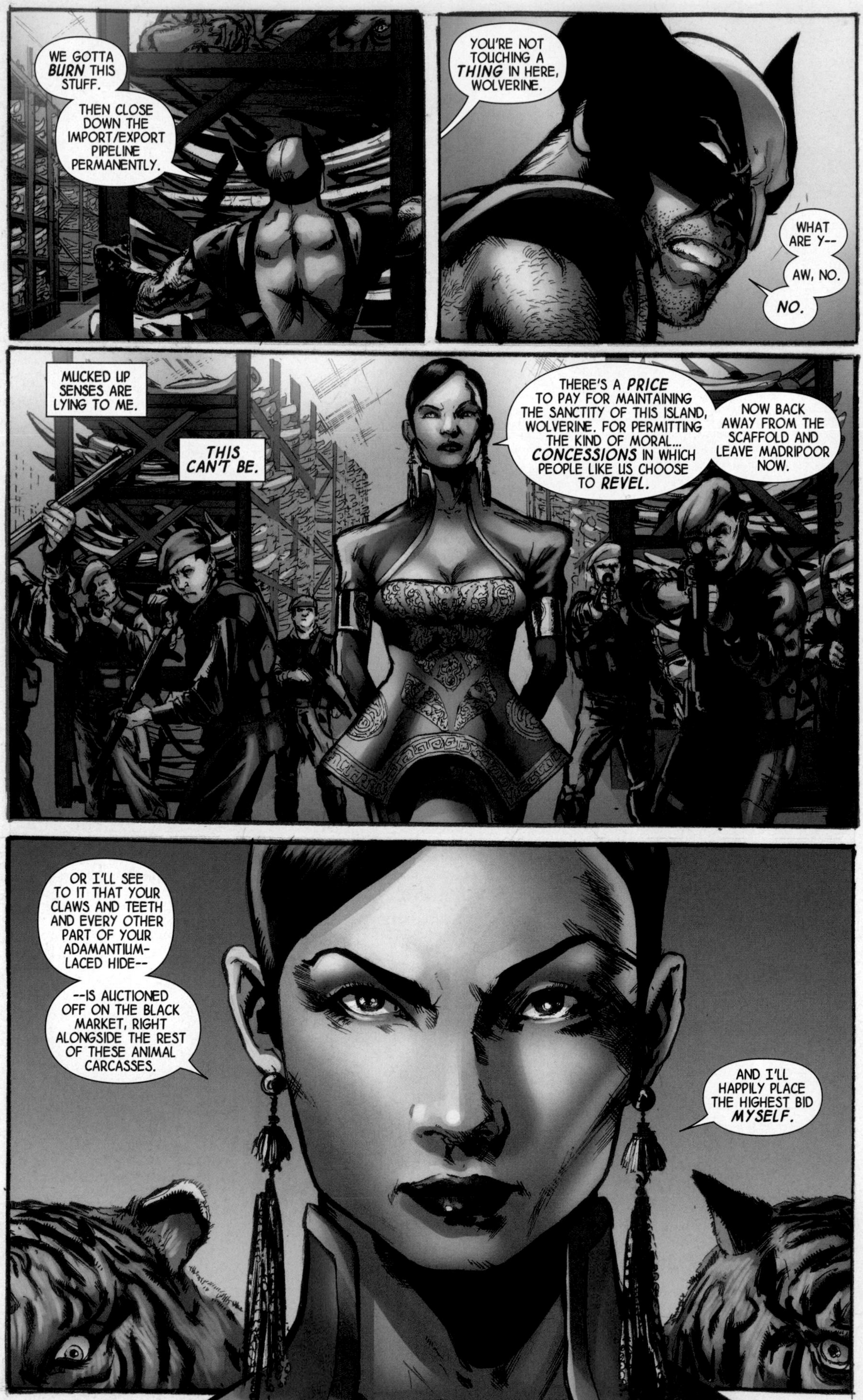
WE GOTTA BURN THIS STUFF.
THEN CLOSE DOWN THE IMPORT/EXPORT PIPELINE PERMANENTLY.
YOU'RE NOT TOUCHING A THING IN HERE, WOLVERINE.
WHAT ARE Y--
AW, NO.
NO.
MUCKED UP SENSES ARE LYING TO ME.
THIS CAN'T BE.
THERE'S A PRICE TO PAY FOR MAINTAINING THE SANCTITY OF THIS ISLAND, WOLVERINE. FOR PERMITTING THE KIND OF MORAL... CONCESSIONS IN WHICH PEOPLE LIKE US CHOOSE TO REVEL.
NOW BACK AWAY FROM THE SCAFFOLD AND LEAVE MADRIPOOR NOW.
OR I'LL SEE TO IT THAT YOUR CLAWS AND TEETH AND EVERY OTHER PART OF YOUR ADAMANTIUM-LACED HIDE--
--IS AUCTIONED OFF ON THE BLACK MARKET, RIGHT ALONGSIDE THE REST OF THESE ANIMAL CARCASSES.
AND I'LL HAPPILY PLACE THE HIGHEST BID MYSELF.

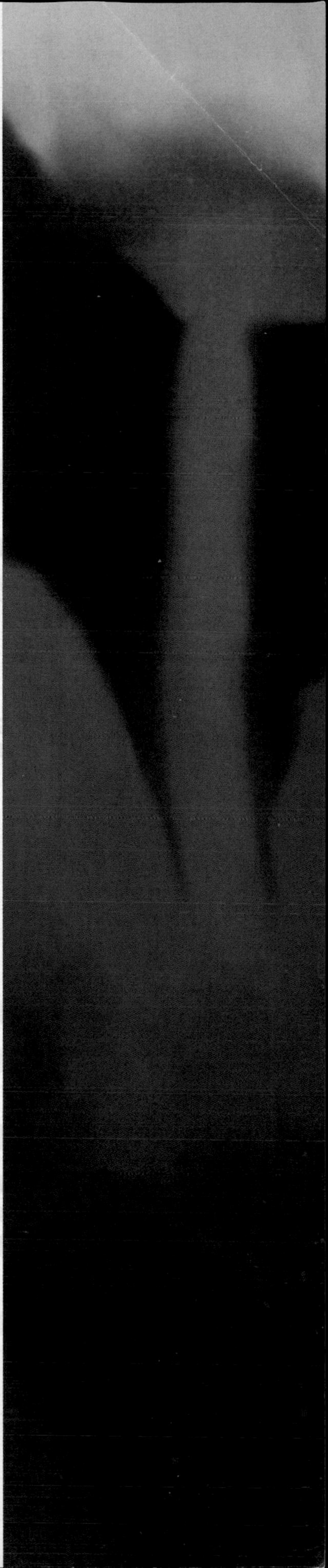

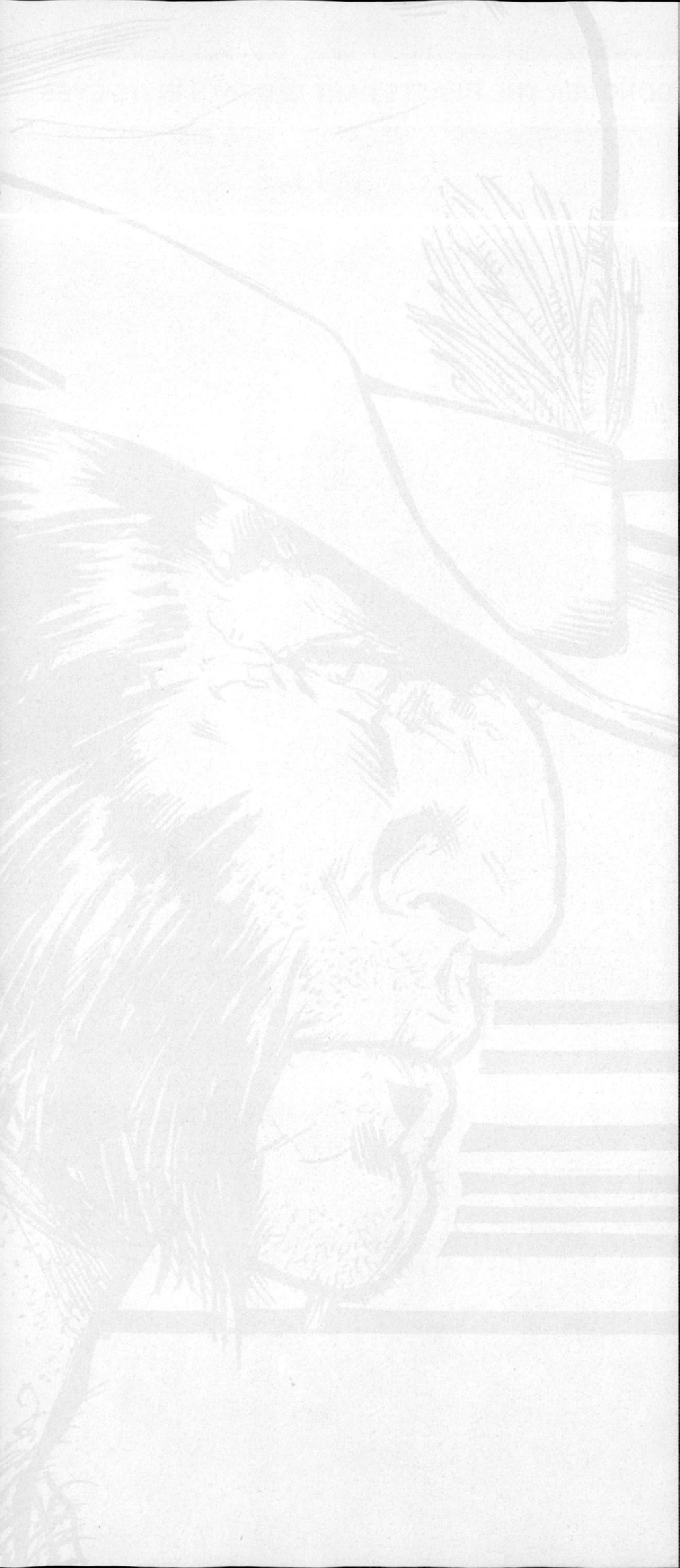

# 13 COME CONQUER THE BEASTS PART 2: DEATH IN ITS EYES

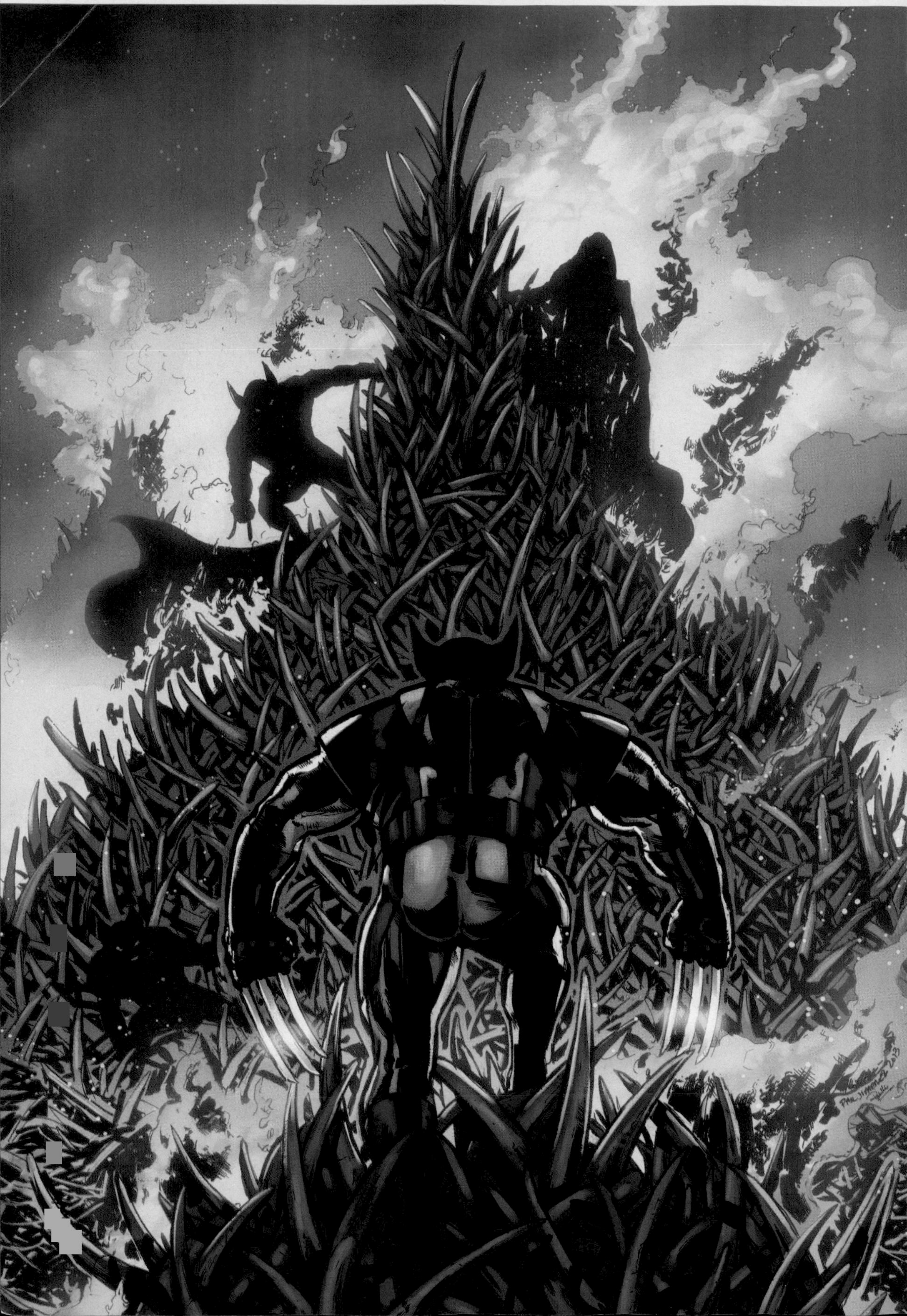

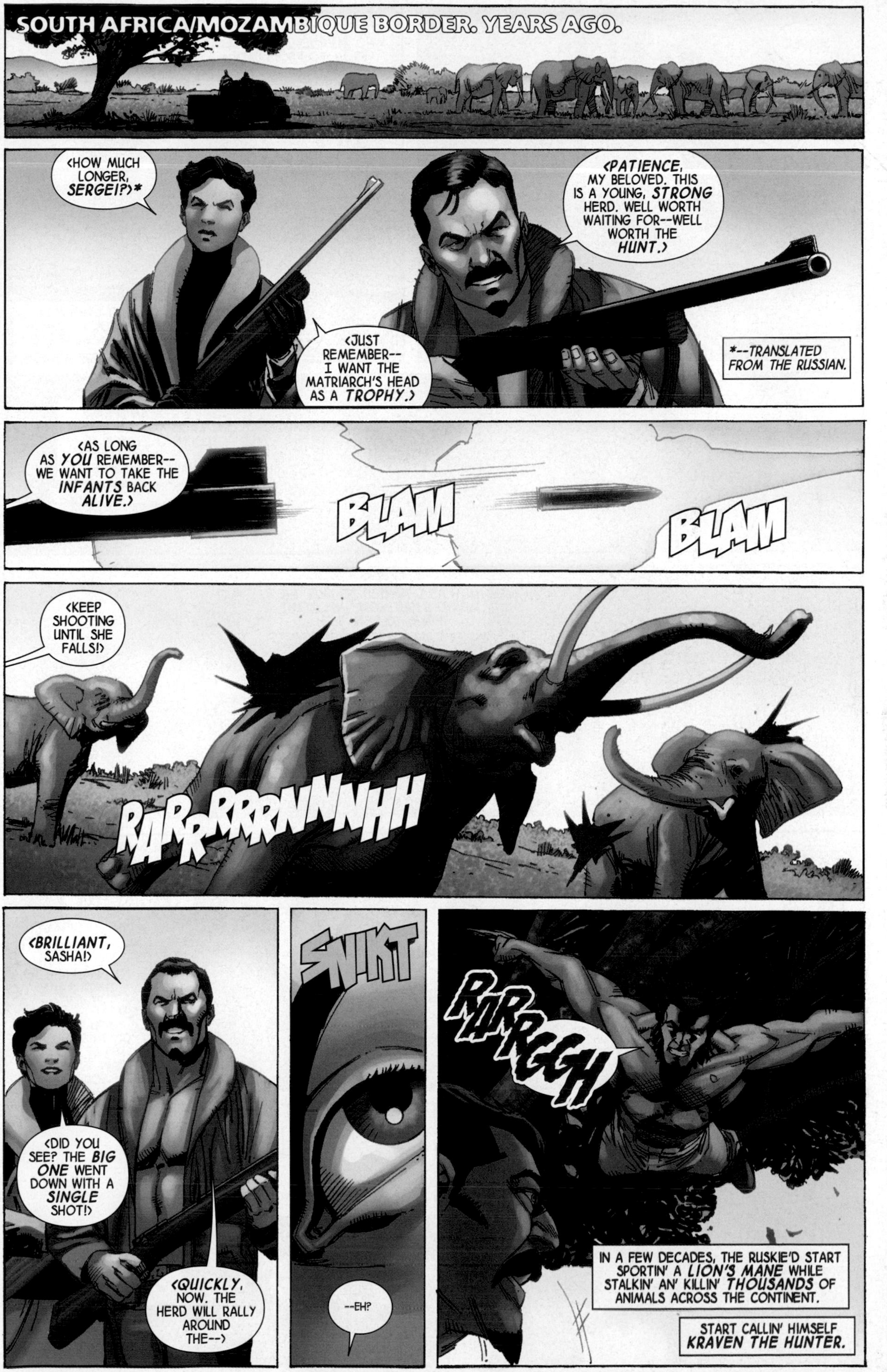
SOUTH AFRICA/MOZAMBIQUE BORDER. YEARS AGO.
<HOW MUCH LONGER, SERGEI?>*
<PATIENCE, MY BELOVED. THIS IS A YOUNG, STRONG HERD. WELL WORTH WAITING FOR--WELL WORTH THE HUNT.>
<JUST REMEMBER-- I WANT THE MATRIARCH'S HEAD AS A TROPHY.>
*--TRANSLATED FROM THE RUSSIAN.
<AS LONG AS YOU REMEMBER-- WE WANT TO TAKE THE INFANTS BACK ALIVE.>
BLAM
BLAM
<KEEP SHOOTING UNTIL SHE FALLS!>
RARRRRRNNNHH
<BRILLIANT, SASHA!>
<DID YOU SEE? THE BIG ONE WENT DOWN WITH A SINGLE SHOT!>
<QUICKLY, NOW. THE HERD WILL RALLY AROUND THE-->
SNIKT
--EH?
RARRGGH
IN A FEW DECADES, THE RUSKIE'D START SPORTIN' A LION'S MANE WHILE STALKIN' AN' KILLIN' THOUSANDS OF ANIMALS ACROSS THE CONTINENT.
START CALLIN' HIMSELF KRAVEN THE HUNTER.

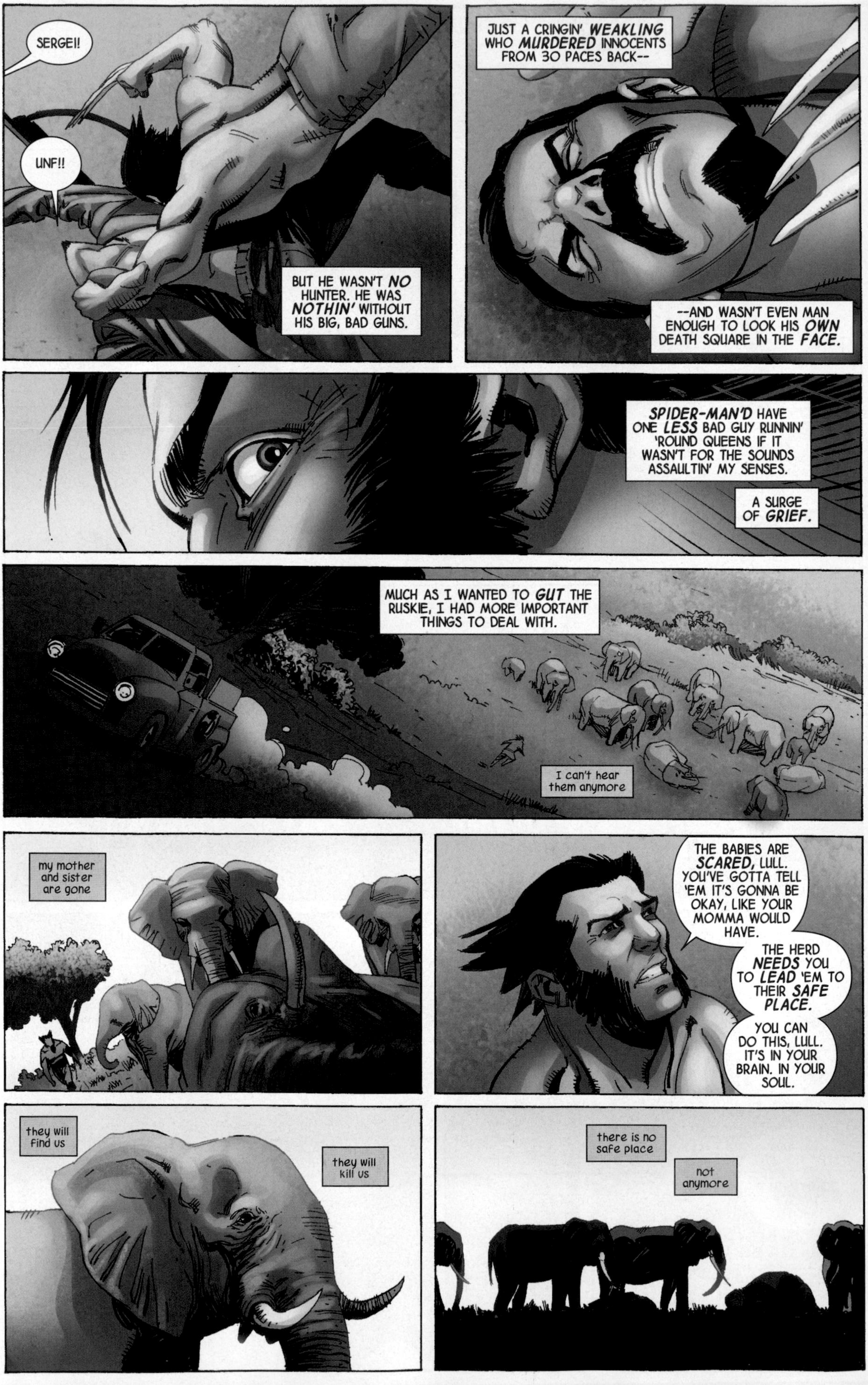
SERGEI!
UNF!!
BUT HE WASN'T NO HUNTER. HE WAS NOTHIN' WITHOUT HIS BIG, BAD GUNS.
JUST A CRINGIN' WEAKLING WHO MURDERED INNOCENTS FROM 30 PACES BACK--
--AND WASN'T EVEN MAN ENOUGH TO LOOK HIS OWN DEATH SQUARE IN THE FACE.
SPIDER-MAN'D HAVE ONE LESS BAD GUY RUNNIN' 'ROUND QUEENS IF IT WASN'T FOR THE SOUNDS ASSAULTIN' MY SENSES.
A SURGE OF GRIEF.
MUCH AS I WANTED TO GUT THE RUSKIE, I HAD MORE IMPORTANT THINGS TO DEAL WITH.
I can't hear them anymore
my mother and sister are gone
THE BABIES ARE SCARED, LULL. YOU'VE GOTTA TELL 'EM IT'S GONNA BE OKAY, LIKE YOUR MOMMA WOULD HAVE.
THE HERD NEEDS YOU TO LEAD 'EM TO THEIR SAFE PLACE.
YOU CAN DO THIS, LULL. IT'S IN YOUR BRAIN. IN YOUR SOUL.
they will find us
they will kill us
there is no safe place
not anymore

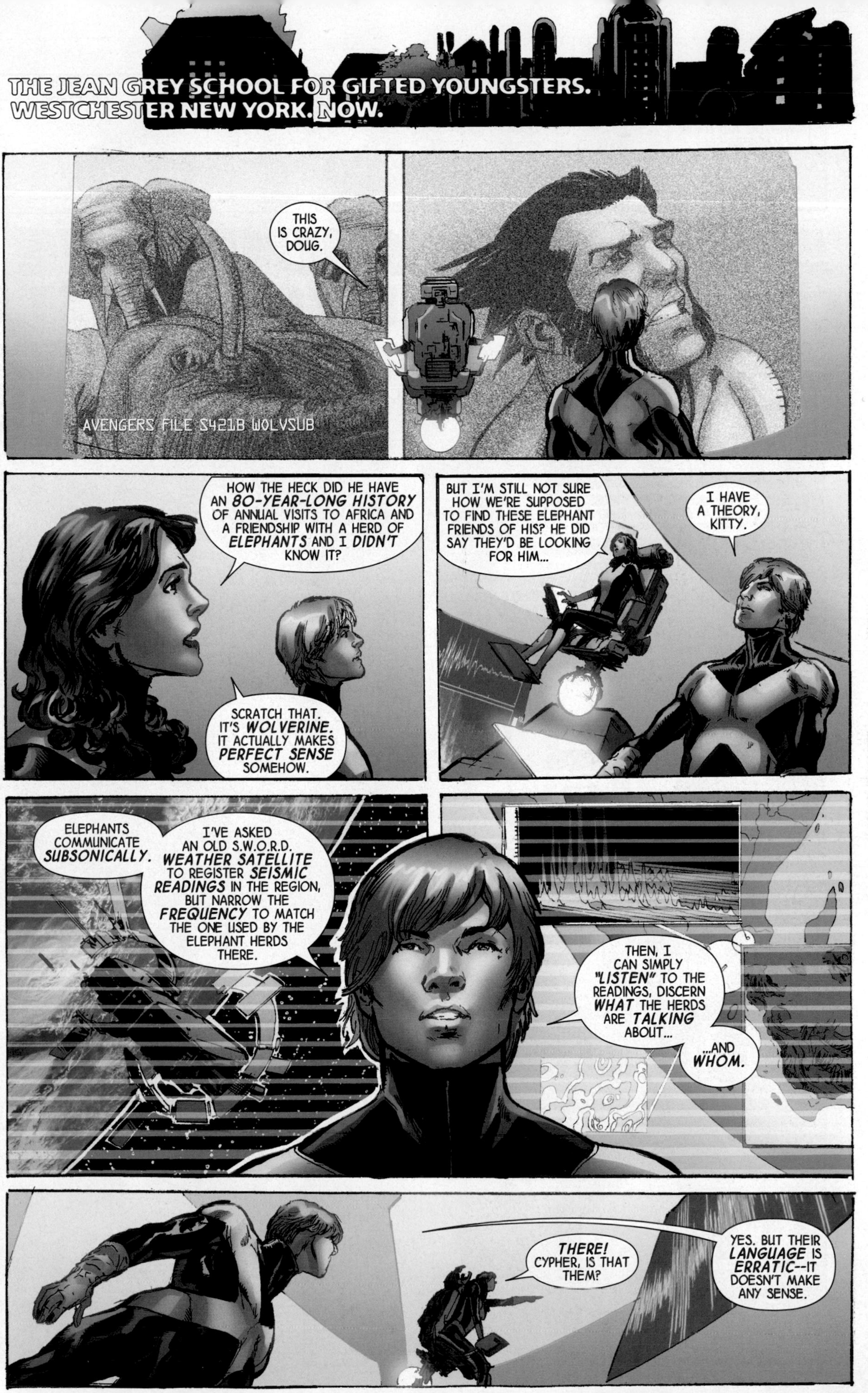
THE JEAN GREY SCHOOL FOR GIFTED YOUNGSTERS. WESTCHESTER NEW YORK. NOW.
THIS IS CRAZY, DOUG.
AVENGERS FILE S421B WOLVSUB
HOW THE HECK DID HE HAVE AN 80-YEAR-LONG HISTORY OF ANNUAL VISITS TO AFRICA AND A FRIENDSHIP WITH A HERD OF ELEPHANTS AND I DIDN'T KNOW IT?
SCRATCH THAT. IT'S WOLVERINE. IT ACTUALLY MAKES PERFECT SENSE SOMEHOW.
BUT I'M STILL NOT SURE HOW WE'RE SUPPOSED TO FIND THESE ELEPHANT FRIENDS OF HIS? HE DID SAY THEY'D BE LOOKING FOR HIM...
I HAVE A THEORY, KITTY.
ELEPHANTS COMMUNICATE SUBSONICALLY.
I'VE ASKED AN OLD S.W.O.R.D. WEATHER SATELLITE TO REGISTER SEISMIC READINGS IN THE REGION, BUT NARROW THE FREQUENCY TO MATCH THE ONE USED BY THE ELEPHANT HERDS THERE.
THEN, I CAN SIMPLY "LISTEN" TO THE READINGS, DISCERN WHAT THE HERDS ARE TALKING ABOUT...
...AND WHOM.
THERE! CYPHER, IS THAT THEM?
YES. BUT THEIR LANGUAGE IS ERRATIC--IT DOESN'T MAKE ANY SENSE.

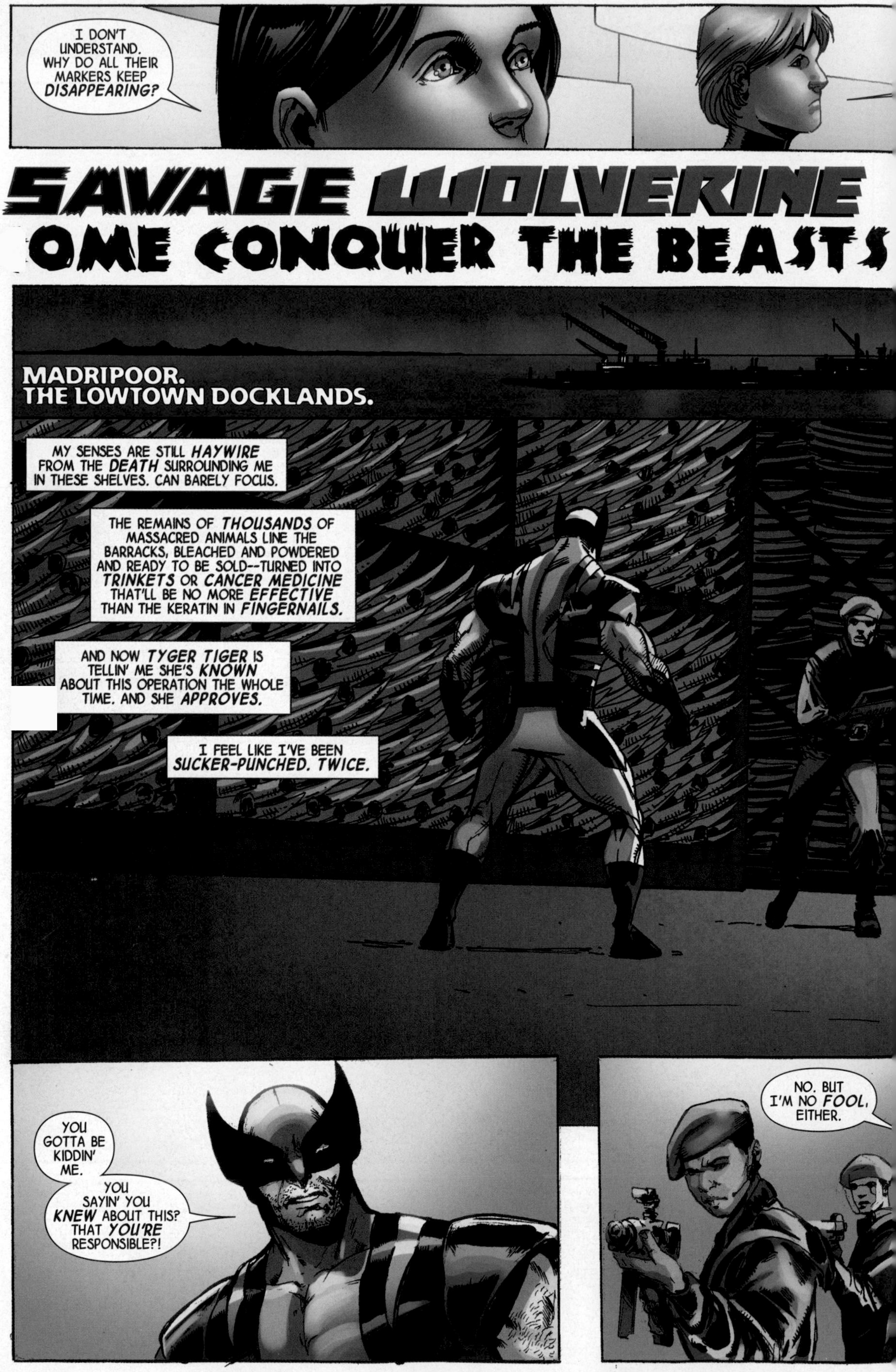
I DON'T UNDERSTAND. WHY DO ALL THEIR MARKERS KEEP DISAPPEARING?
SAVAGE WOLVERINE
OME CONQUER THE BEASTS
MADRIPOOR. THE LOWTOWN DOCKLANDS.
MY SENSES ARE STILL HAYWIRE FROM THE DEATH SURROUNDING ME IN THESE SHELVES. CAN BARELY FOCUS.
THE REMAINS OF THOUSANDS OF MASSACRED ANIMALS LINE THE BARRACKS, BLEACHED AND POWDERED AND READY TO BE SOLD--TURNED INTO TRINKETS OR CANCER MEDICINE THAT'LL BE NO MORE EFFECTIVE THAN THE KERATIN IN FINGERNAILS.
AND NOW TYGER TIGER IS TELLIN' ME SHE'S KNOWN ABOUT THIS OPERATION THE WHOLE TIME. AND SHE APPROVES.
I FEEL LIKE I'VE BEEN SUCKER-PUNCHED. TWICE.
YOU GOTTA BE KIDDIN' ME.
YOU SAYIN' YOU KNEW ABOUT THIS? THAT YOU'RE RESPONSIBLE?!
NO. BUT I'M NO FOOL, EITHER.

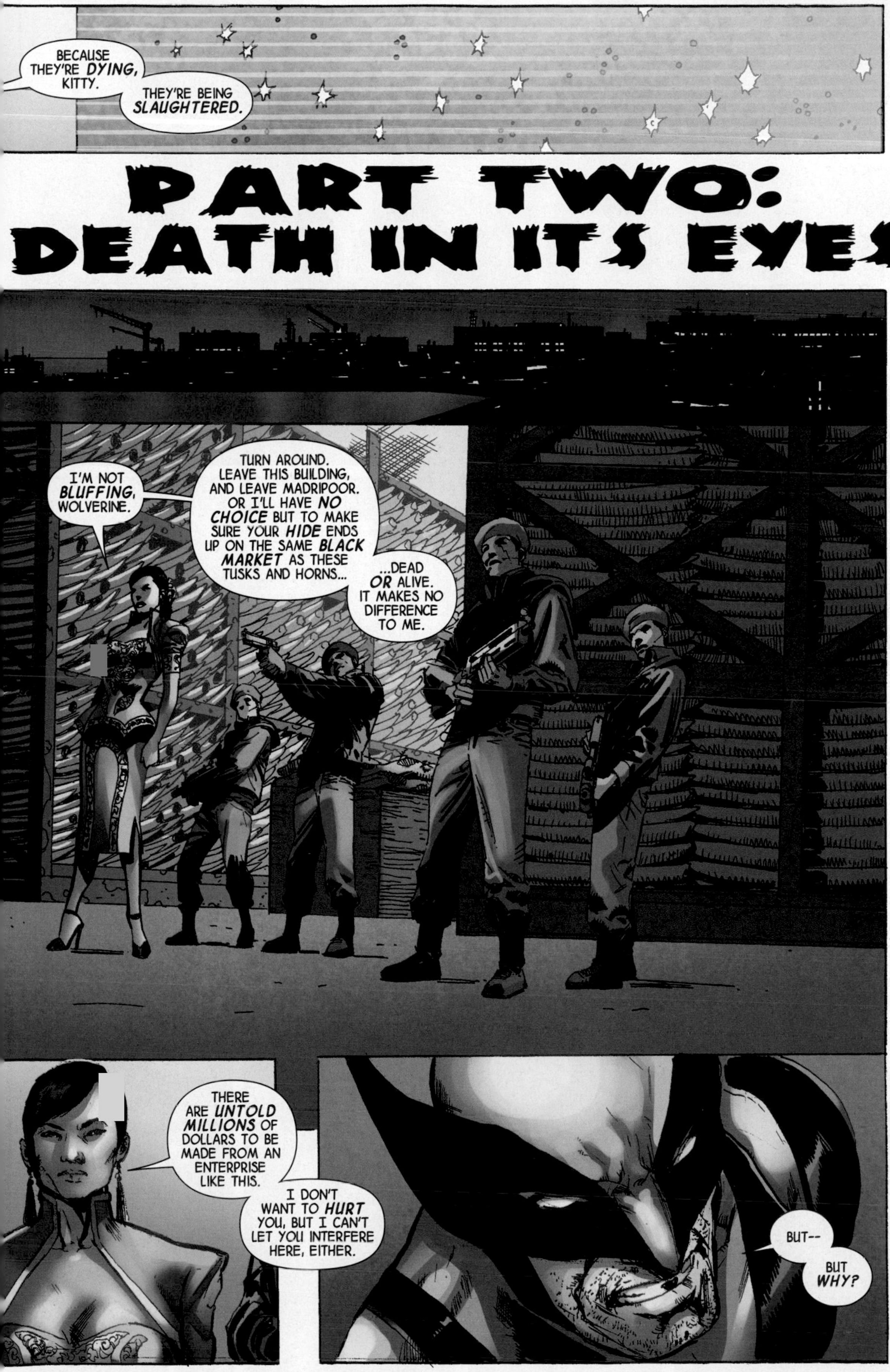
BECAUSE THEY'RE DYING, KITTY.
THEY'RE BEING SLAUGHTERED.
PART TWO: DEATH IN ITS EYES
I'M NOT BLUFFING, WOLVERINE.
TURN AROUND. LEAVE THIS BUILDING, AND LEAVE MADRIPOOR. OR I'LL HAVE NO CHOICE BUT TO MAKE SURE YOUR HIDE ENDS UP ON THE SAME BLACK MARKET AS THESE TUSKS AND HORNS...
...DEAD OR ALIVE. IT MAKES NO DIFFERENCE TO ME.
THERE ARE UNTOLD MILLIONS OF DOLLARS TO BE MADE FROM AN ENTERPRISE LIKE THIS.
I DON'T WANT TO HURT YOU, BUT I CAN'T LET YOU INTERFERE HERE, EITHER.
BUT--
BUT WHY?

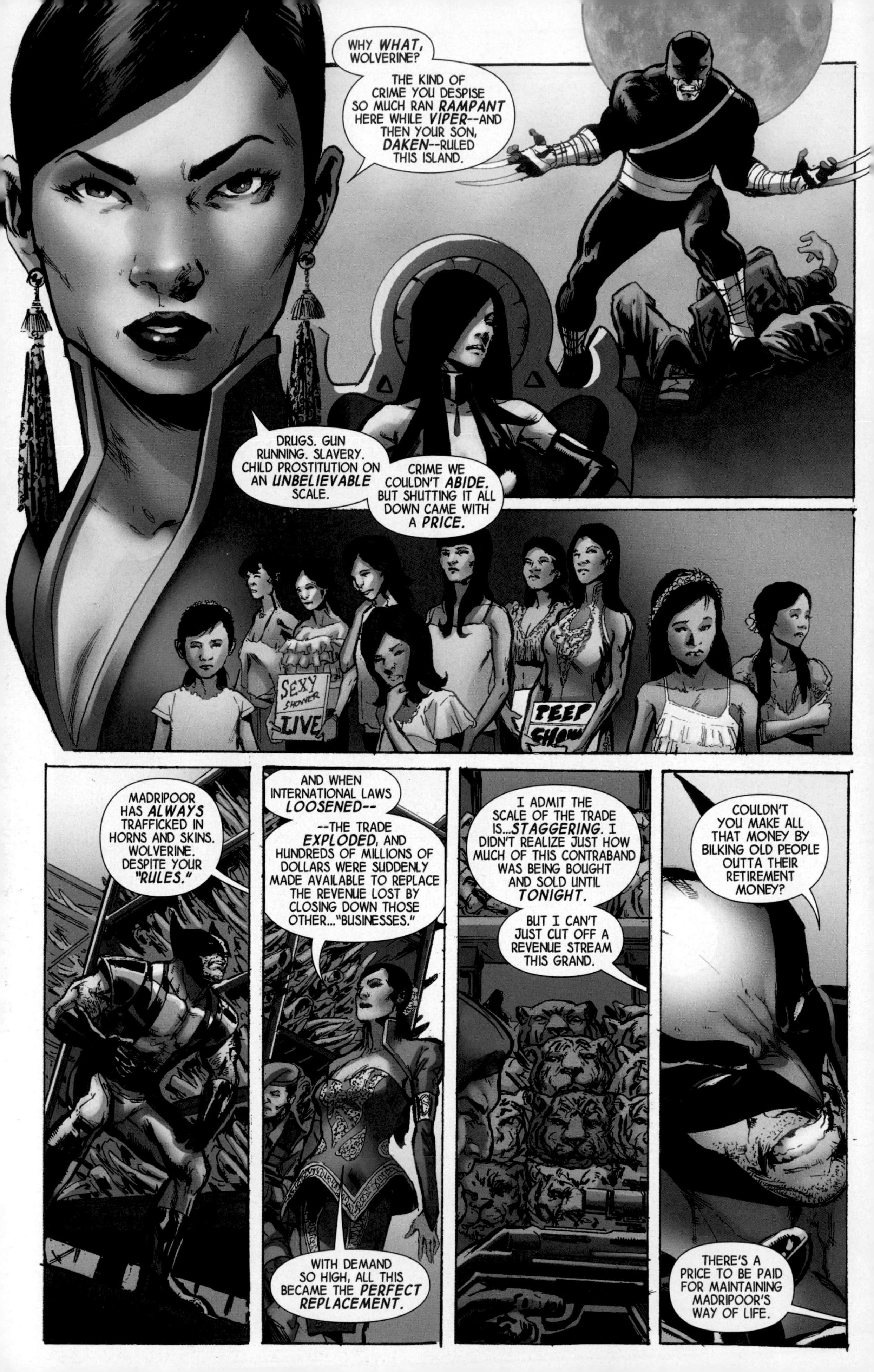
WHY WHAT, WOLVERINE?
THE KIND OF CRIME YOU DESPISE SO MUCH RAN RAMPANT HERE WHILE VIPER--AND THEN YOUR SON, DAKEN--RULED THIS ISLAND.
DRUGS. GUN RUNNING. SLAVERY. CHILD PROSTITUTION ON AN UNBELIEVABLE SCALE.
CRIME WE COULDN'T ABIDE. BUT SHUTTING IT ALL DOWN CAME WITH A PRICE.
SEXY SHOWER LIVE
PEEP SHOW
MADRIPOOR HAS ALWAYS TRAFFICKED IN HORNS AND SKINS. WOLVERINE. DESPITE YOUR "RULES."
AND WHEN INTERNATIONAL LAWS LOOSENED--
--THE TRADE EXPLODED, AND HUNDREDS OF MILLIONS OF DOLLARS WERE SUDDENLY MADE AVAILABLE TO REPLACE THE REVENUE LOST BY CLOSING DOWN THOSE OTHER..."BUSINESSES."
WITH DEMAND SO HIGH, ALL THIS BECAME THE PERFECT REPLACEMENT.
I ADMIT THE SCALE OF THE TRADE IS...STAGGERING. I DIDN'T REALIZE JUST HOW MUCH OF THIS CONTRABAND WAS BEING BOUGHT AND SOLD UNTIL TONIGHT.
BUT I CAN'T JUST CUT OFF A REVENUE STREAM THIS GRAND.
COULDN'T YOU MAKE ALL THAT MONEY BY BILKING OLD PEOPLE OUTTA THEIR RETIREMENT MONEY?
THERE'S A PRICE TO BE PAID FOR MAINTAINING MADRIPOOR'S WAY OF LIFE.

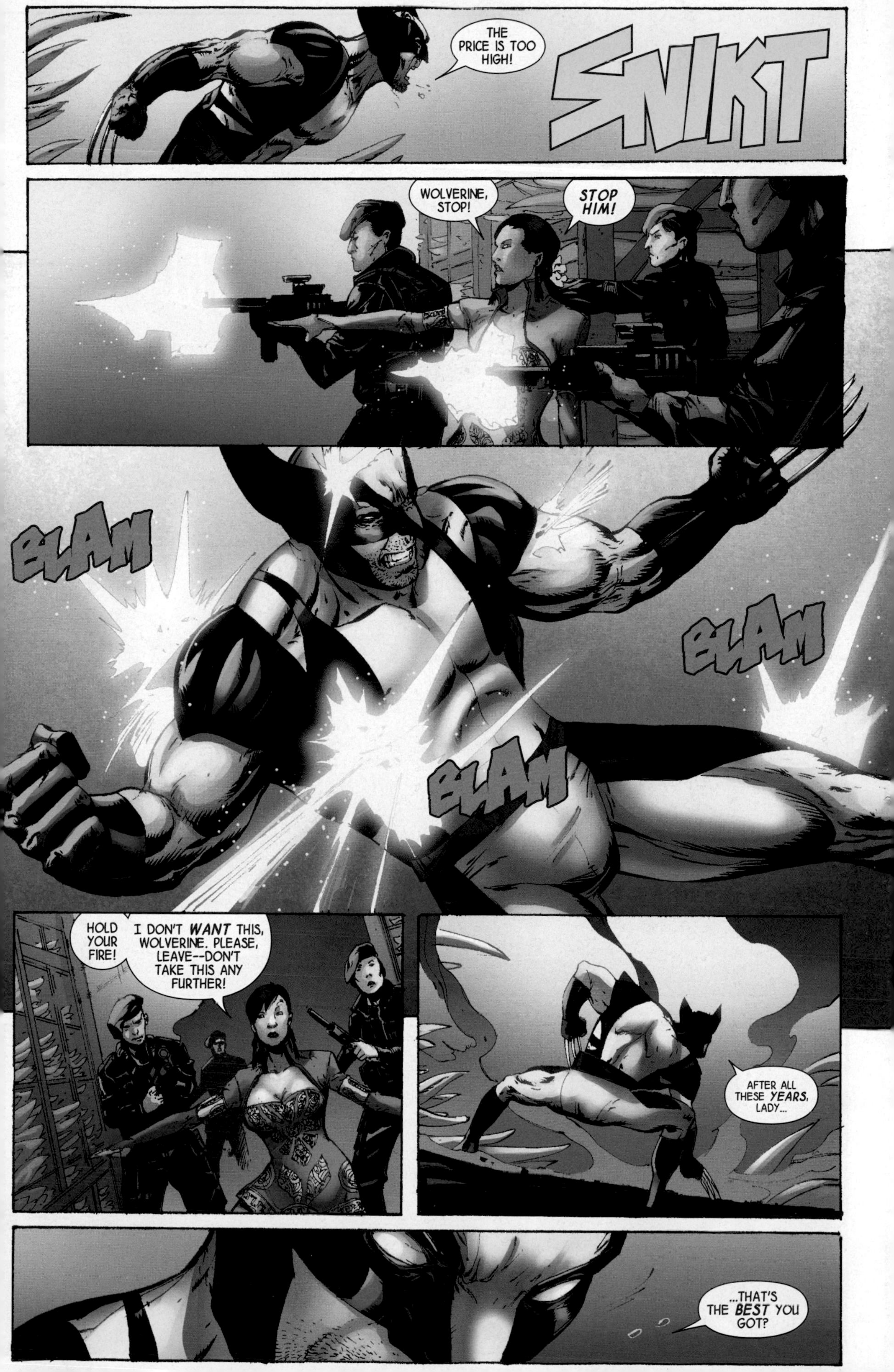
THE PRICE IS TOO HIGH!
SNIKT
WOLVERINE, STOP!
STOP HIM!
BLAM
BLAM
BLAM
HOLD YOUR FIRE!
I DON'T WANT THIS, WOLVERINE. PLEASE, LEAVE--DON'T TAKE THIS ANY FURTHER!
AFTER ALL THESE YEARS, LADY...
...THAT'S THE BEST YOU GOT?

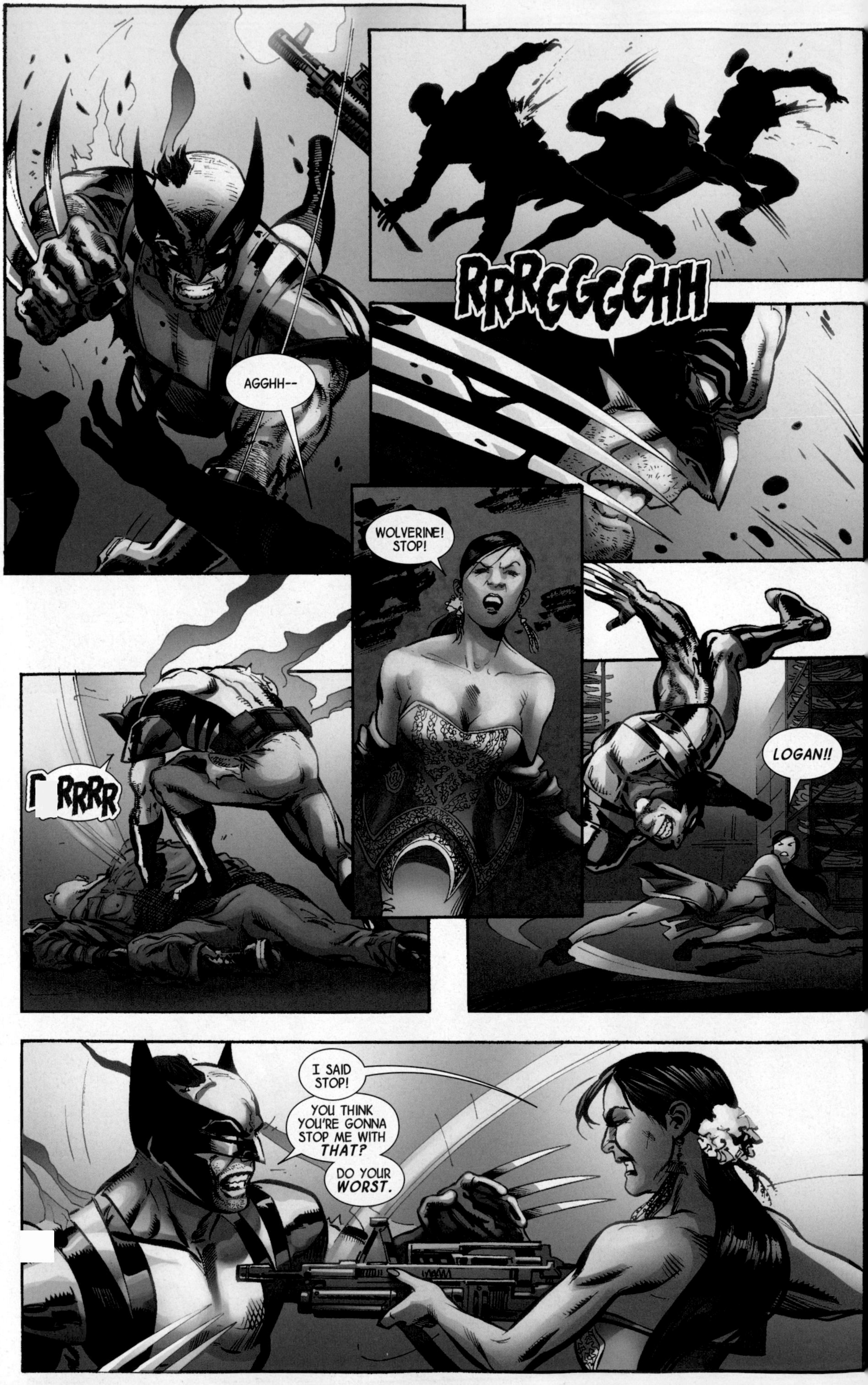
AGGHH--
RRRGGGGHH
WOLVERINE! STOP!
RRRR
LOGAN!!
I SAID STOP!
YOU THINK YOU'RE GONNA STOP ME WITH *THAT?*
DO YOUR *WORST.*

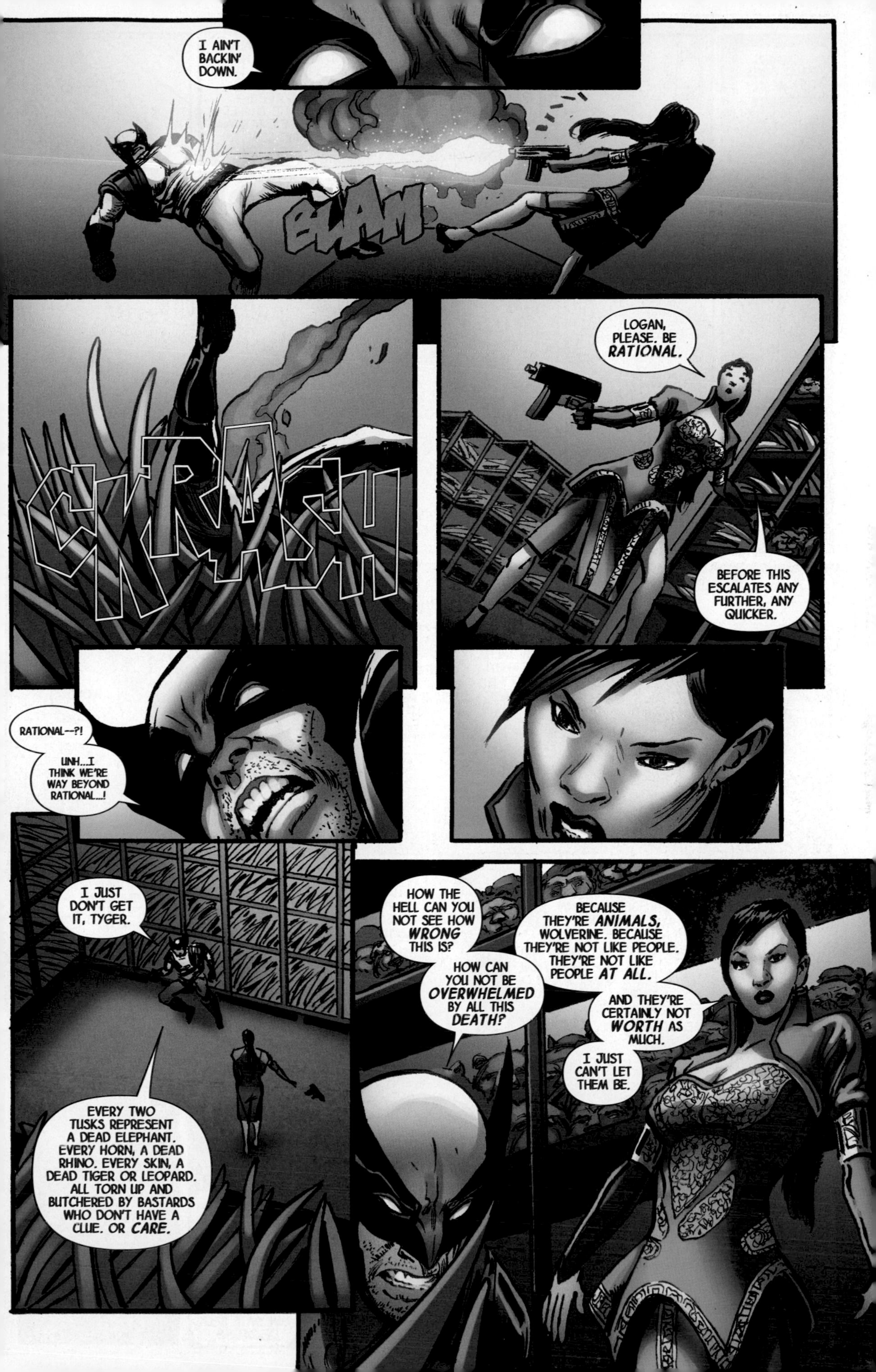

I AIN'T BACKIN' DOWN.
BLAM
CKRASH
LOGAN, PLEASE. BE RATIONAL.
BEFORE THIS ESCALATES ANY FURTHER, ANY QUICKER.
RATIONAL--?!
UNH...I THINK WE'RE WAY BEYOND RATIONAL...!
I JUST DON'T GET IT, TYGER.
EVERY TWO TUSKS REPRESENT A DEAD ELEPHANT. EVERY HORN, A DEAD RHINO. EVERY SKIN, A DEAD TIGER OR LEOPARD. ALL TORN UP AND BUTCHERED BY BASTARDS WHO DON'T HAVE A CLUE. OR CARE.
HOW THE HELL CAN YOU NOT SEE HOW WRONG THIS IS?
HOW CAN YOU NOT BE OVERWHELMED BY ALL THIS DEATH?
BECAUSE THEY'RE ANIMALS, WOLVERINE. BECAUSE THEY'RE NOT LIKE PEOPLE. THEY'RE NOT LIKE PEOPLE AT ALL.
AND THEY'RE CERTAINLY NOT WORTH AS MUCH.
I JUST CAN'T LET THEM BE.

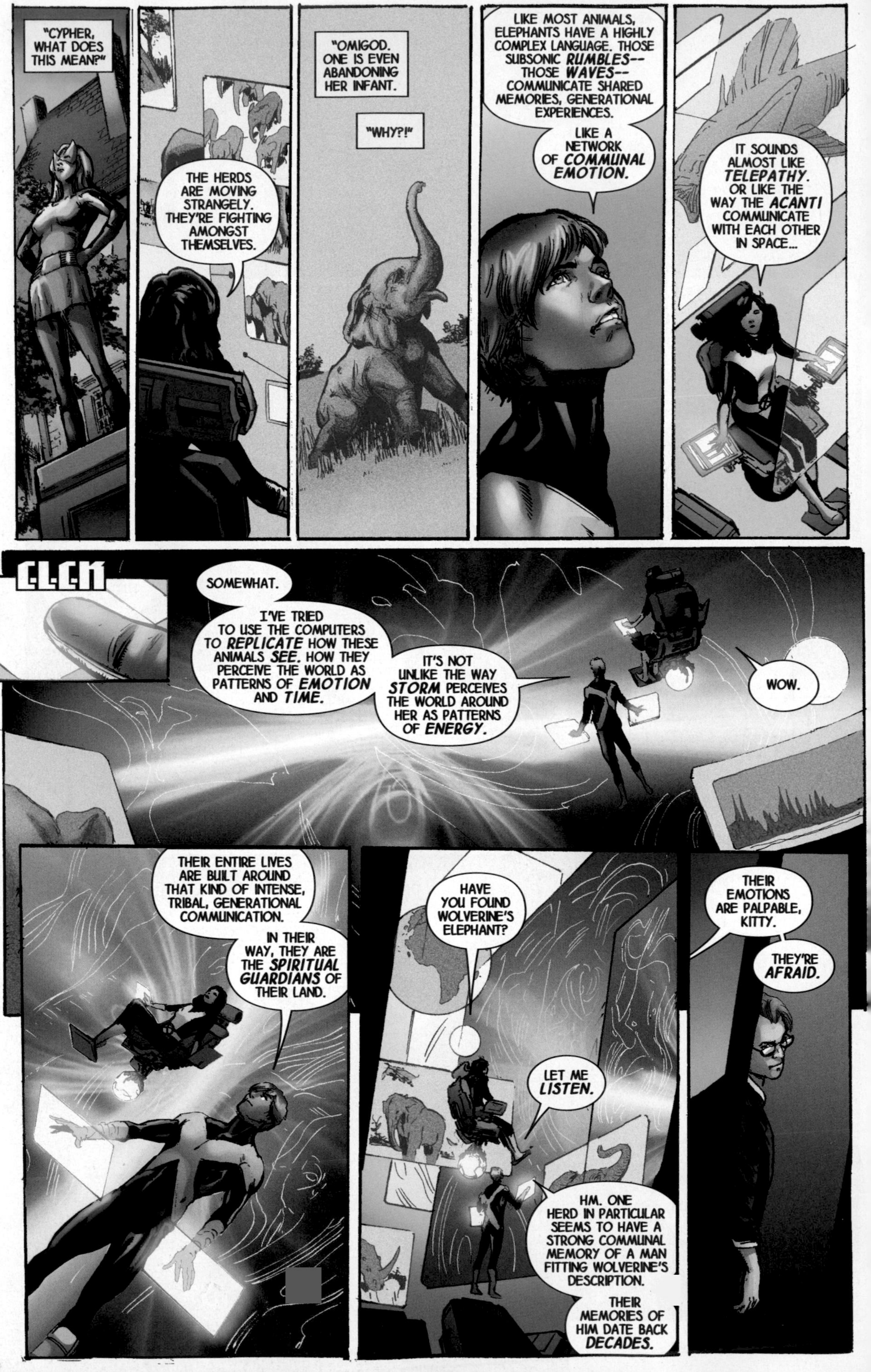
"CYPHER, WHAT DOES THIS MEAN?"
THE HERDS ARE MOVING STRANGELY. THEY'RE FIGHTING AMONGST THEMSELVES.
"OMIGOD. ONE IS EVEN ABANDONING HER INFANT.
"WHY?!"
LIKE MOST ANIMALS, ELEPHANTS HAVE A HIGHLY COMPLEX LANGUAGE. THOSE SUBSONIC RUMBLES-- THOSE WAVES-- COMMUNICATE SHARED MEMORIES, GENERATIONAL EXPERIENCES.
LIKE A NETWORK OF COMMUNAL EMOTION.
IT SOUNDS ALMOST LIKE TELEPATHY. OR LIKE THE WAY THE ACANTI COMMUNICATE WITH EACH OTHER IN SPACE...
CLCK
SOMEWHAT.
I'VE TRIED TO USE THE COMPUTERS TO REPLICATE HOW THESE ANIMALS SEE. HOW THEY PERCEIVE THE WORLD AS PATTERNS OF EMOTION AND TIME.
IT'S NOT UNLIKE THE WAY STORM PERCEIVES THE WORLD AROUND HER AS PATTERNS OF ENERGY.
WOW.
THEIR ENTIRE LIVES ARE BUILT AROUND THAT KIND OF INTENSE, TRIBAL, GENERATIONAL COMMUNICATION.
IN THEIR WAY, THEY ARE THE SPIRITUAL GUARDIANS OF THEIR LAND.
HAVE YOU FOUND WOLVERINE'S ELEPHANT?
LET ME LISTEN.
HM. ONE HERD IN PARTICULAR SEEMS TO HAVE A STRONG COMMUNAL MEMORY OF A MAN FITTING WOLVERINE'S DESCRIPTION.
THEIR MEMORIES OF HIM DATE BACK DECADES.
THEIR EMOTIONS ARE PALPABLE, KITTY.
THEY'RE AFRAID.

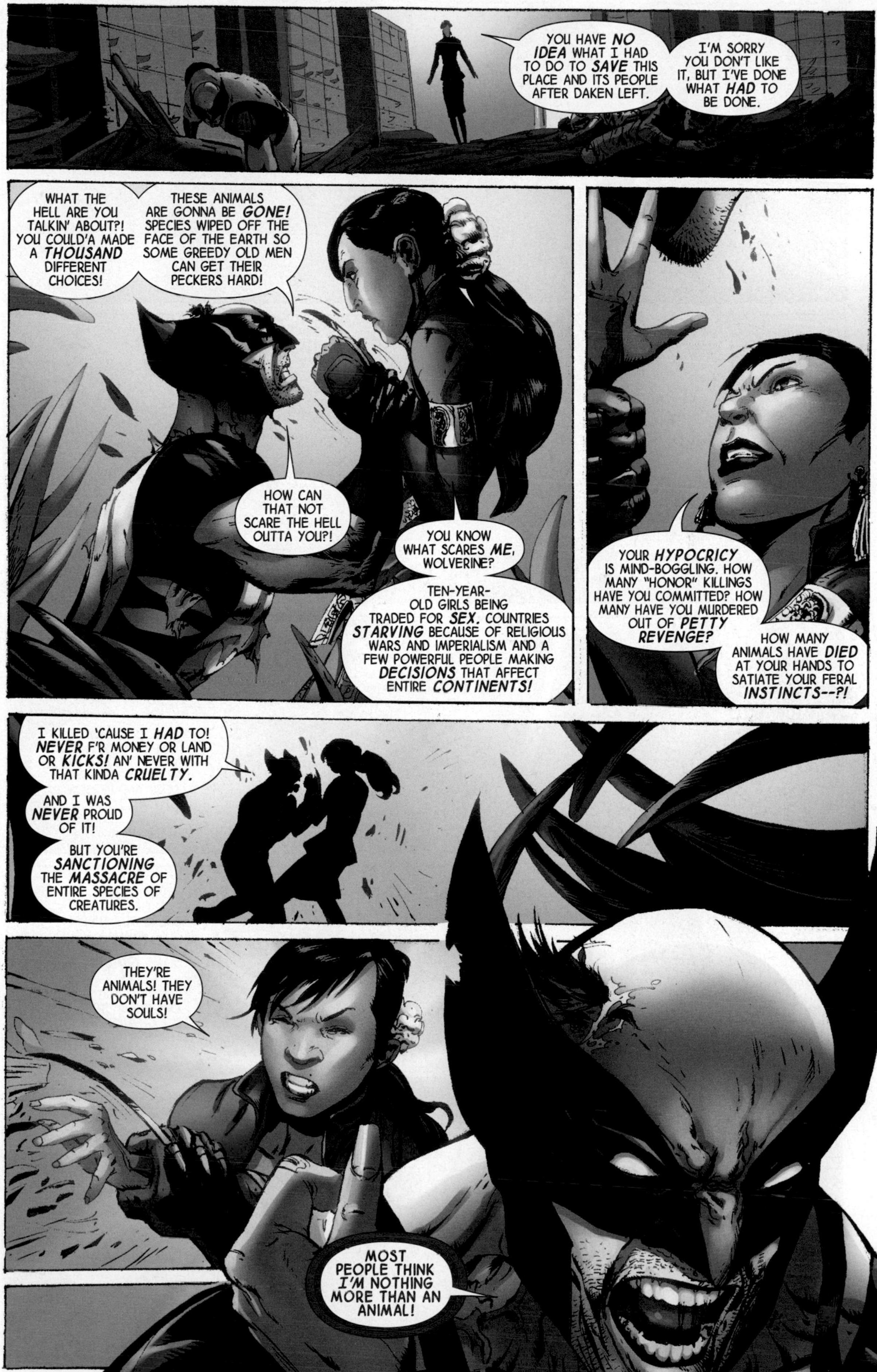

YOU HAVE NO IDEA WHAT I HAD TO DO TO SAVE THIS PLACE AND ITS PEOPLE AFTER DAKEN LEFT.
I'M SORRY YOU DON'T LIKE IT, BUT I'VE DONE WHAT HAD TO BE DONE.
WHAT THE HELL ARE YOU TALKIN' ABOUT?! YOU COULD'A MADE A THOUSAND DIFFERENT CHOICES!
THESE ANIMALS ARE GONNA BE GONE! SPECIES WIPED OFF THE FACE OF THE EARTH SO SOME GREEDY OLD MEN CAN GET THEIR PECKERS HARD!
HOW CAN THAT NOT SCARE THE HELL OUTTA YOU?!
YOU KNOW WHAT SCARES ME, WOLVERINE?
TEN-YEAR-OLD GIRLS BEING TRADED FOR SEX. COUNTRIES STARVING BECAUSE OF RELIGIOUS WARS AND IMPERIALISM AND A FEW POWERFUL PEOPLE MAKING DECISIONS THAT AFFECT ENTIRE CONTINENTS!
YOUR HYPOCRICY IS MIND-BOGGLING. HOW MANY "HONOR" KILLINGS HAVE YOU COMMITTED? HOW MANY HAVE YOU MURDERED OUT OF PETTY REVENGE?
HOW MANY ANIMALS HAVE DIED AT YOUR HANDS TO SATIATE YOUR FERAL INSTINCTS--?!
I KILLED 'CAUSE I HAD TO! NEVER F'R MONEY OR LAND OR KICKS! AN' NEVER WITH THAT KINDA CRUELTY.
AND I WAS NEVER PROUD OF IT!
BUT YOU'RE SANCTIONING THE MASSACRE OF ENTIRE SPECIES OF CREATURES.
THEY'RE ANIMALS! THEY DON'T HAVE SOULS!
MOST PEOPLE THINK I'M NOTHING MORE THAN AN ANIMAL!

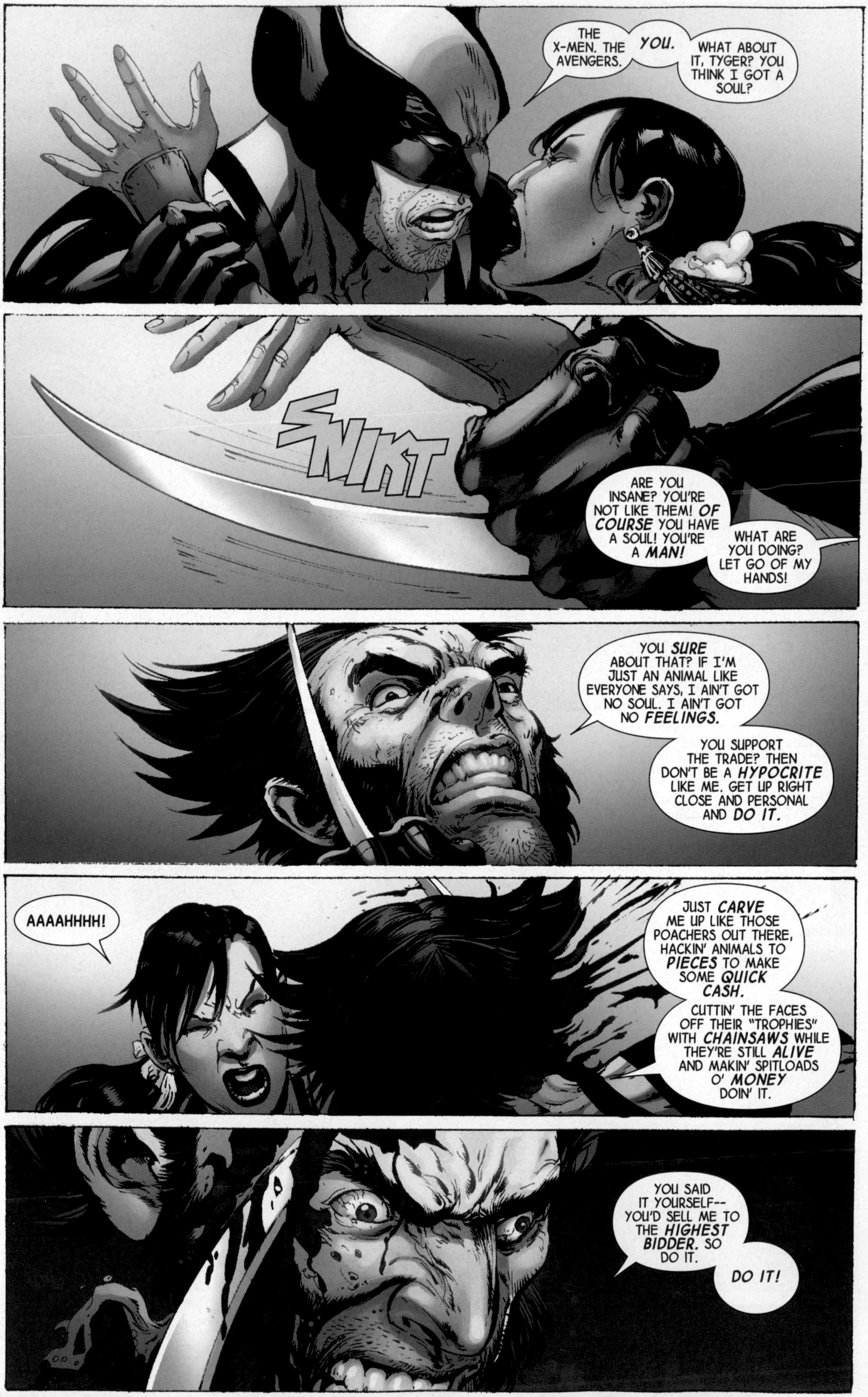
THE X-MEN. THE AVENGERS.
YOU.
WHAT ABOUT IT, TYGER? YOU THINK I GOT A SOUL?
SNIKT
ARE YOU INSANE? YOU'RE NOT LIKE THEM! OF COURSE YOU HAVE A SOUL! YOU'RE A MAN!
WHAT ARE YOU DOING? LET GO OF MY HANDS!
YOU SURE ABOUT THAT? IF I'M JUST AN ANIMAL LIKE EVERYONE SAYS, I AIN'T GOT NO SOUL. I AIN'T GOT NO FEELINGS.
YOU SUPPORT THE TRADE? THEN DON'T BE A HYPOCRITE LIKE ME. GET UP RIGHT CLOSE AND PERSONAL AND DO IT.
AAAAHHHH!
JUST CARVE ME UP LIKE THOSE POACHERS OUT THERE, HACKIN' ANIMALS TO PIECES TO MAKE SOME QUICK CASH.
CUTTIN' THE FACES OFF THEIR "TROPHIES" WITH CHAINSAWS WHILE THEY'RE STILL ALIVE AND MAKIN' SPITLOADS O' MONEY DOIN' IT.
YOU SAID IT YOURSELF-- YOU'D SELL ME TO THE HIGHEST BIDDER. SO DO IT.
DO IT!

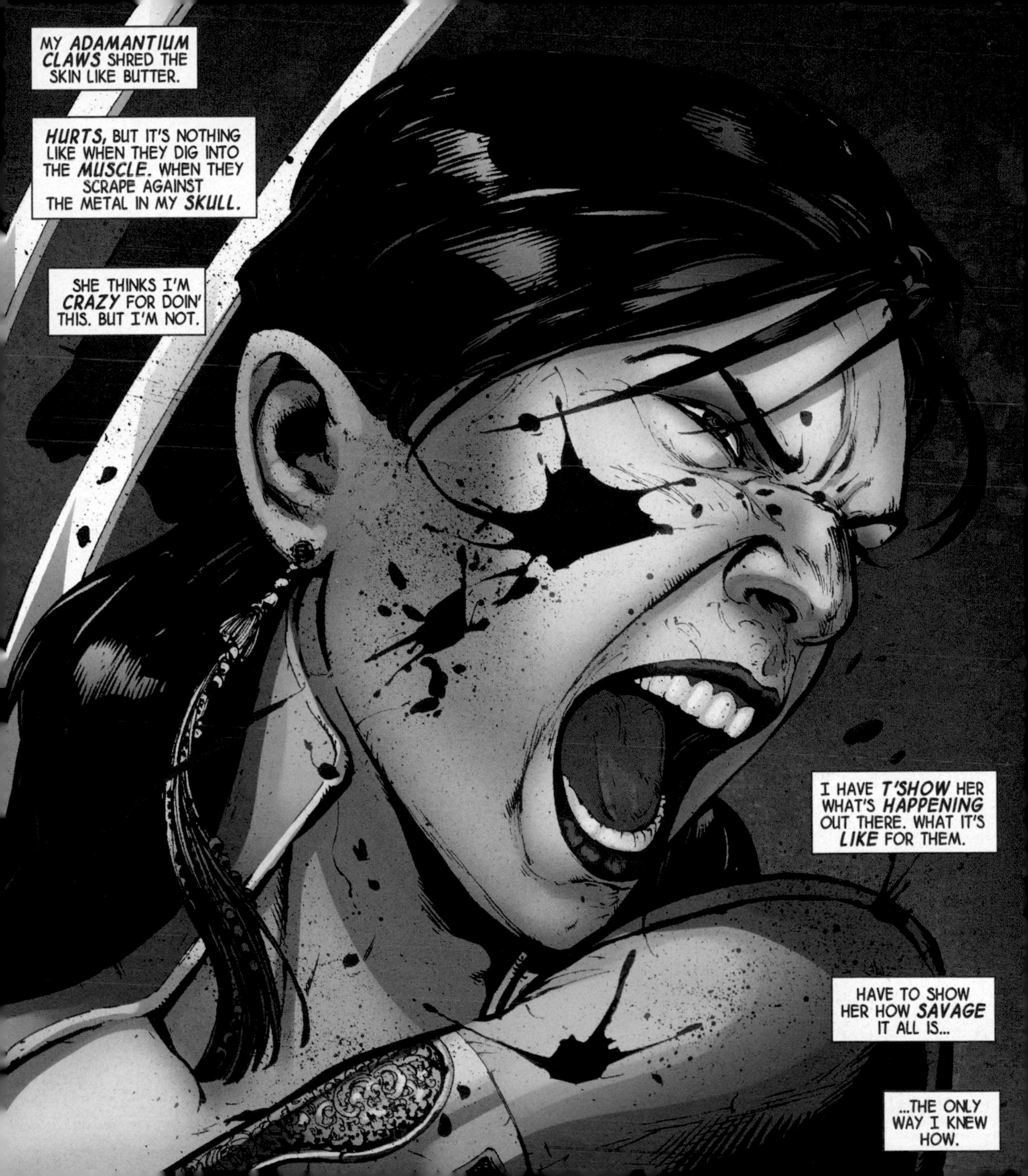
MY ADAMANTIUM CLAWS SHRED THE SKIN LIKE BUTTER.
HURTS, BUT IT'S NOTHING LIKE WHEN THEY DIG INTO THE MUSCLE. WHEN THEY SCRAPE AGAINST THE METAL IN MY SKULL.
SHE THINKS I'M CRAZY FOR DOIN' THIS. BUT I'M NOT.
I HAVE T'SHOW HER WHAT'S HAPPENING OUT THERE. WHAT IT'S LIKE FOR THEM.
HAVE TO SHOW HER HOW SAVAGE IT ALL IS...
...THE ONLY WAY I KNEW HOW.

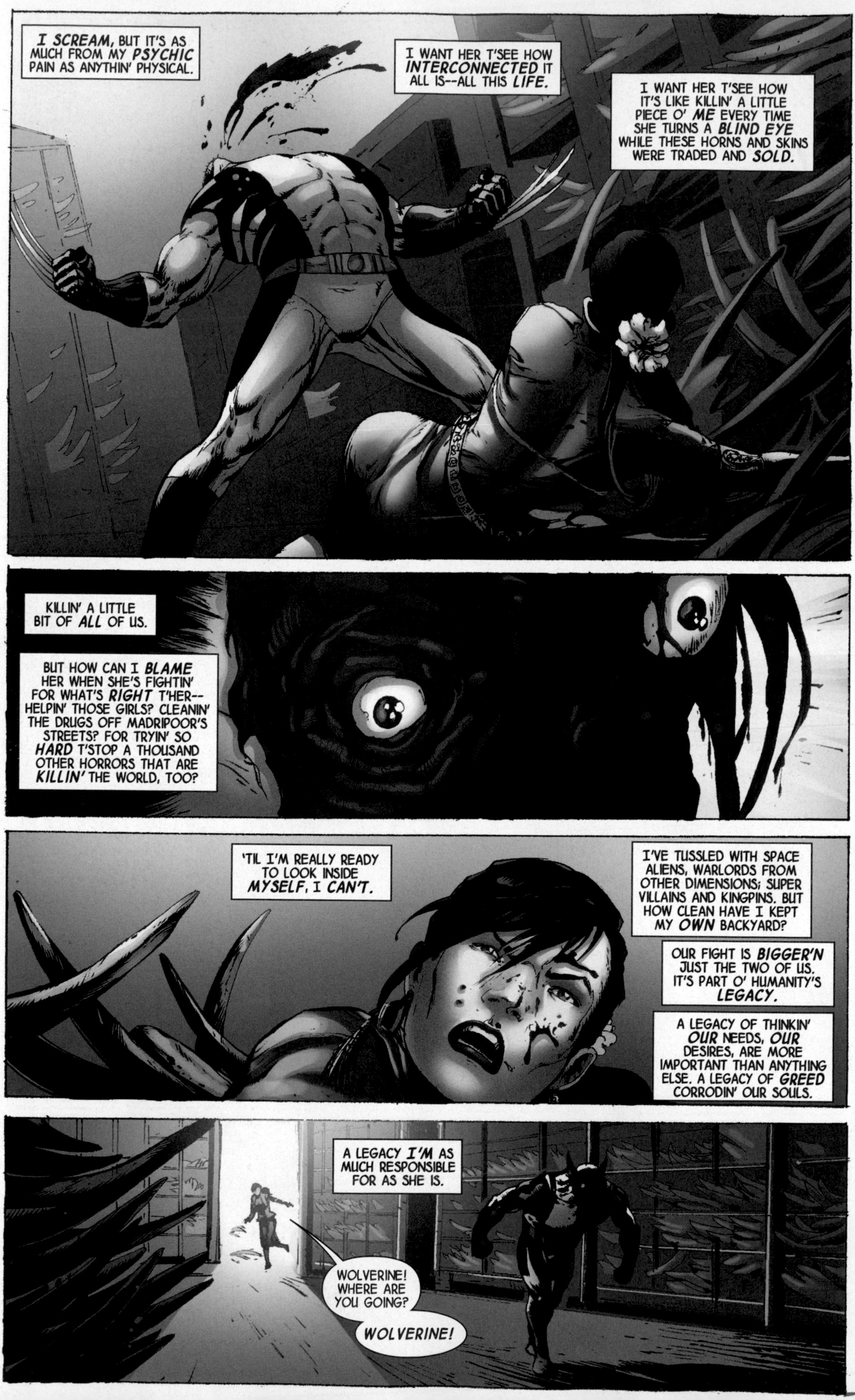
I SCREAM, BUT IT'S AS MUCH FROM MY PSYCHIC PAIN AS ANYTHIN' PHYSICAL.
I WANT HER T'SEE HOW INTERCONNECTED IT ALL IS--ALL THIS LIFE.
I WANT HER T'SEE HOW IT'S LIKE KILLIN' A LITTLE PIECE O' ME EVERY TIME SHE TURNS A BLIND EYE WHILE THESE HORNS AND SKINS WERE TRADED AND SOLD.
KILLIN' A LITTLE BIT OF ALL OF US.
BUT HOW CAN I BLAME HER WHEN SHE'S FIGHTIN' FOR WHAT'S RIGHT T'HER--HELPIN' THOSE GIRLS? CLEANIN' THE DRUGS OFF MADRIPOOR'S STREETS? FOR TRYIN' SO HARD T'STOP A THOUSAND OTHER HORRORS THAT ARE KILLIN' THE WORLD, TOO?
'TIL I'M REALLY READY TO LOOK INSIDE MYSELF, I CAN'T.
I'VE TUSSLED WITH SPACE ALIENS, WARLORDS FROM OTHER DIMENSIONS; SUPER VILLAINS AND KINGPINS. BUT HOW CLEAN HAVE I KEPT MY OWN BACKYARD?
OUR FIGHT IS BIGGER'N JUST THE TWO OF US. IT'S PART O' HUMANITY'S LEGACY.
A LEGACY OF THINKIN' OUR NEEDS, OUR DESIRES, ARE MORE IMPORTANT THAN ANYTHING ELSE. A LEGACY OF GREED CORRODIN' OUR SOULS.
A LEGACY I'M AS MUCH RESPONSIBLE FOR AS SHE IS.
WOLVERINE! WHERE ARE YOU GOING?
WOLVERINE!

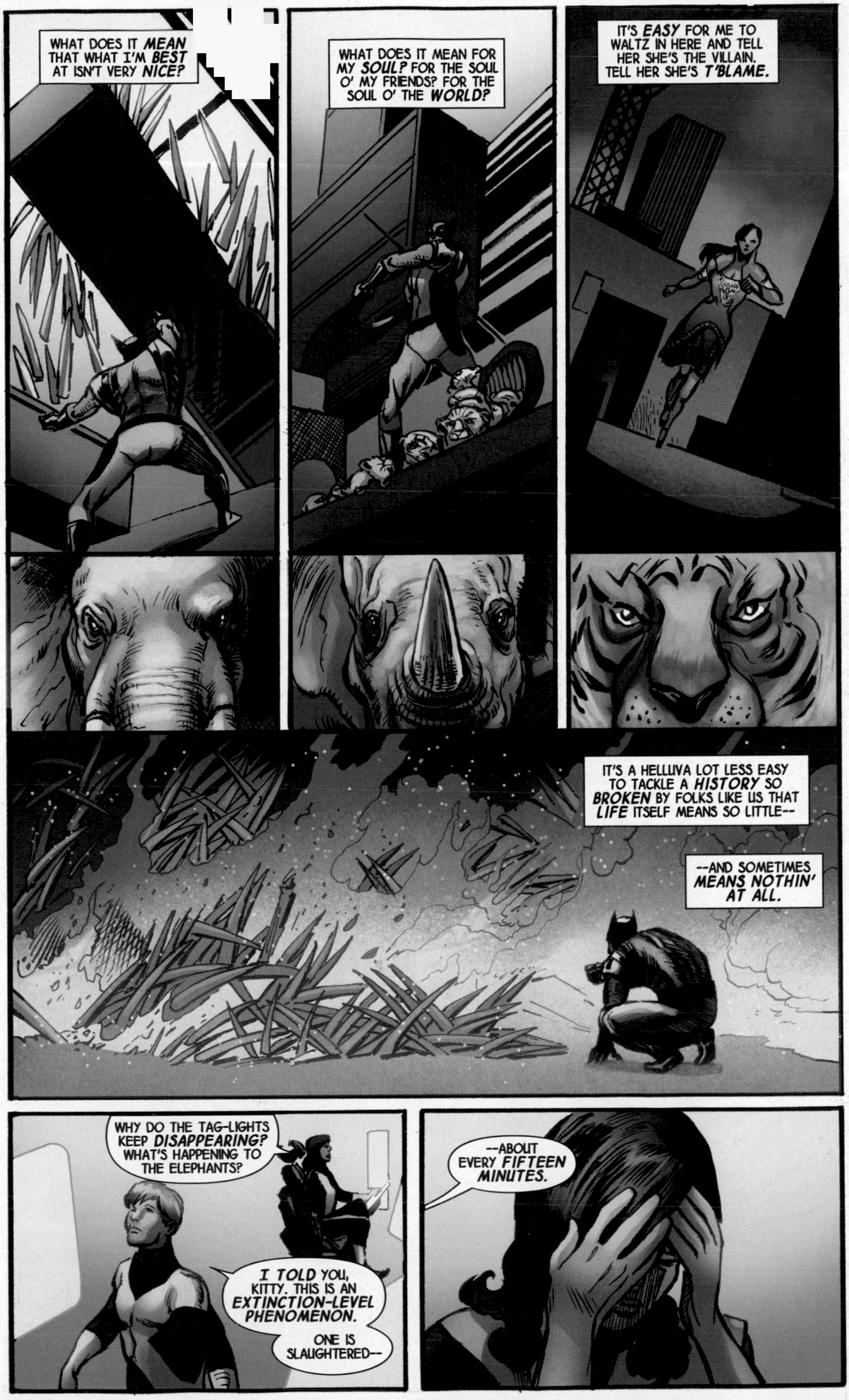

WHAT DOES IT MEAN THAT WHAT I'M BEST AT ISN'T VERY NICE?
WHAT DOES IT MEAN FOR MY SOUL? FOR THE SOUL O' MY FRIENDS? FOR THE SOUL O' THE WORLD?
IT'S EASY FOR ME TO WALTZ IN HERE AND TELL HER SHE'S THE VILLAIN. TELL HER SHE'S T'BLAME.
IT'S A HELLUVA LOT LESS EASY TO TACKLE A HISTORY SO BROKEN BY FOLKS LIKE US THAT LIFE ITSELF MEANS SO LITTLE--
--AND SOMETIMES MEANS NOTHIN' AT ALL.
WHY DO THE TAG-LIGHTS KEEP DISAPPEARING? WHAT'S HAPPENING TO THE ELEPHANTS?
I TOLD YOU, KITTY. THIS IS AN EXTINCTION-LEVEL PHENOMENON.
ONE IS SLAUGHTERED--
--ABOUT EVERY FIFTEEN MINUTES.

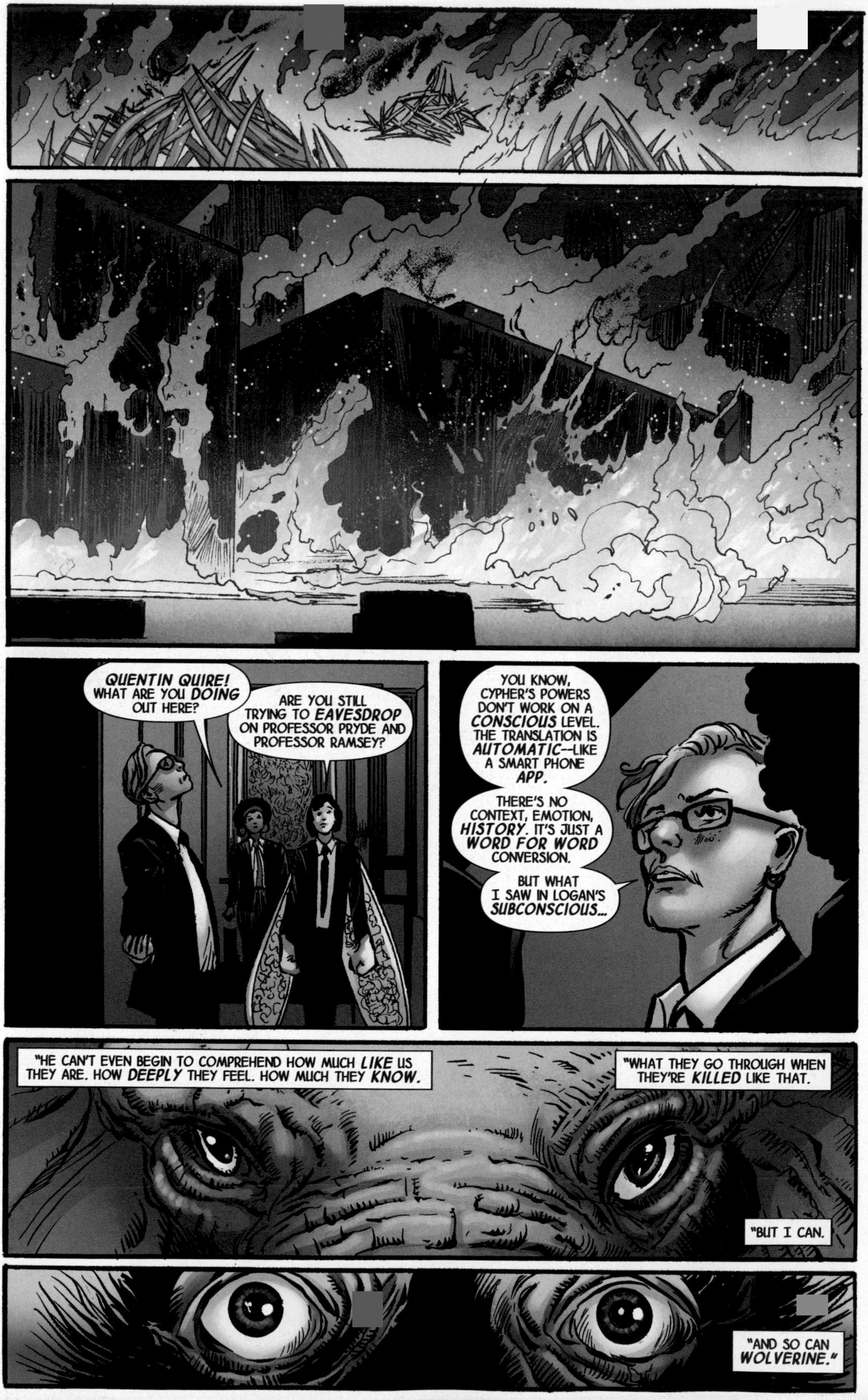
QUENTIN QUIRE! WHAT ARE YOU DOING OUT HERE?
ARE YOU STILL TRYING TO EAVESDROP ON PROFESSOR PRYDE AND PROFESSOR RAMSEY?
YOU KNOW, CYPHER'S POWERS DON'T WORK ON A CONSCIOUS LEVEL. THE TRANSLATION IS AUTOMATIC--LIKE A SMART PHONE APP.
THERE'S NO CONTEXT, EMOTION, HISTORY. IT'S JUST A WORD FOR WORD CONVERSION.
BUT WHAT I SAW IN LOGAN'S SUBCONSCIOUS...
"HE CAN'T EVEN BEGIN TO COMPREHEND HOW MUCH LIKE US THEY ARE. HOW DEEPLY THEY FEEL. HOW MUCH THEY KNOW.
"WHAT THEY GO THROUGH WHEN THEY'RE KILLED LIKE THAT.
"BUT I CAN.
"AND SO CAN WOLVERINE."

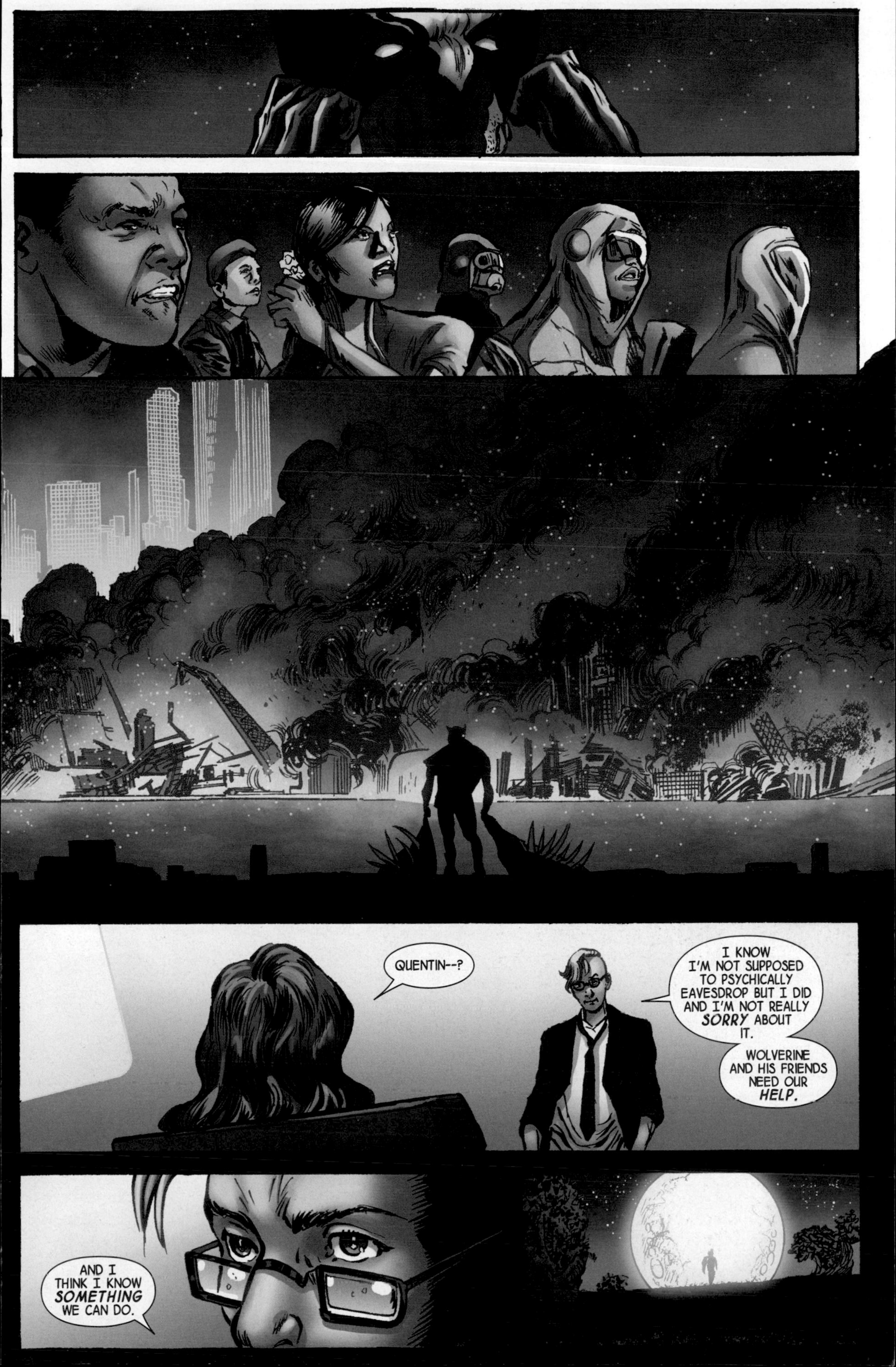
QUENTIN--?
I KNOW I'M NOT SUPPOSED TO PSYCHICALLY EAVESDROP BUT I DID AND I'M NOT REALLY SORRY ABOUT IT.
WOLVERINE AND HIS FRIENDS NEED OUR HELP.
AND I THINK I KNOW SOMETHING WE CAN DO.

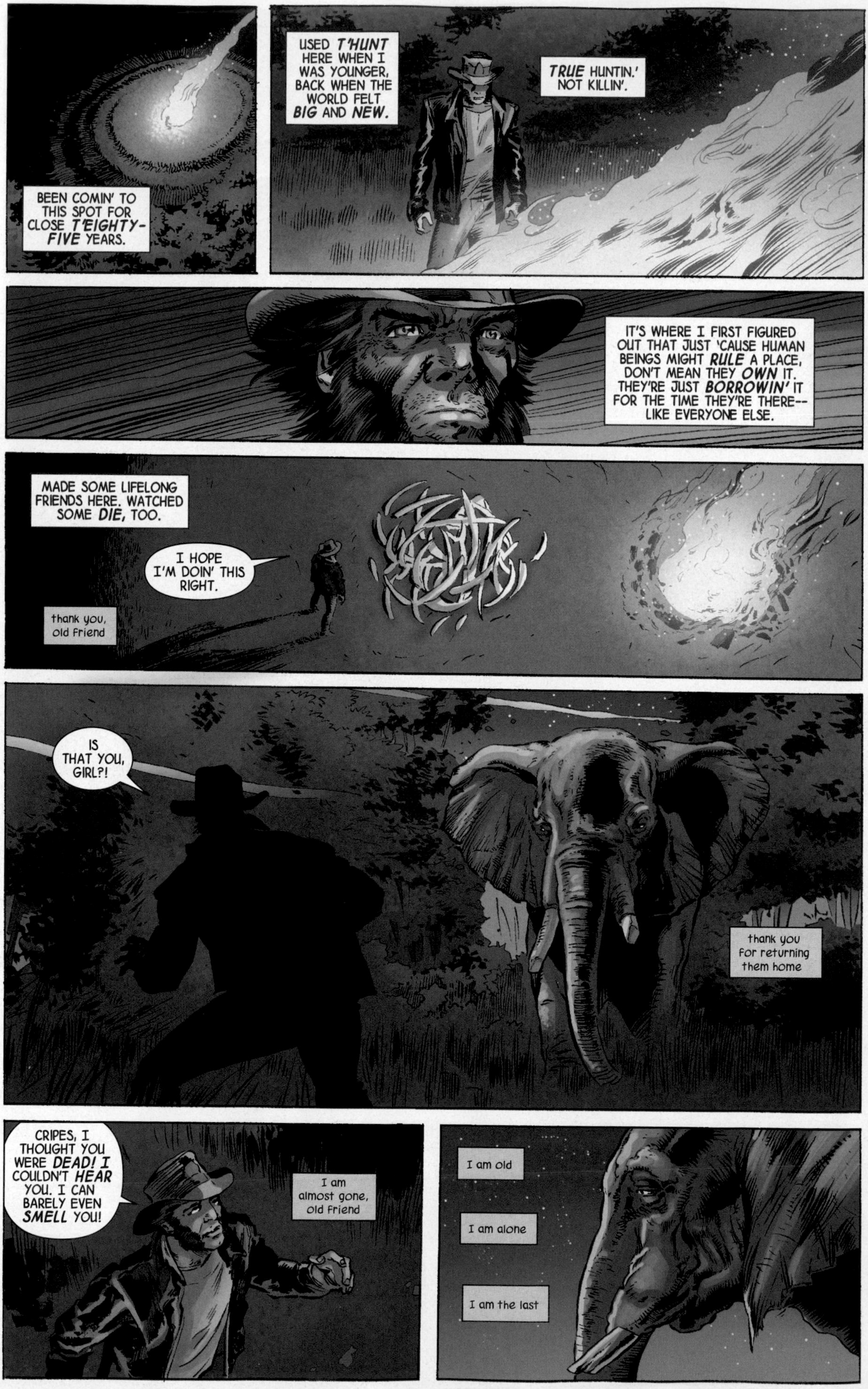
BEEN COMIN' TO THIS SPOT FOR CLOSE T'EIGHTY-FIVE YEARS.
USED T'HUNT HERE WHEN I WAS YOUNGER, BACK WHEN THE WORLD FELT BIG AND NEW.
TRUE HUNTIN.' NOT KILLIN'.
IT'S WHERE I FIRST FIGURED OUT THAT JUST 'CAUSE HUMAN BEINGS MIGHT RULE A PLACE, DON'T MEAN THEY OWN IT. THEY'RE JUST BORROWIN' IT FOR THE TIME THEY'RE THERE--LIKE EVERYONE ELSE.
MADE SOME LIFELONG FRIENDS HERE. WATCHED SOME DIE, TOO.
I HOPE I'M DOIN' THIS RIGHT.
thank you, old friend
IS THAT YOU, GIRL?!
thank you for returning them home
CRIPES, I THOUGHT YOU WERE DEAD! I COULDN'T HEAR YOU. I CAN BARELY EVEN SMELL YOU!
I am almost gone, old friend
I am old
I am alone
I am the last

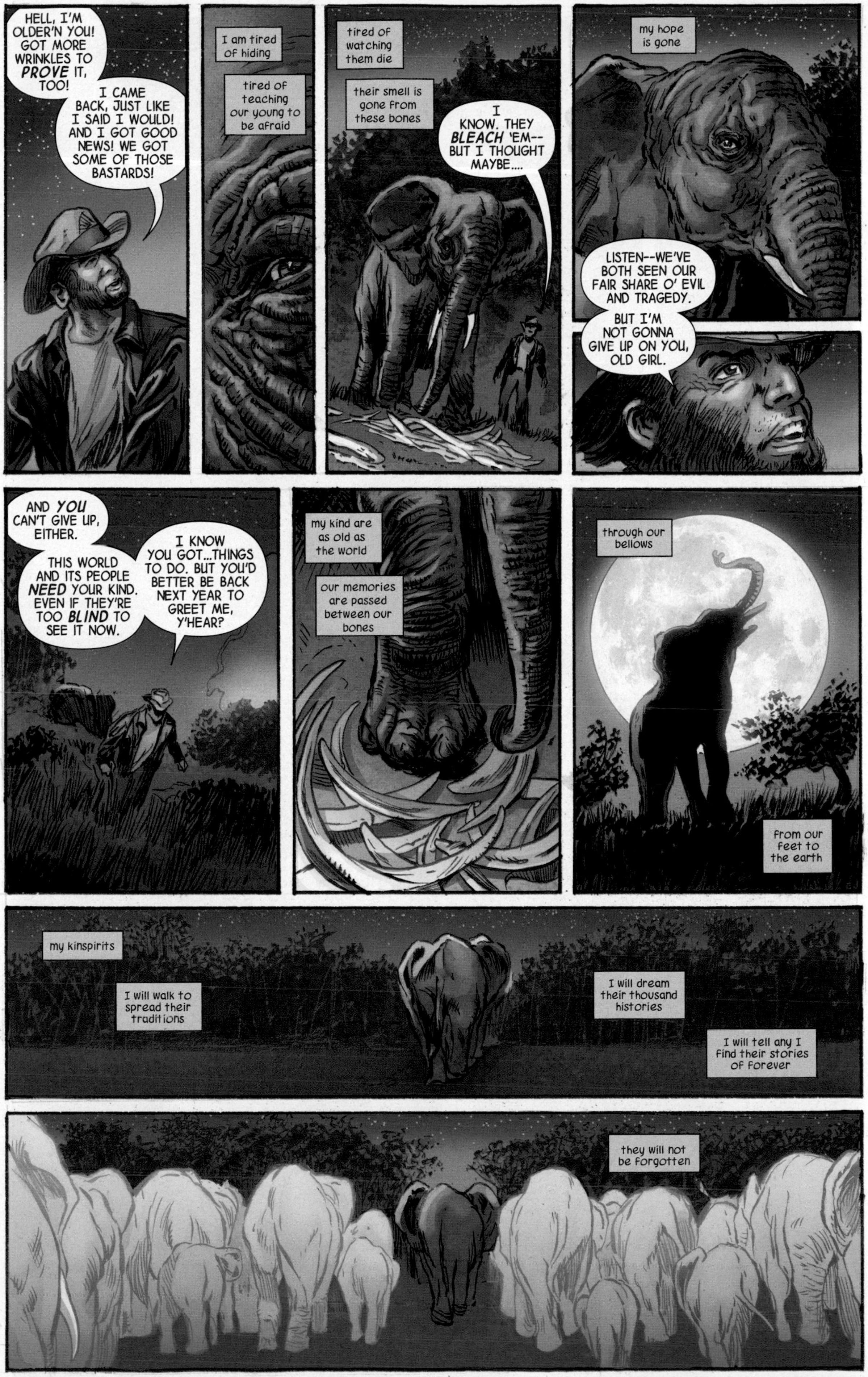

HELL, I'M OLDER'N YOU! GOT MORE WRINKLES TO PROVE IT, TOO!
I CAME BACK, JUST LIKE I SAID I WOULD! AND I GOT GOOD NEWS! WE GOT SOME OF THOSE BASTARDS!
I am tired of hiding
tired of teaching our young to be afraid
tired of watching them die
their smell is gone from these bones
I KNOW. THEY BLEACH 'EM-- BUT I THOUGHT MAYBE....
my hope is gone
LISTEN--WE'VE BOTH SEEN OUR FAIR SHARE O' EVIL AND TRAGEDY.
BUT I'M NOT GONNA GIVE UP ON YOU, OLD GIRL.
AND YOU CAN'T GIVE UP, EITHER.
THIS WORLD AND ITS PEOPLE NEED YOUR KIND. EVEN IF THEY'RE TOO BLIND TO SEE IT NOW.
I KNOW YOU GOT...THINGS TO DO. BUT YOU'D BETTER BE BACK NEXT YEAR TO GREET ME, Y'HEAR?
my kind are as old as the world
our memories are passed between our bones
through our bellows
from our feet to the earth
my kinspirits
I will walk to spread their traditions
I will dream their thousand histories
I will tell any I find their stories of forever
they will not be forgotten

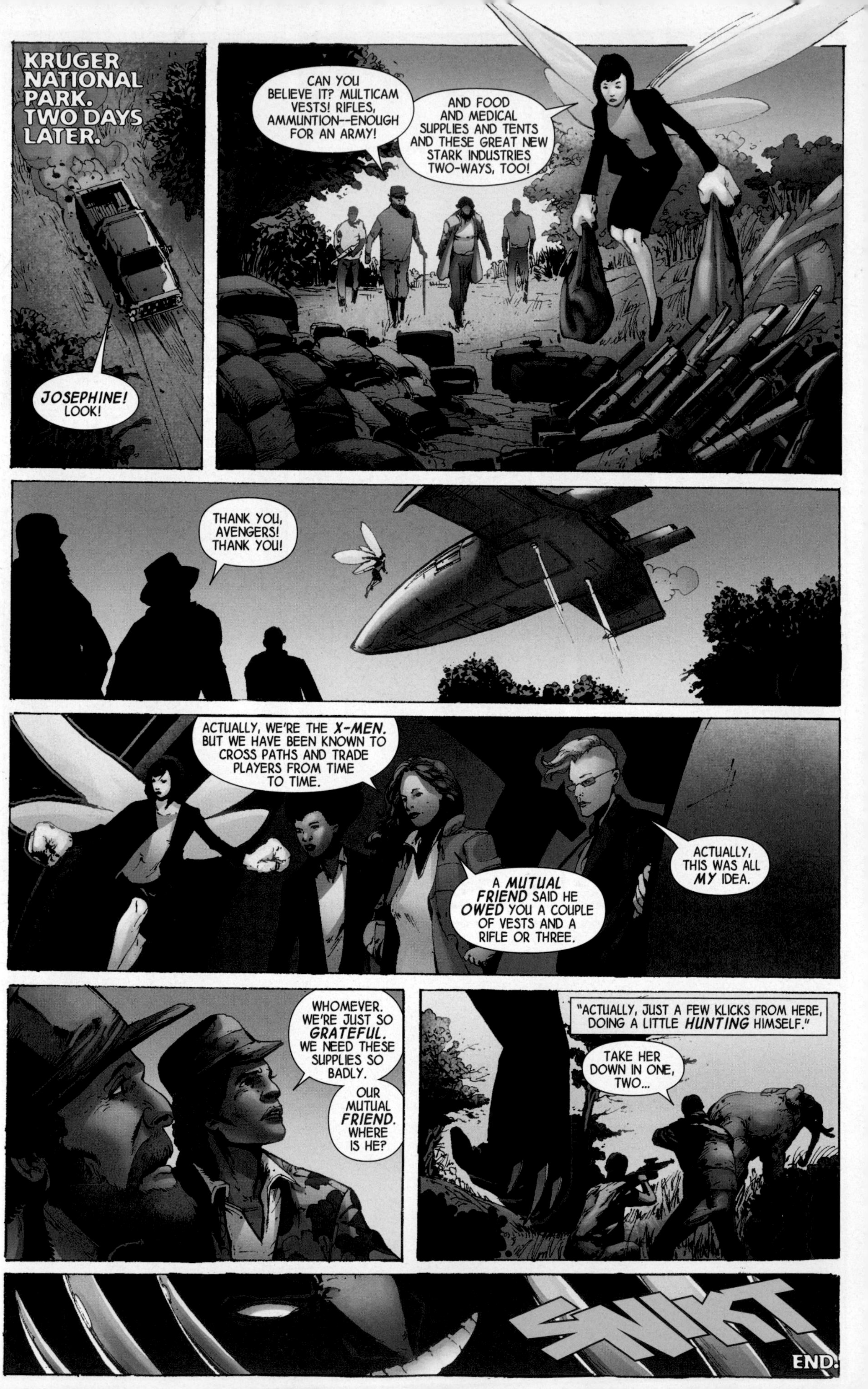
KRUGER NATIONAL PARK. TWO DAYS LATER.
JOSEPHINE! LOOK!
CAN YOU BELIEVE IT? MULTICAM VESTS! RIFLES, AMMUNTION--ENOUGH FOR AN ARMY!
AND FOOD AND MEDICAL SUPPLIES AND TENTS AND THESE GREAT NEW STARK INDUSTRIES TWO-WAYS, TOO!
THANK YOU, AVENGERS! THANK YOU!
ACTUALLY, WE'RE THE X-MEN. BUT WE HAVE BEEN KNOWN TO CROSS PATHS AND TRADE PLAYERS FROM TIME TO TIME.
A MUTUAL FRIEND SAID HE OWED YOU A COUPLE OF VESTS AND A RIFLE OR THREE.
ACTUALLY, THIS WAS ALL MY IDEA.
WHOMEVER. WE'RE JUST SO GRATEFUL. WE NEED THESE SUPPLIES SO BADLY.
OUR MUTUAL FRIEND. WHERE IS HE?
"ACTUALLY, JUST A FEW KLICKS FROM HERE, DOING A LITTLE HUNTING HIMSELF."
TAKE HER DOWN IN ONE, TWO...
SNIKT
END.

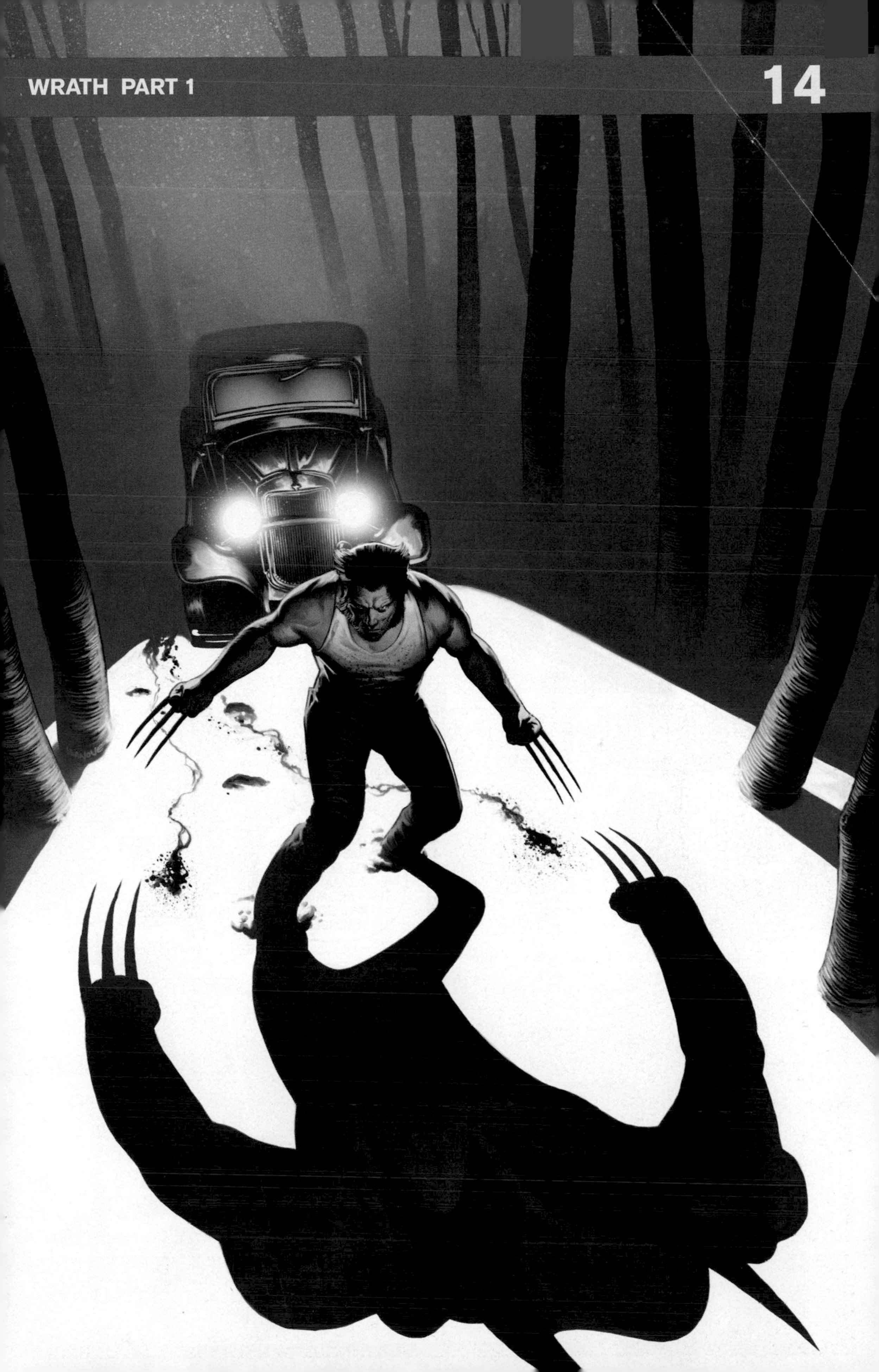
WRATH PART 1
14

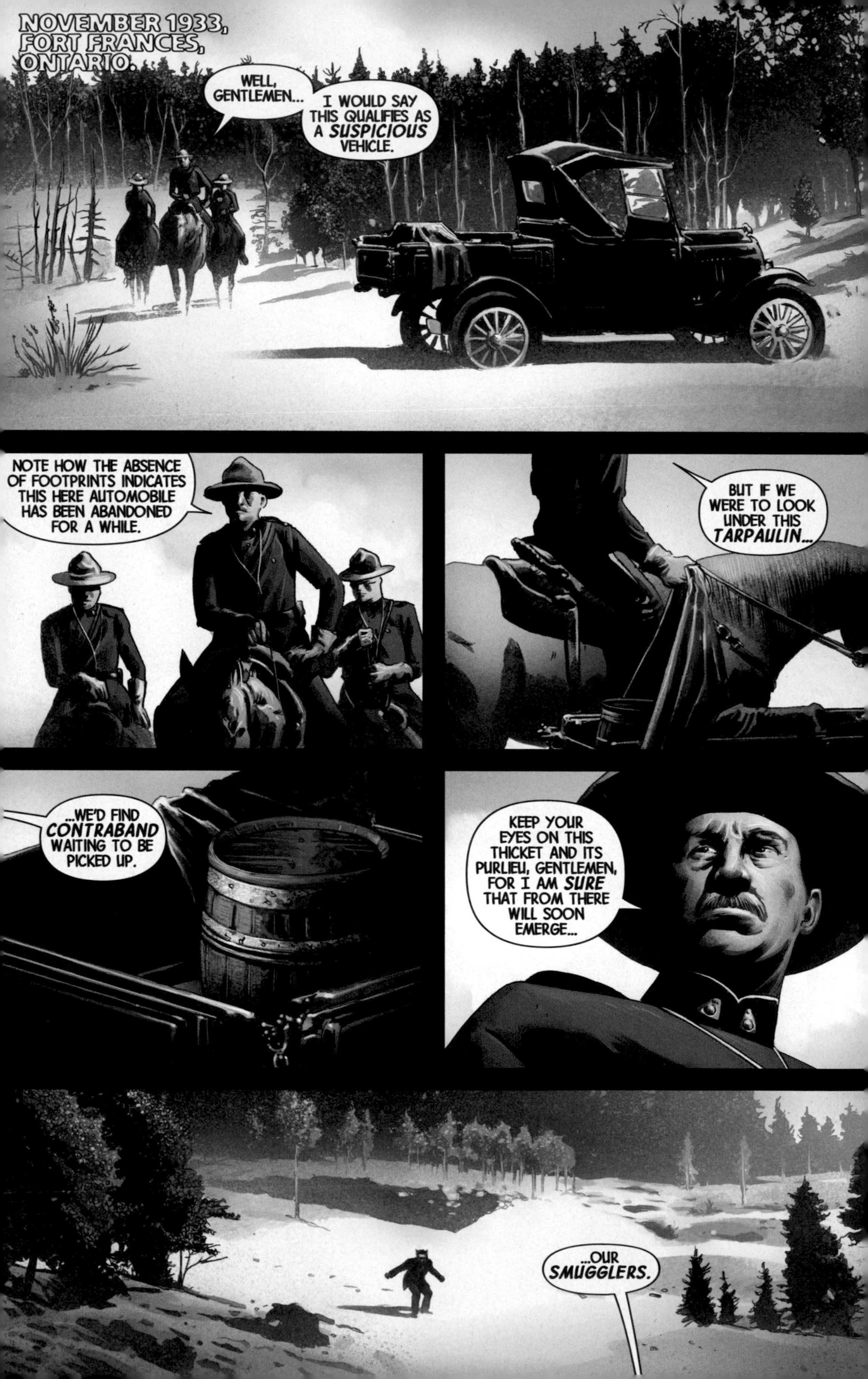
NOVEMBER 1933, FORT FRANCES, ONTARIO.
WELL, GENTLEMEN...
I WOULD SAY THIS QUALIFIES AS A SUSPICIOUS VEHICLE.
NOTE HOW THE ABSENCE OF FOOTPRINTS INDICATES THIS HERE AUTOMOBILE HAS BEEN ABANDONED FOR A WHILE.
BUT IF WE WERE TO LOOK UNDER THIS TARPAULIN...
...WE'D FIND CONTRABAND WAITING TO BE PICKED UP.
KEEP YOUR EYES ON THIS THICKET AND ITS PURLIEU, GENTLEMEN, FOR I AM SURE THAT FROM THERE WILL SOON EMERGE...
...OUR SMUGGLERS.

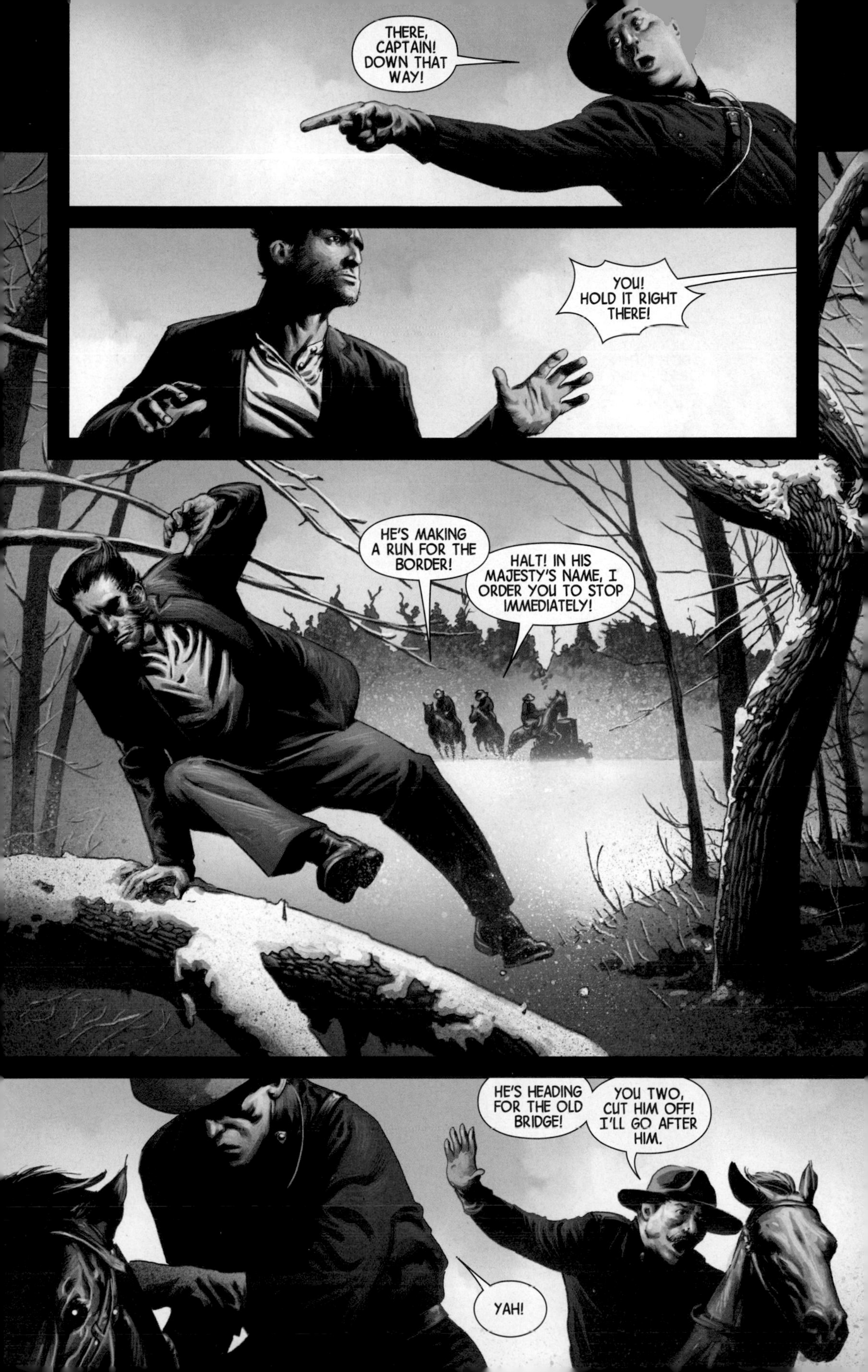
THERE, CAPTAIN! DOWN THAT WAY!
YOU! HOLD IT RIGHT THERE!
HE'S MAKING A RUN FOR THE BORDER!
HALT! IN HIS MAJESTY'S NAME, I ORDER YOU TO STOP IMMEDIATELY!
HE'S HEADING FOR THE OLD BRIDGE!
YOU TWO, CUT HIM OFF! I'LL GO AFTER HIM.
YAH!

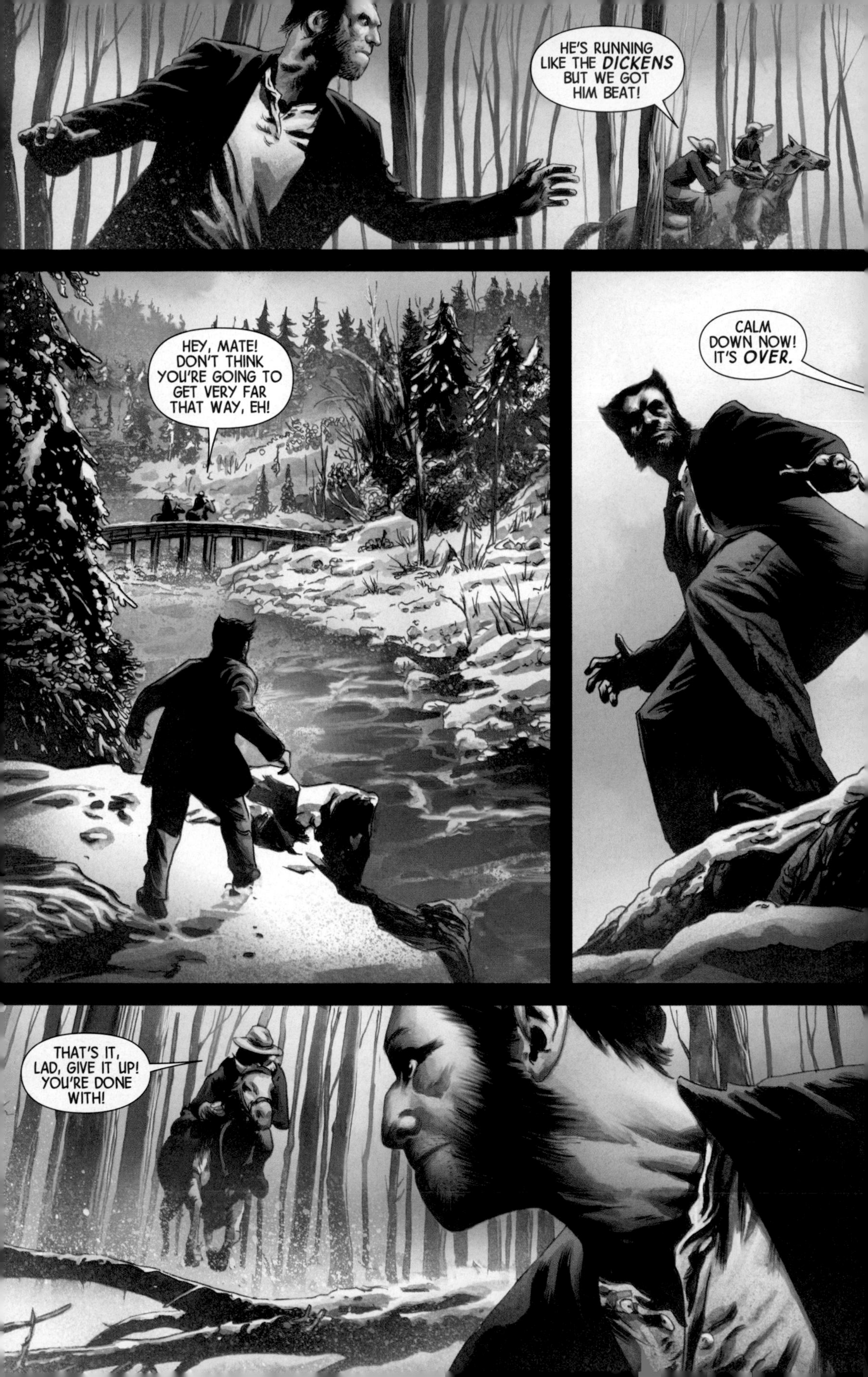
HE'S RUNNING LIKE THE DICKENS BUT WE GOT HIM BEAT!
HEY, MATE! DON'T THINK YOU'RE GOING TO GET VERY FAR THAT WAY, EH!
CALM DOWN NOW! IT'S OVER.
THAT'S IT, LAD, GIVE IT UP! YOU'RE DONE WITH!

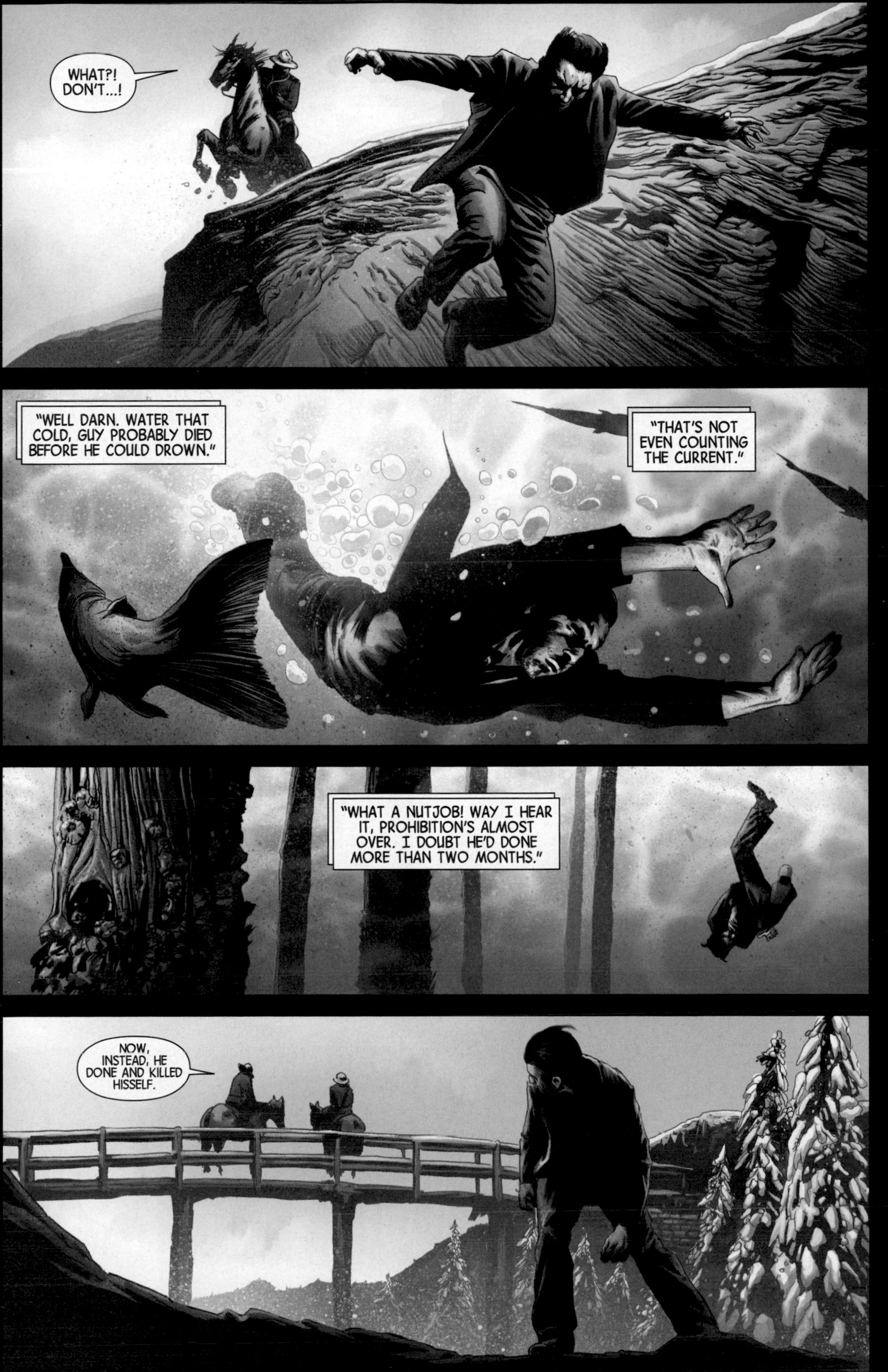
WHAT?! DON'T...!
"WELL DARN. WATER THAT COLD, GUY PROBABLY DIED BEFORE HE COULD DROWN."
"THAT'S NOT EVEN COUNTING THE CURRENT."
"WHAT A NUTJOB! WAY I HEAR IT, PROHIBITION'S ALMOST OVER. I DOUBT HE'D DONE MORE THAN TWO MONTHS."
NOW, INSTEAD, HE DONE AND KILLED HISSELF.

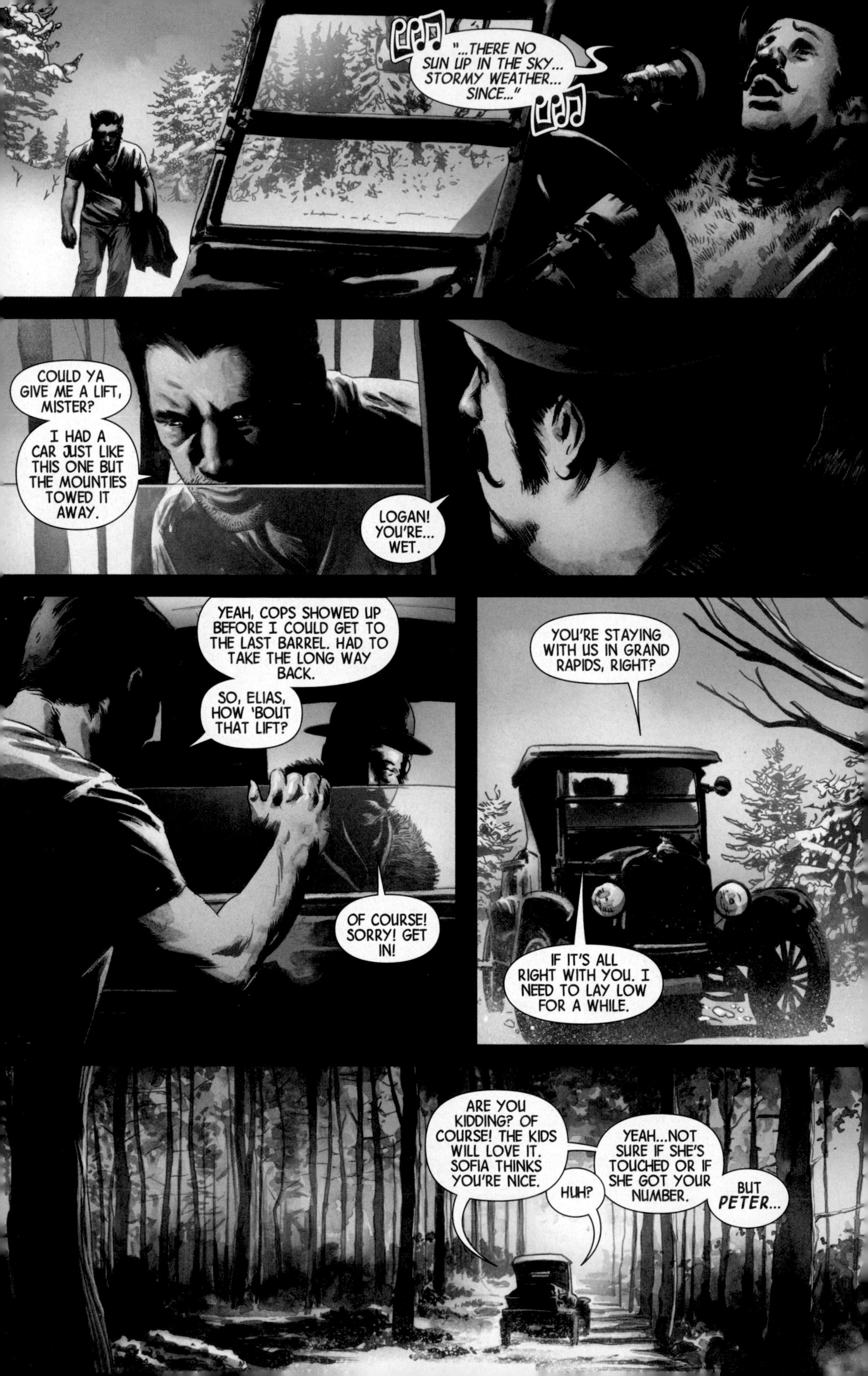

"...THERE NO SUN UP IN THE SKY... STORMY WEATHER... SINCE..."
COULD YA GIVE ME A LIFT, MISTER?
I HAD A CAR JUST LIKE THIS ONE BUT THE MOUNTIES TOWED IT AWAY.
LOGAN! YOU'RE... WET.
YEAH, COPS SHOWED UP BEFORE I COULD GET TO THE LAST BARREL. HAD TO TAKE THE LONG WAY BACK.
SO, ELIAS, HOW 'BOUT THAT LIFT?
OF COURSE! SORRY! GET IN!
YOU'RE STAYING WITH US IN GRAND RAPIDS, RIGHT?
IF IT'S ALL RIGHT WITH YOU. I NEED TO LAY LOW FOR A WHILE.
ARE YOU KIDDING? OF COURSE! THE KIDS WILL LOVE IT. SOFIA THINKS YOU'RE NICE.
HUH?
YEAH...NOT SURE IF SHE'S TOUCHED OR IF SHE GOT YOUR NUMBER.
BUT *PETER*...

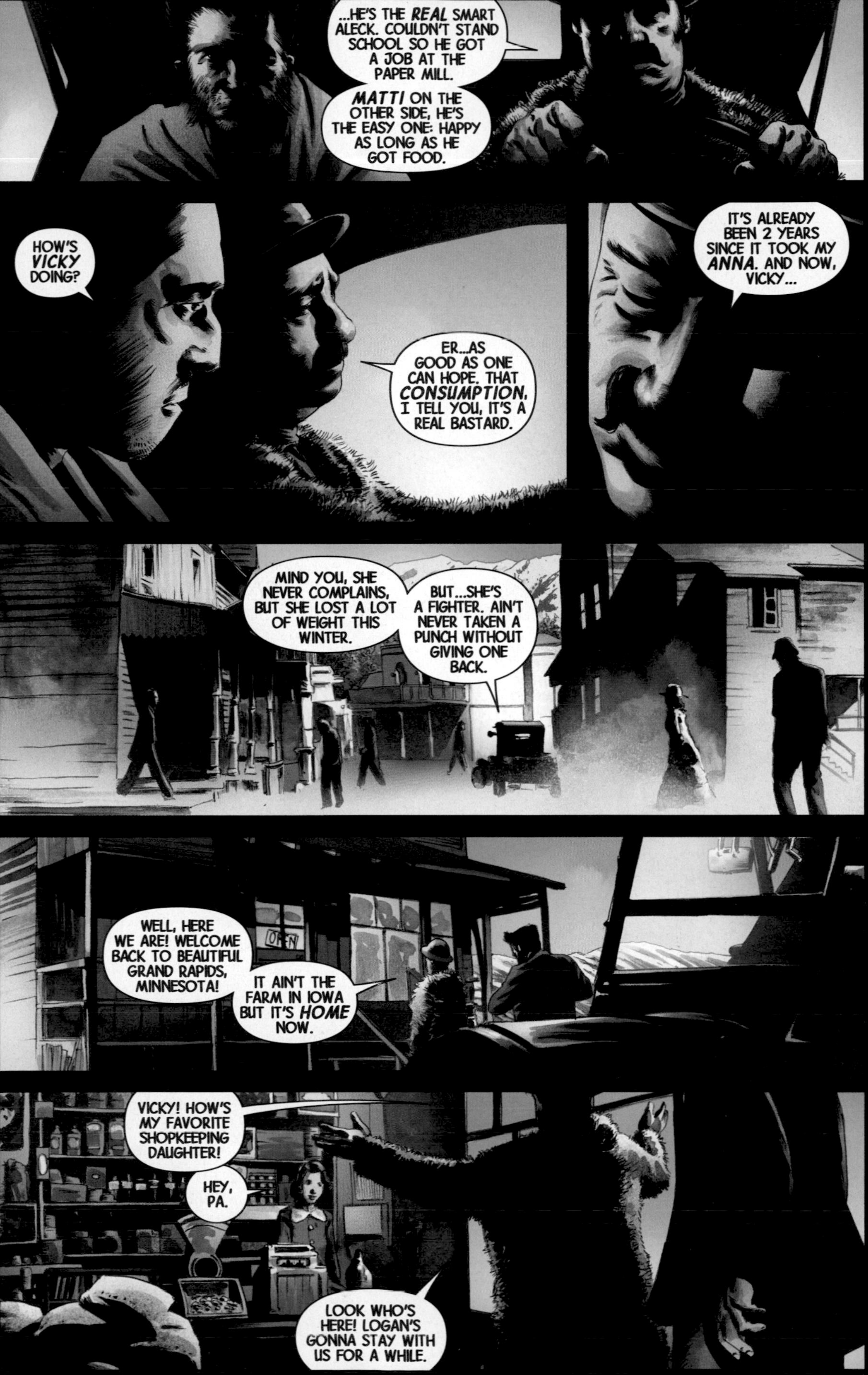
...HE'S THE REAL SMART ALECK. COULDN'T STAND SCHOOL SO HE GOT A JOB AT THE PAPER MILL.
MATT! ON THE OTHER SIDE, HE'S THE EASY ONE: HAPPY AS LONG AS HE GOT FOOD.
HOW'S VICKY DOING?
ER...AS GOOD AS ONE CAN HOPE. THAT CONSUMPTION, I TELL YOU, IT'S A REAL BASTARD.
IT'S ALREADY BEEN 2 YEARS SINCE IT TOOK MY ANNA. AND NOW, VICKY...
MIND YOU, SHE NEVER COMPLAINS, BUT SHE LOST A LOT OF WEIGHT THIS WINTER.
BUT...SHE'S A FIGHTER. AIN'T NEVER TAKEN A PUNCH WITHOUT GIVING ONE BACK.
WELL, HERE WE ARE! WELCOME BACK TO BEAUTIFUL GRAND RAPIDS, MINNESOTA!
IT AIN'T THE FARM IN IOWA BUT IT'S HOME NOW.
OPEN
VICKY! HOW'S MY FAVORITE SHOPKEEPING DAUGHTER!
HEY, PA.
LOOK WHO'S HERE! LOGAN'S GONNA STAY WITH US FOR A WHILE.

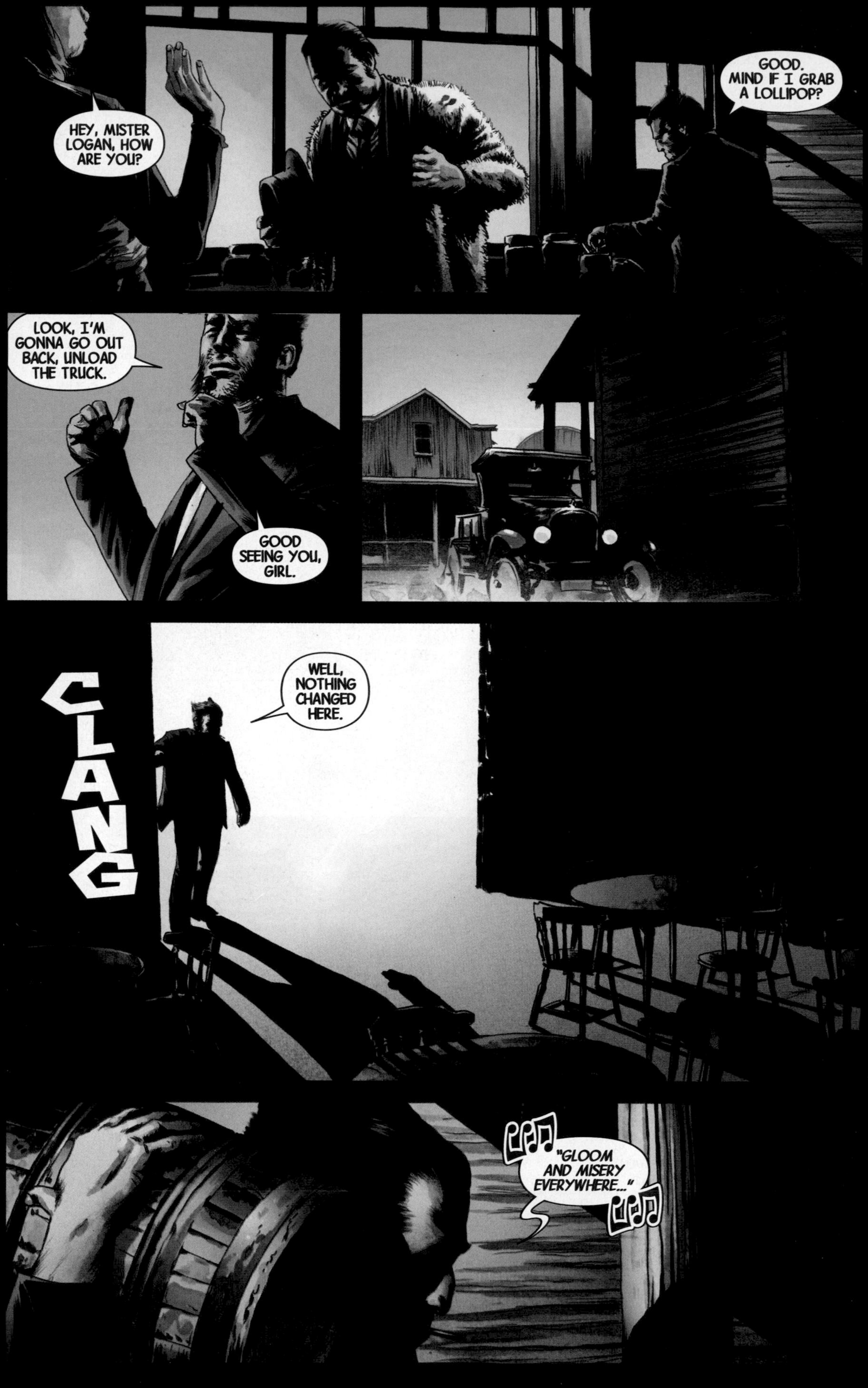
HEY, MISTER LOGAN, HOW ARE YOU?
GOOD. MIND IF I GRAB A LOLLIPOP?
LOOK, I'M GONNA GO OUT BACK, UNLOAD THE TRUCK.
GOOD SEEING YOU, GIRL.
CLANG
WELL, NOTHING CHANGED HERE.
"GLOOM AND MISERY EVERYWHERE..."

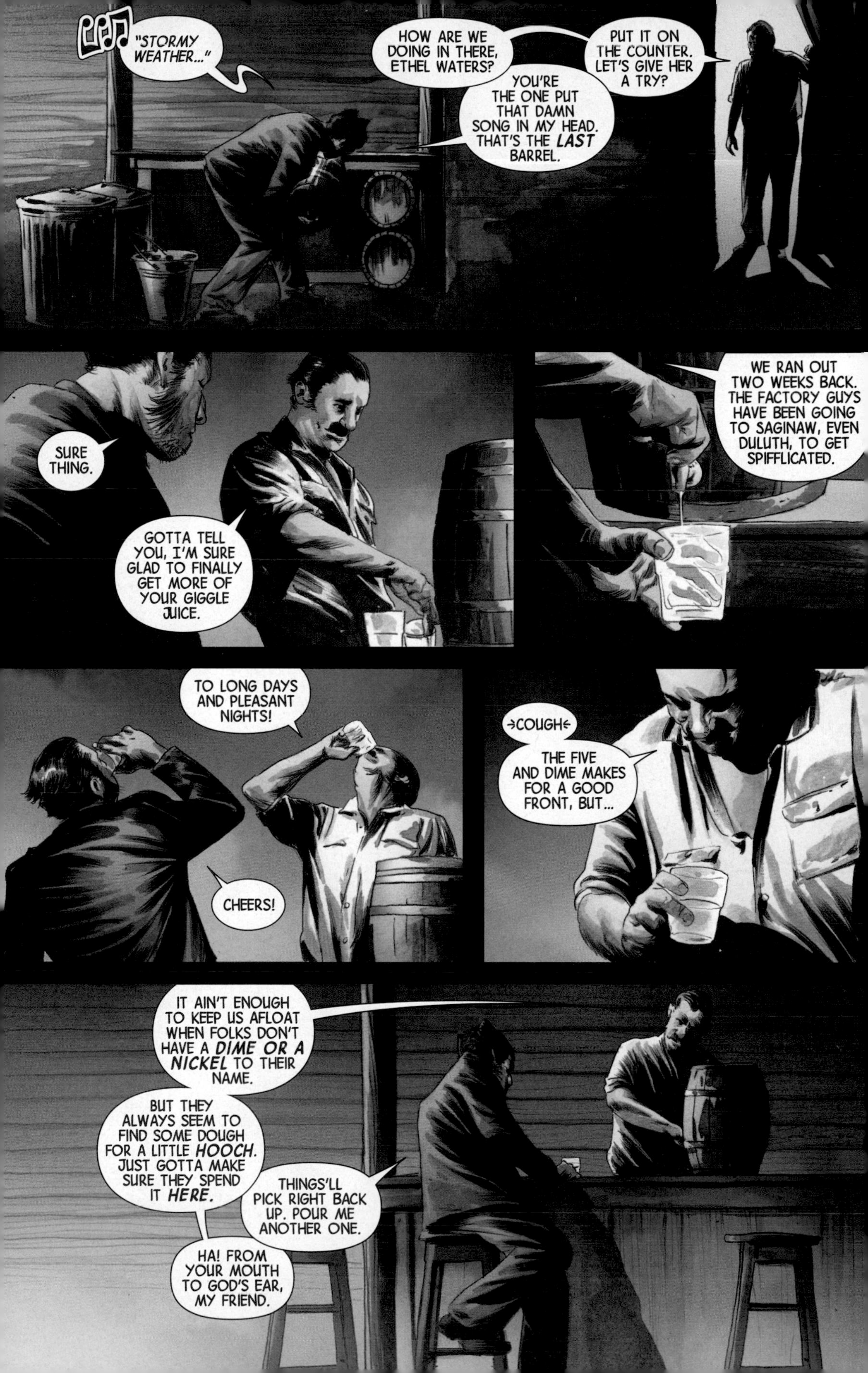
"STORMY WEATHER..."
HOW ARE WE DOING IN THERE, ETHEL WATERS?
PUT IT ON THE COUNTER. LET'S GIVE HER A TRY?
YOU'RE THE ONE PUT THAT DAMN SONG IN MY HEAD. THAT'S THE *LAST* BARREL.
SURE THING.
GOTTA TELL YOU, I'M SURE GLAD TO FINALLY GET MORE OF YOUR GIGGLE JUICE.
WE RAN OUT TWO WEEKS BACK. THE FACTORY GUYS HAVE BEEN GOING TO SAGINAW, EVEN DULUTH, TO GET SPIFFLICATED.
TO LONG DAYS AND PLEASANT NIGHTS!
CHEERS!
COUGH
THE FIVE AND DIME MAKES FOR A GOOD FRONT, BUT...
IT AIN'T ENOUGH TO KEEP US AFLOAT WHEN FOLKS DON'T HAVE A *DIME OR A NICKEL* TO THEIR NAME.
BUT THEY ALWAYS SEEM TO FIND SOME DOUGH FOR A LITTLE *HOOCH*. JUST GOTTA MAKE SURE THEY SPEND IT *HERE.*
THINGS'LL PICK RIGHT BACK UP. POUR ME ANOTHER ONE.
HA! FROM YOUR MOUTH TO GOD'S EAR, MY FRIEND.

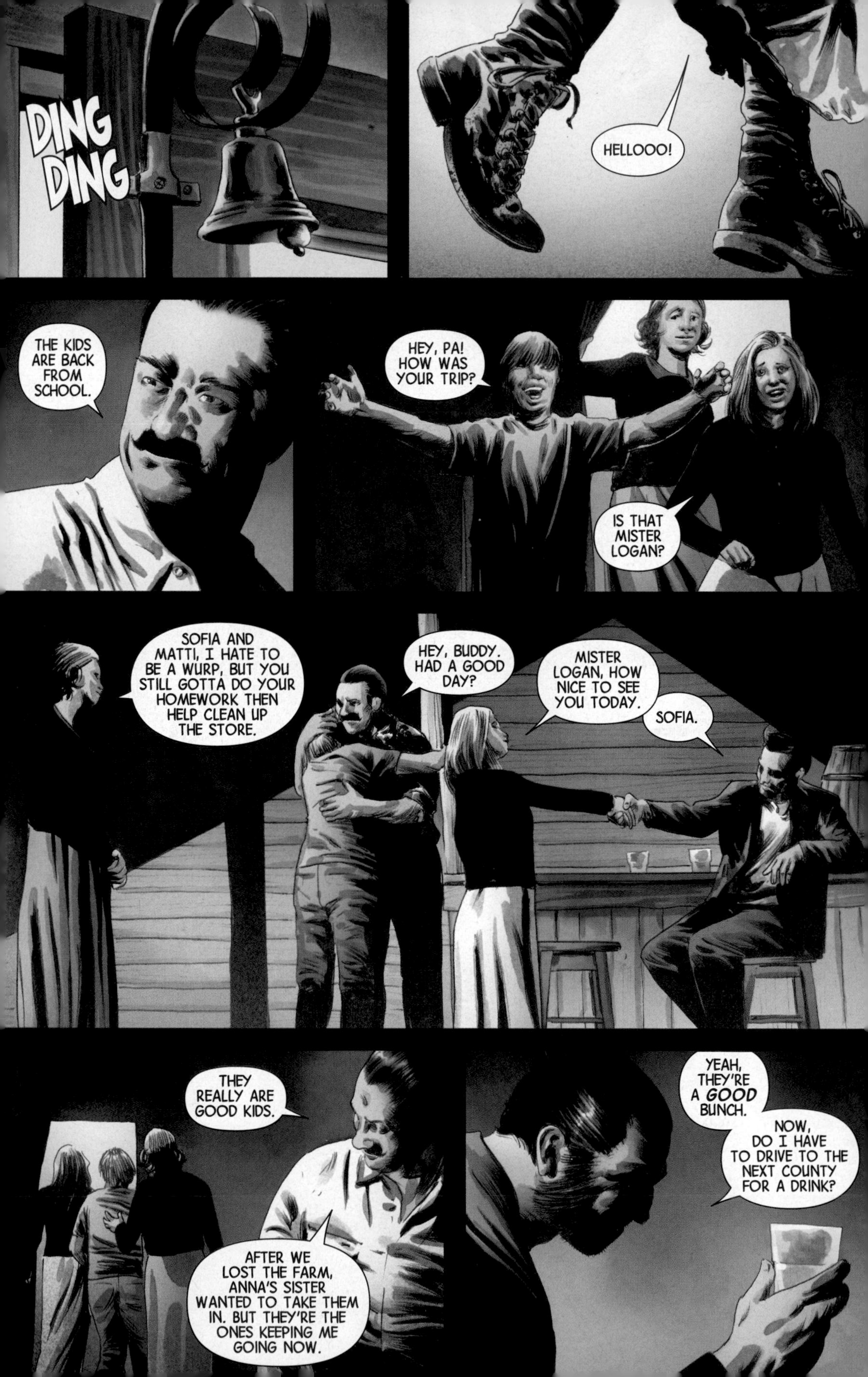
DING DING
HELLOOO!
THE KIDS ARE BACK FROM SCHOOL.
HEY, PA! HOW WAS YOUR TRIP?
IS THAT MISTER LOGAN?
SOFIA AND MATTI, I HATE TO BE A WURP, BUT YOU STILL GOTTA DO YOUR HOMEWORK THEN HELP CLEAN UP THE STORE.
HEY, BUDDY. HAD A GOOD DAY?
MISTER LOGAN, HOW NICE TO SEE YOU TODAY.
SOFIA.
THEY REALLY ARE GOOD KIDS.
AFTER WE LOST THE FARM, ANNA'S SISTER WANTED TO TAKE THEM IN. BUT THEY'RE THE ONES KEEPING ME GOING NOW.
YEAH, THEY'RE A *GOOD* BUNCH.
NOW, DO I HAVE TO DRIVE TO THE NEXT COUNTY FOR A DRINK?

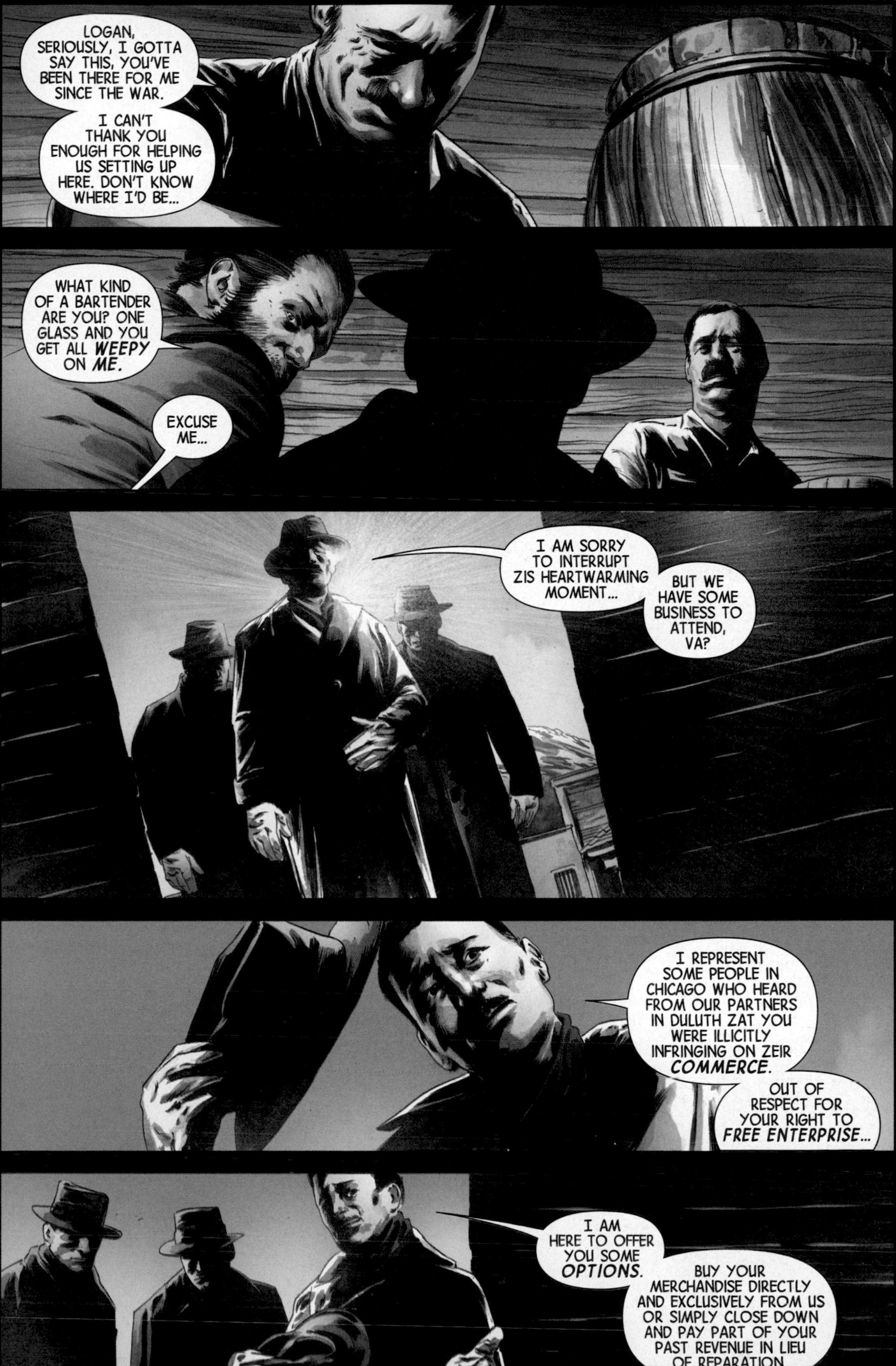
LOGAN, SERIOUSLY, I GOTTA SAY THIS, YOU'VE BEEN THERE FOR ME SINCE THE WAR.
I CAN'T THANK YOU ENOUGH FOR HELPING US SETTING UP HERE. DON'T KNOW WHERE I'D BE...
WHAT KIND OF A BARTENDER ARE YOU? ONE GLASS AND YOU GET ALL WEEPY ON ME.
EXCUSE ME...
I AM SORRY TO INTERRUPT ZIS HEARTWARMING MOMENT...
BUT WE HAVE SOME BUSINESS TO ATTEND, VA?
I REPRESENT SOME PEOPLE IN CHICAGO WHO HEARD FROM OUR PARTNERS IN DULUTH ZAT YOU WERE ILLICITLY INFRINGING ON ZEIR COMMERCE.
OUT OF RESPECT FOR YOUR RIGHT TO FREE ENTERPRISE...
I AM HERE TO OFFER YOU SOME OPTIONS.
BUY YOUR MERCHANDISE DIRECTLY AND EXCLUSIVELY FROM US OR SIMPLY CLOSE DOWN AND PAY PART OF YOUR PAST REVENUE IN LIEU OF REPARATION.

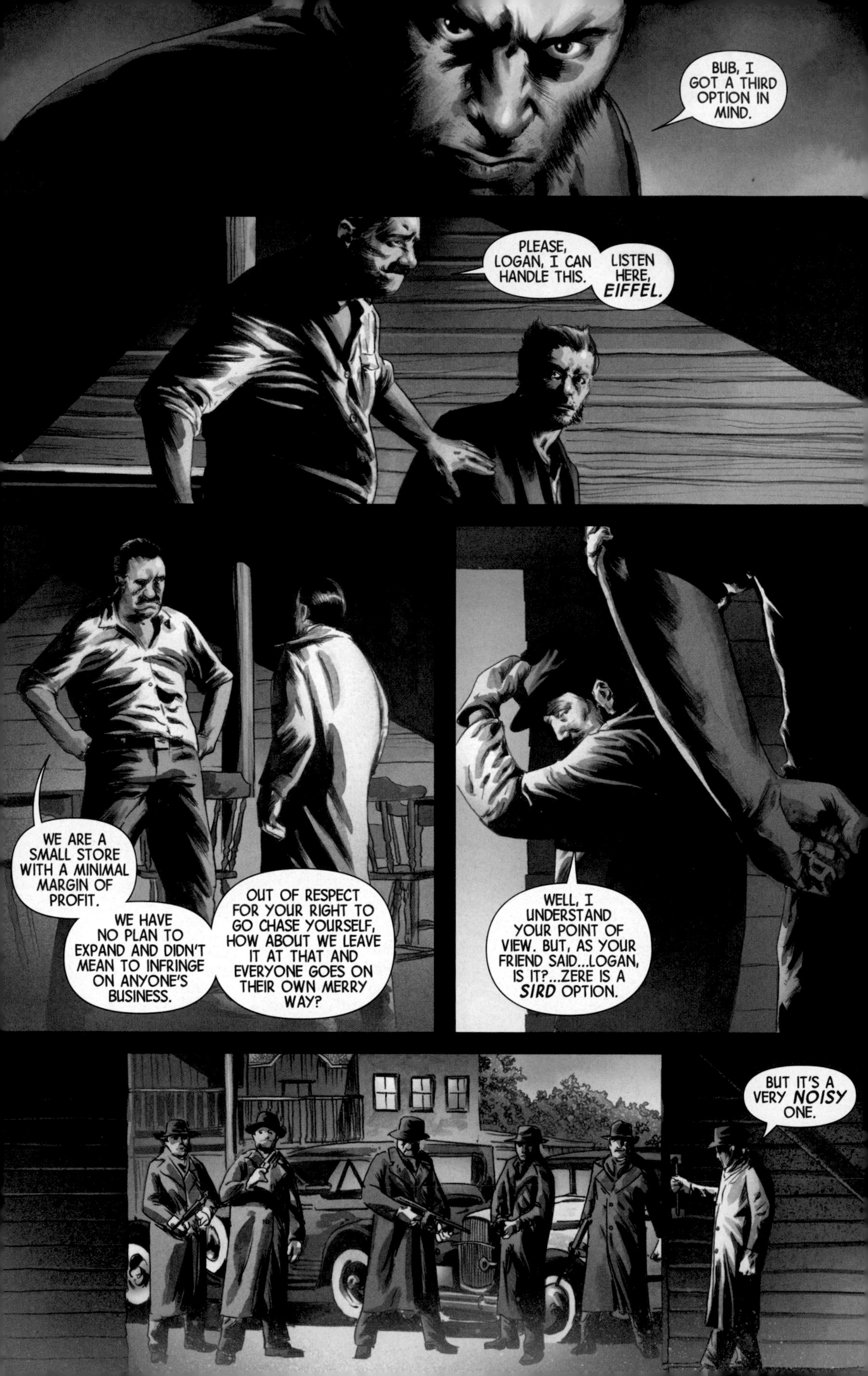
BUB, I GOT A THIRD OPTION IN MIND.
PLEASE, LOGAN, I CAN HANDLE THIS.
LISTEN HERE, EIFFEL.
WE ARE A SMALL STORE WITH A MINIMAL MARGIN OF PROFIT.
WE HAVE NO PLAN TO EXPAND AND DIDN'T MEAN TO INFRINGE ON ANYONE'S BUSINESS.
OUT OF RESPECT FOR YOUR RIGHT TO GO CHASE YOURSELF, HOW ABOUT WE LEAVE IT AT THAT AND EVERYONE GOES ON THEIR OWN MERRY WAY?
WELL, I UNDERSTAND YOUR POINT OF VIEW. BUT, AS YOUR FRIEND SAID...LOGAN, IS IT?...ZERE IS A SIRD OPTION.
BUT IT'S A VERY NOISY ONE.

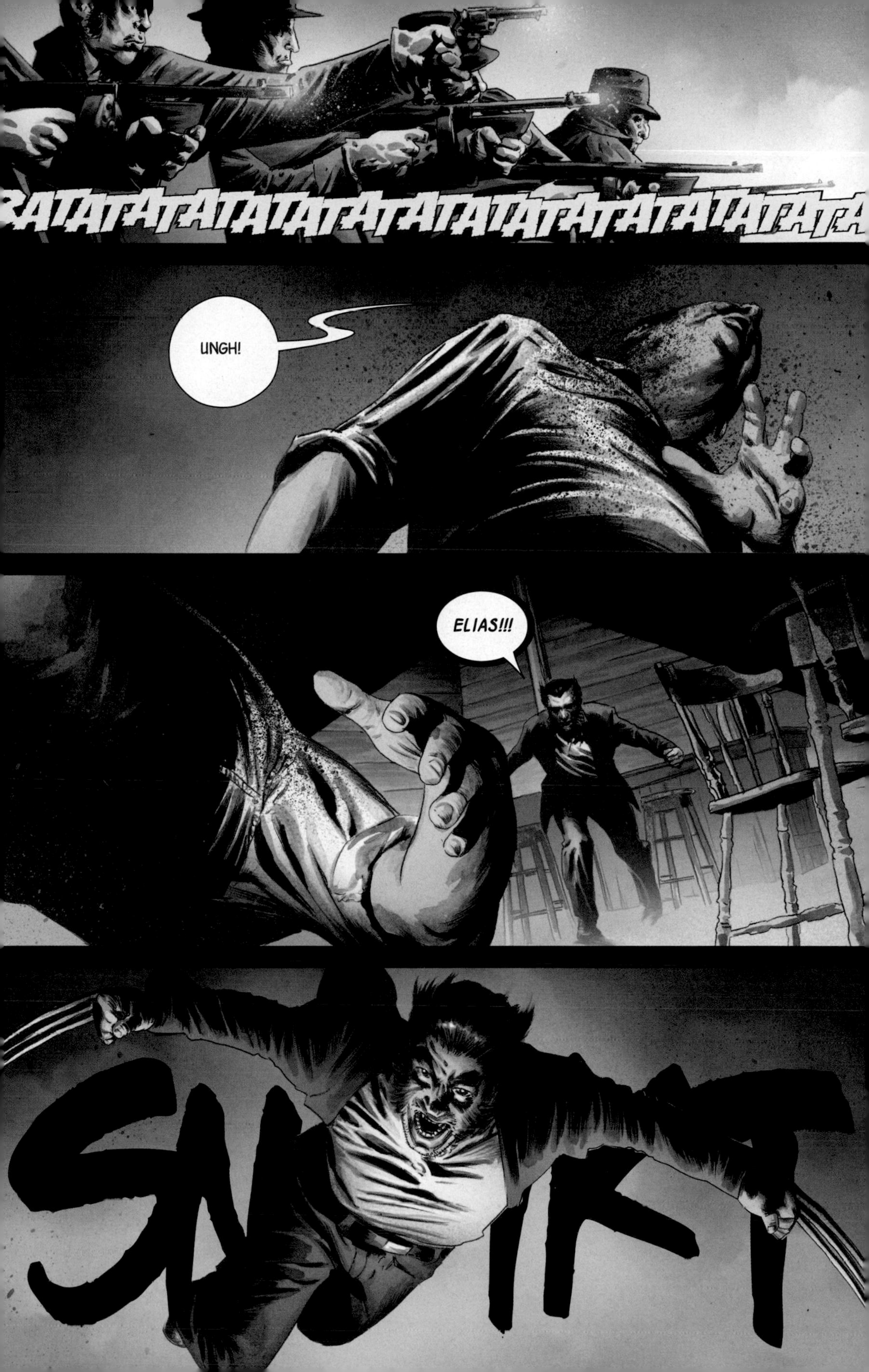
RATATATATATATATATATATATATATATATATA
UNGH!
ELIAS!!!

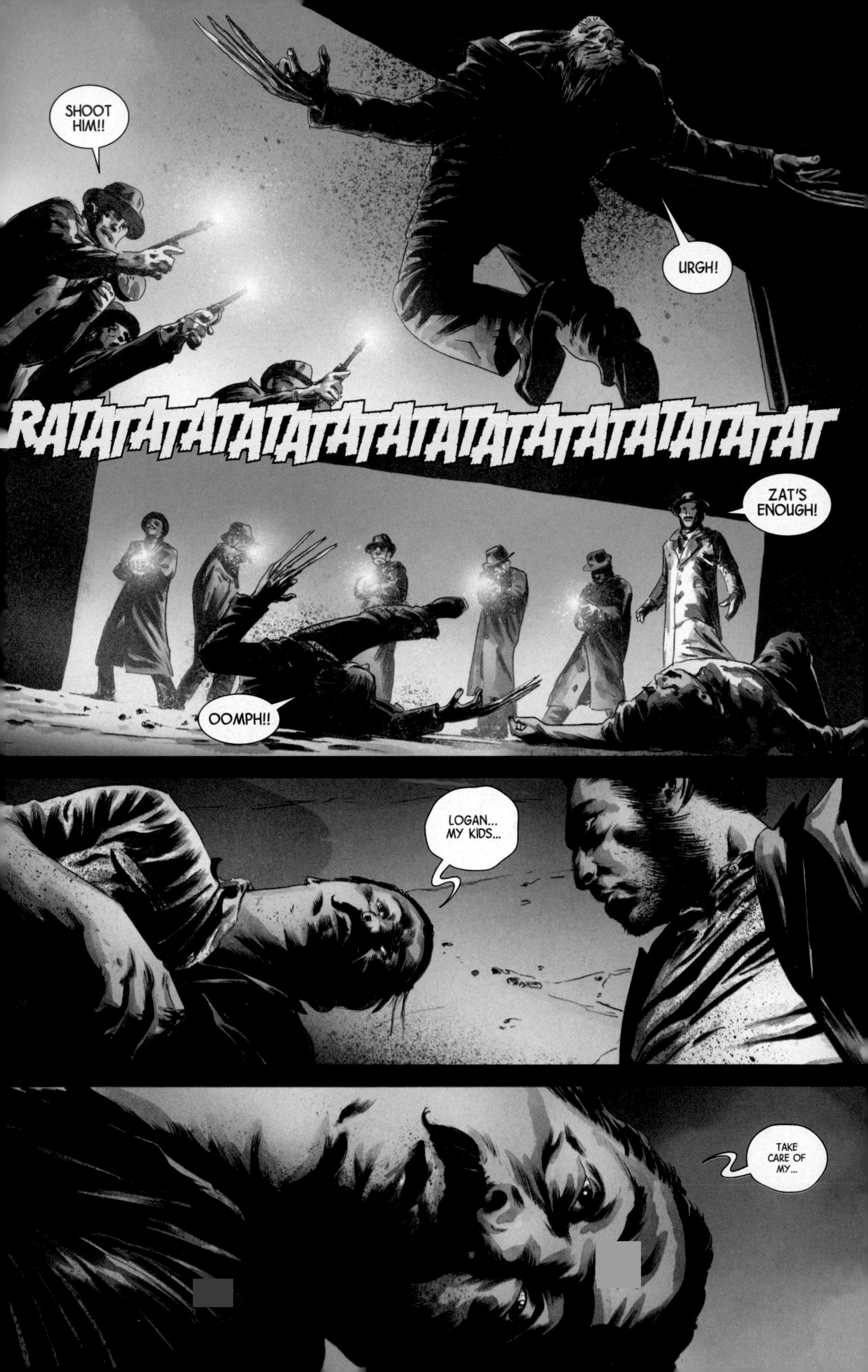
SHOOT HIM!!
URGH!
RATATATATATATATATATATATATATATATATATAT
ZAT'S ENOUGH!
OOMPH!!
LOGAN... MY KIDS...
TAKE CARE OF MY...

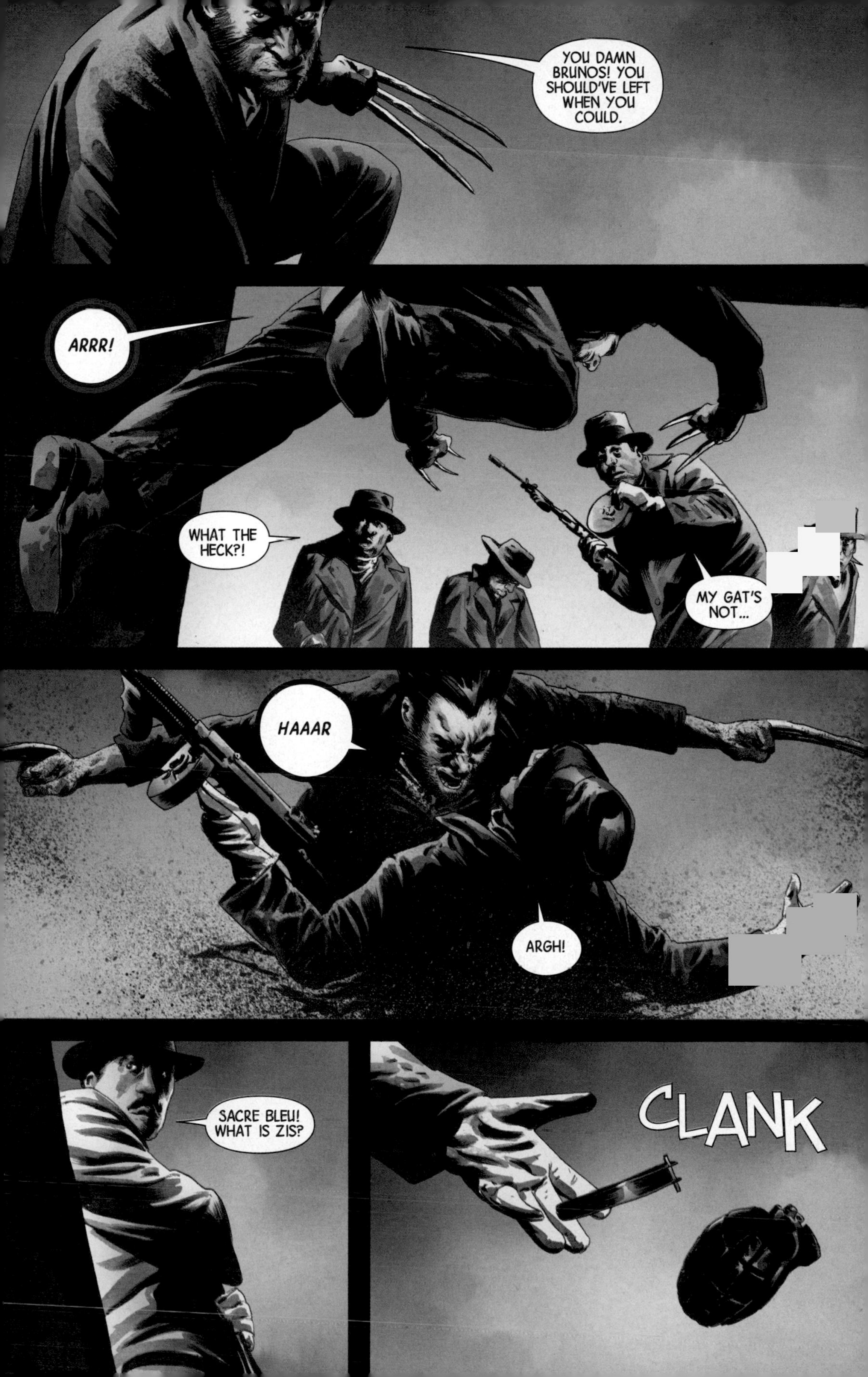
YOU DAMN BRUNOS! YOU SHOULD'VE LEFT WHEN YOU COULD.
ARRR!
WHAT THE HECK?!
MY GAT'S NOT...
HAAAR
ARGH!
SACRE BLEU! WHAT IS ZIS?
CLANK

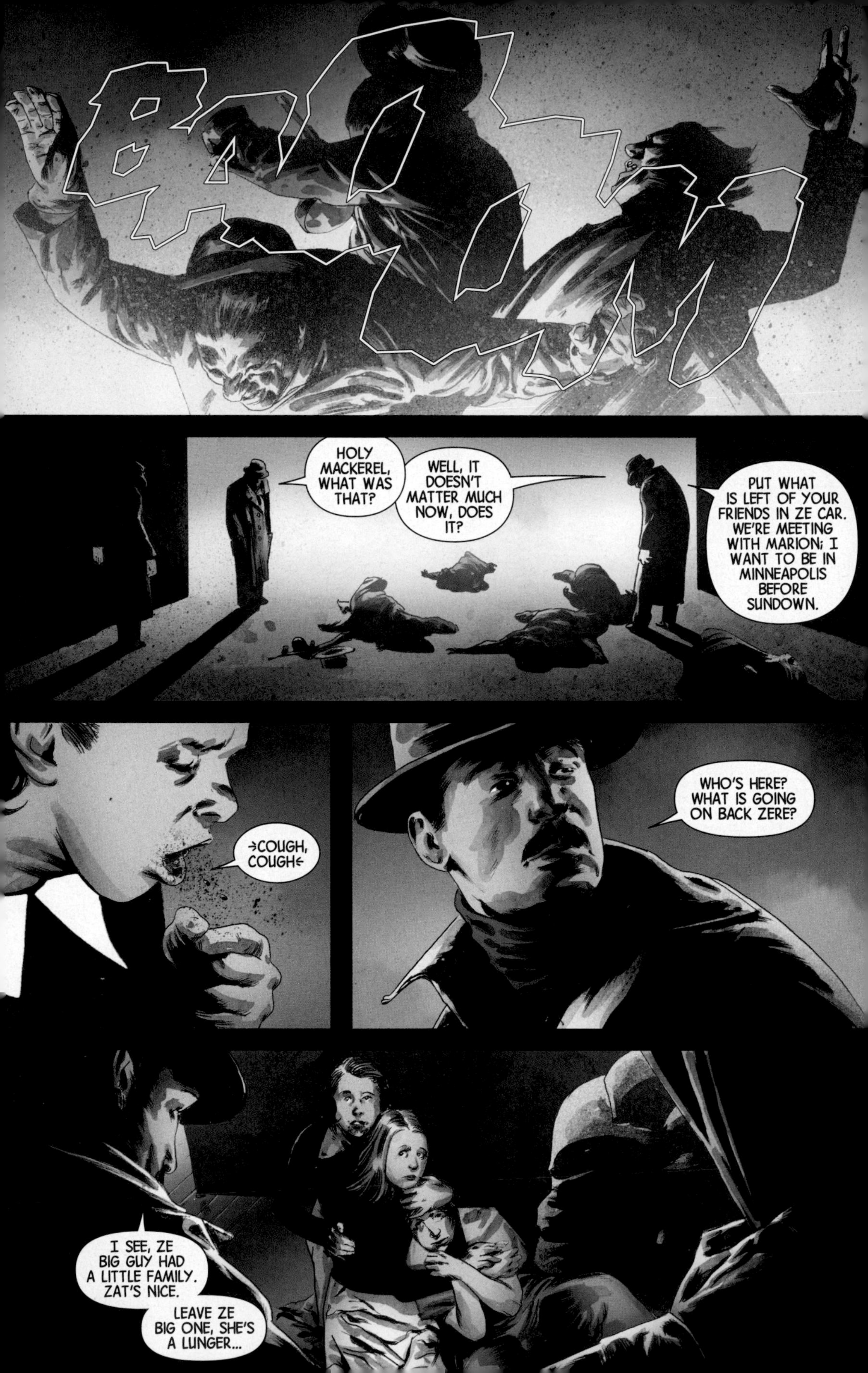
BALOOM
HOLY MACKEREL, WHAT WAS THAT?
WELL, IT DOESN'T MATTER MUCH NOW, DOES IT?
PUT WHAT IS LEFT OF YOUR FRIENDS IN ZE CAR. WE'RE MEETING WITH MARION; I WANT TO BE IN MINNEAPOLIS BEFORE SUNDOWN.
→COUGH, COUGH←
WHO'S HERE? WHAT IS GOING ON BACK ZERE?
I SEE, ZE BIG GUY HAD A LITTLE FAMILY. ZAT'S NICE.
LEAVE ZE BIG ONE, SHE'S A LUNGER...

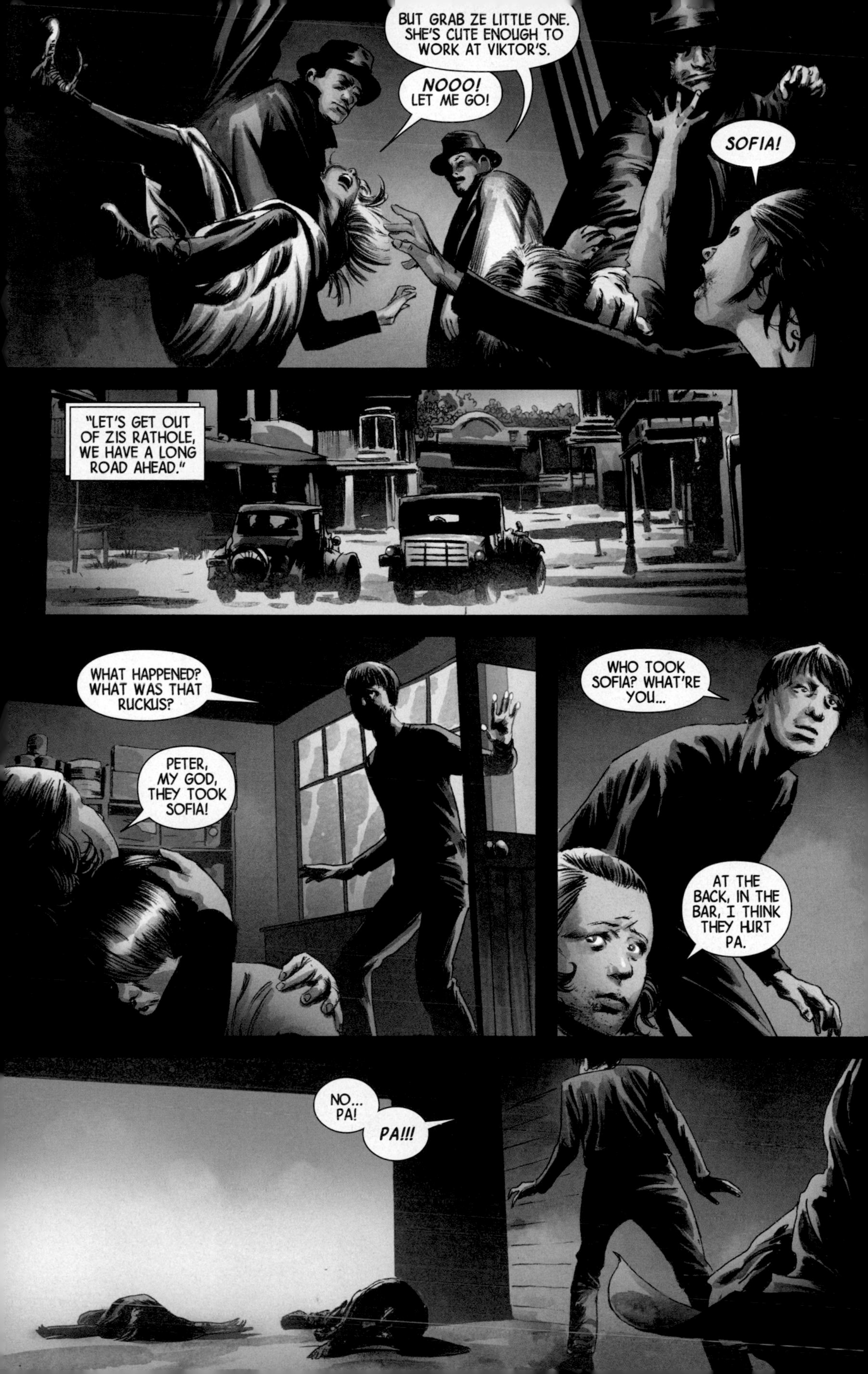
NOOO! LET ME GO!
BUT GRAB ZE LITTLE ONE. SHE'S CUTE ENOUGH TO WORK AT VIKTOR'S.
SOFIA!
"LET'S GET OUT OF ZIS RATHOLE, WE HAVE A LONG ROAD AHEAD."
WHAT HAPPENED? WHAT WAS THAT RUCKUS?
PETER, MY GOD, THEY TOOK SOFIA!
WHO TOOK SOFIA? WHAT'RE YOU...
AT THE BACK, IN THE BAR, I THINK THEY HURT PA.
NO... PA!
PA!!!

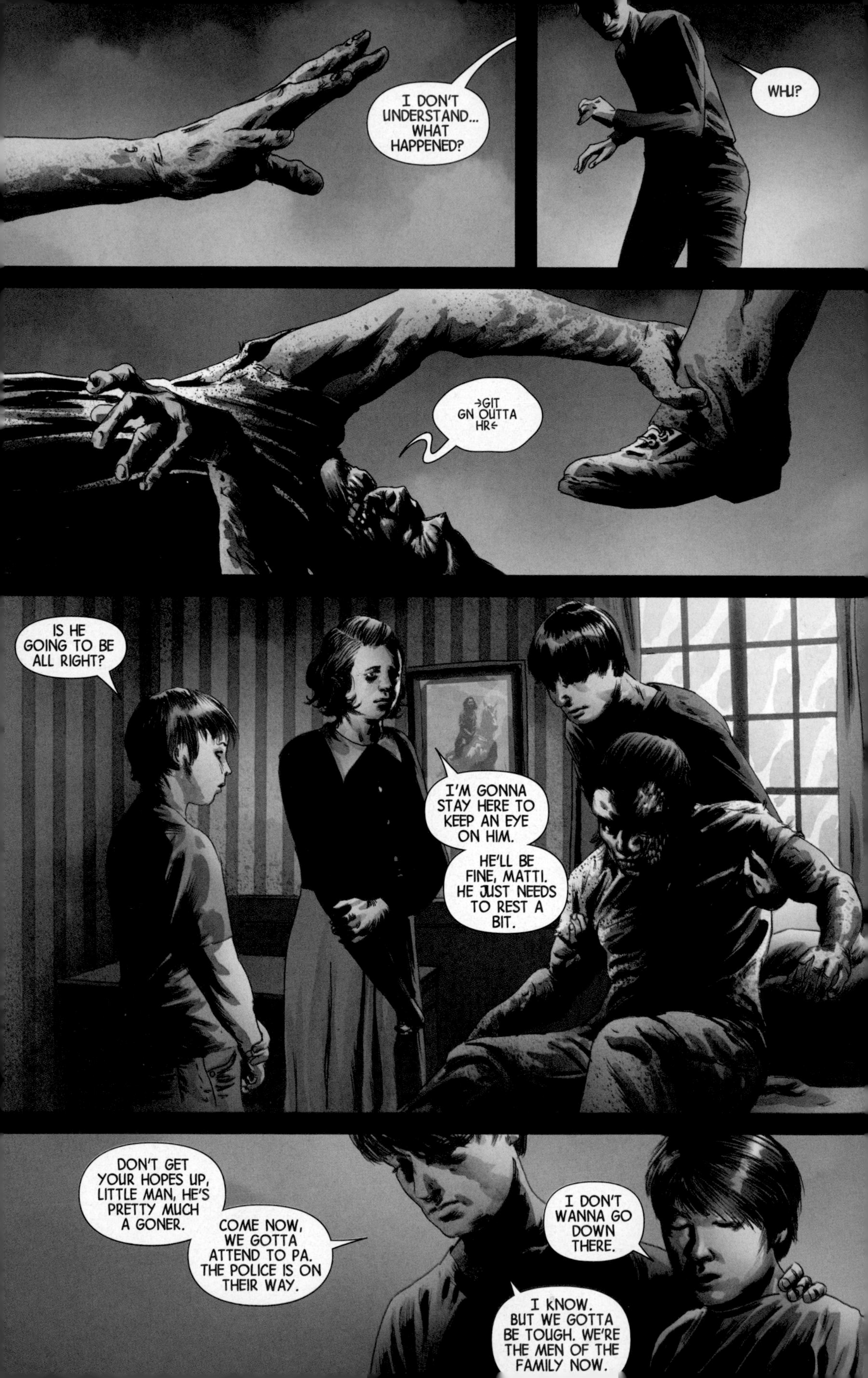
I DON'T UNDERSTAND... WHAT HAPPENED?
WHU?
→GIT GN OUTTA HR←
IS HE GOING TO BE ALL RIGHT?
I'M GONNA STAY HERE TO KEEP AN EYE ON HIM.
HE'LL BE FINE, MATTI. HE JUST NEEDS TO REST A BIT.
DON'T GET YOUR HOPES UP, LITTLE MAN, HE'S PRETTY MUCH A GONER.
COME NOW, WE GOTTA ATTEND TO PA. THE POLICE IS ON THEIR WAY.
I DON'T WANNA GO DOWN THERE.
I KNOW. BUT WE GOTTA BE TOUGH. WE'RE THE MEN OF THE FAMILY NOW.

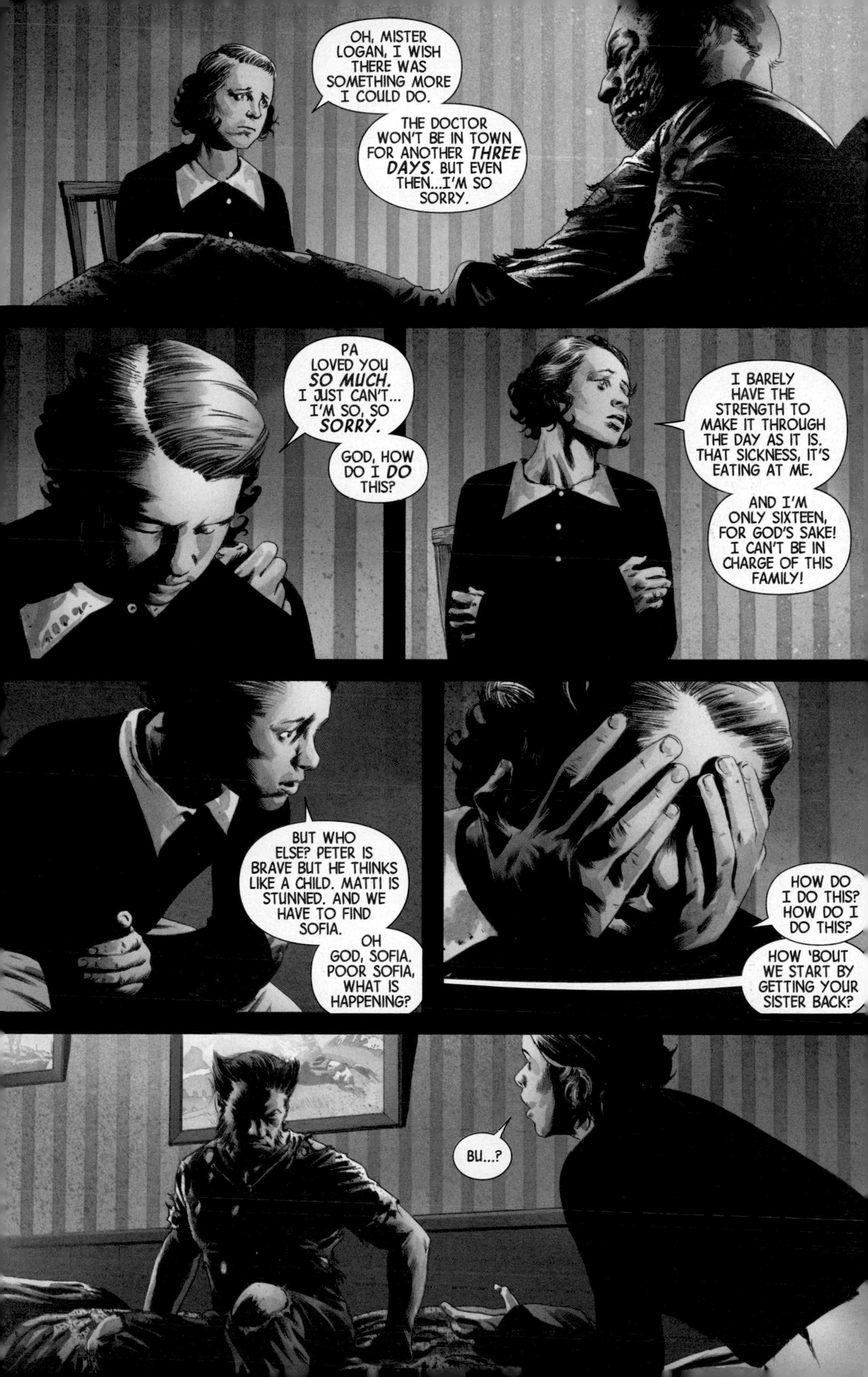
OH, MISTER LOGAN, I WISH THERE WAS SOMETHING MORE I COULD DO.
THE DOCTOR WON'T BE IN TOWN FOR ANOTHER THREE DAYS. BUT EVEN THEN...I'M SO SORRY.
PA LOVED YOU SO MUCH. I JUST CAN'T... I'M SO, SO SORRY.
GOD, HOW DO I DO THIS?
I BARELY HAVE THE STRENGTH TO MAKE IT THROUGH THE DAY AS IT IS. THAT SICKNESS, IT'S EATING AT ME.
AND I'M ONLY SIXTEEN, FOR GOD'S SAKE! I CAN'T BE IN CHARGE OF THIS FAMILY!
BUT WHO ELSE? PETER IS BRAVE BUT HE THINKS LIKE A CHILD. MATTI IS STUNNED. AND WE HAVE TO FIND SOFIA.
OH GOD, SOFIA. POOR SOFIA, WHAT IS HAPPENING?
HOW DO I DO THIS? HOW DO I DO THIS?
HOW 'BOUT WE START BY GETTING YOUR SISTER BACK?
BU...?

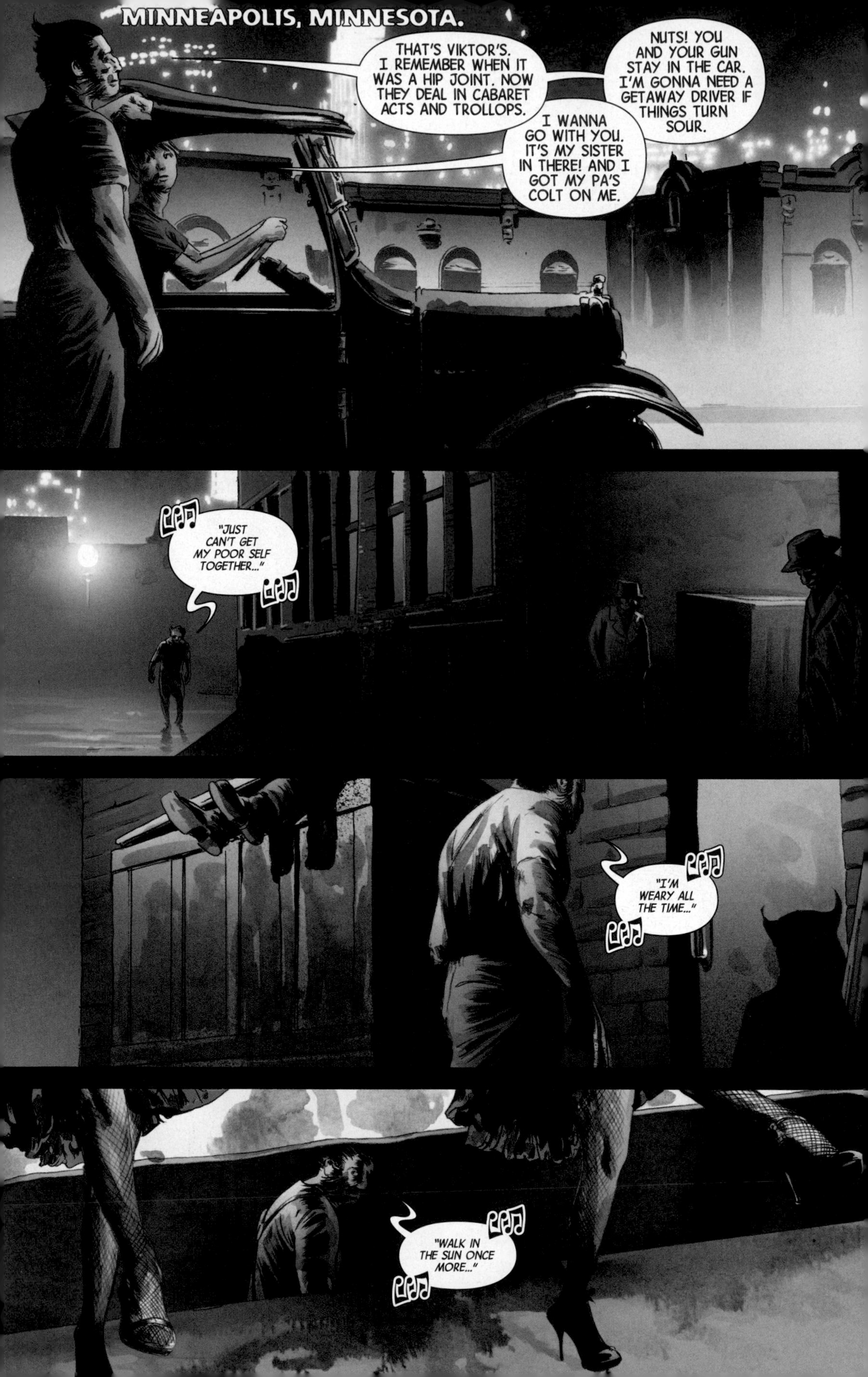
MINNEAPOLIS, MINNESOTA.
THAT'S VIKTOR'S. I REMEMBER WHEN IT WAS A HIP JOINT. NOW THEY DEAL IN CABARET ACTS AND TROLLOPS.
I WANNA GO WITH YOU. IT'S MY SISTER IN THERE! AND I GOT MY PA'S COLT ON ME.
NUTS! YOU AND YOUR GUN STAY IN THE CAR. I'M GONNA NEED A GETAWAY DRIVER IF THINGS TURN SOUR.
"JUST CAN'T GET MY POOR SELF TOGETHER..."
"I'M WEARY ALL THE TIME..."
"WALK IN THE SUN ONCE MORE..."

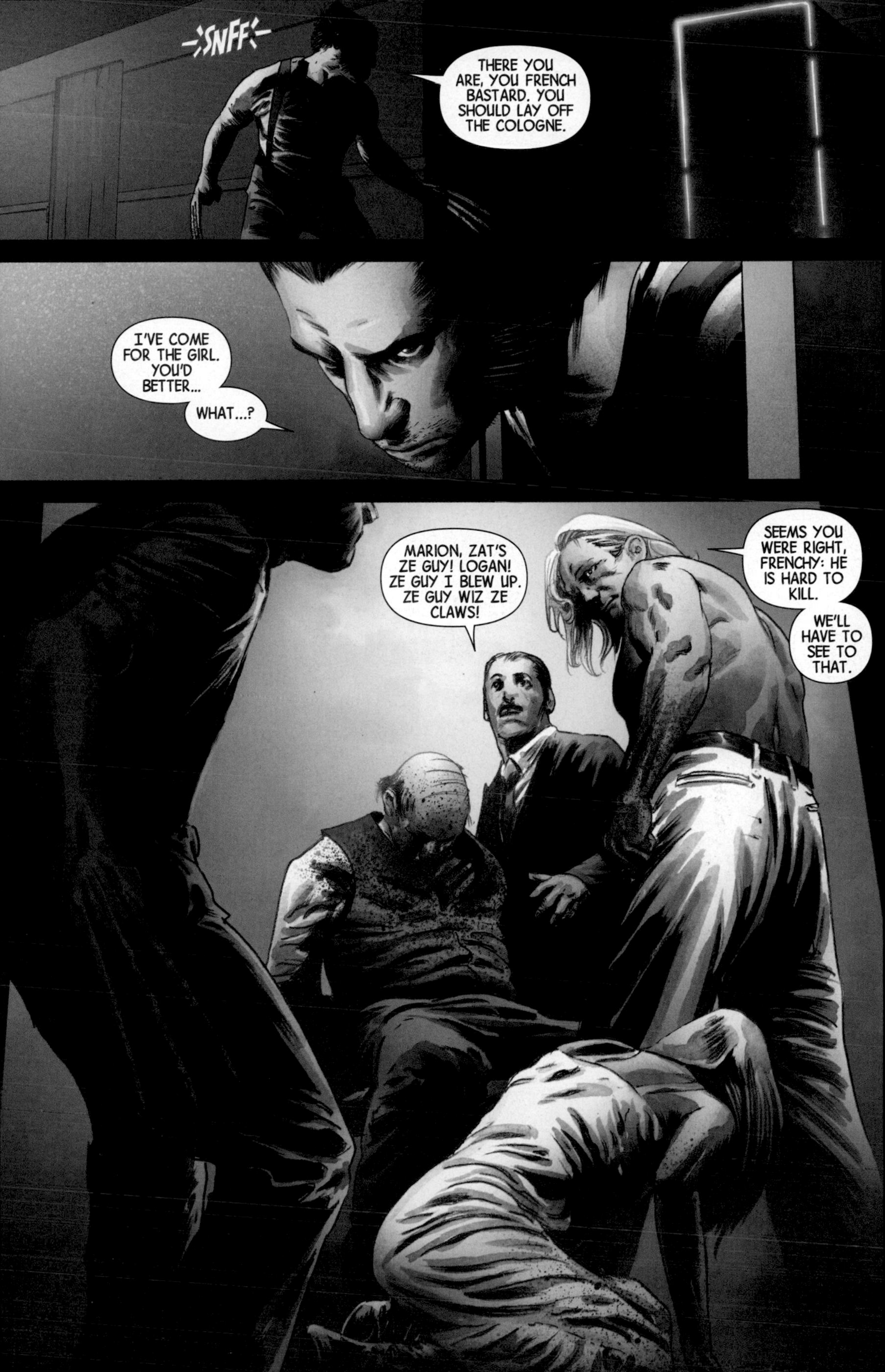
SNFF
THERE YOU ARE, YOU FRENCH BASTARD. YOU SHOULD LAY OFF THE COLOGNE.
I'VE COME FOR THE GIRL. YOU'D BETTER...
WHAT...?
MARION, ZAT'S ZE GUY! LOGAN! ZE GUY I BLEW UP. ZE GUY WIZ ZE CLAWS!
SEEMS YOU WERE RIGHT, FRENCHY: HE IS HARD TO KILL.
WE'LL HAVE TO SEE TO THAT.

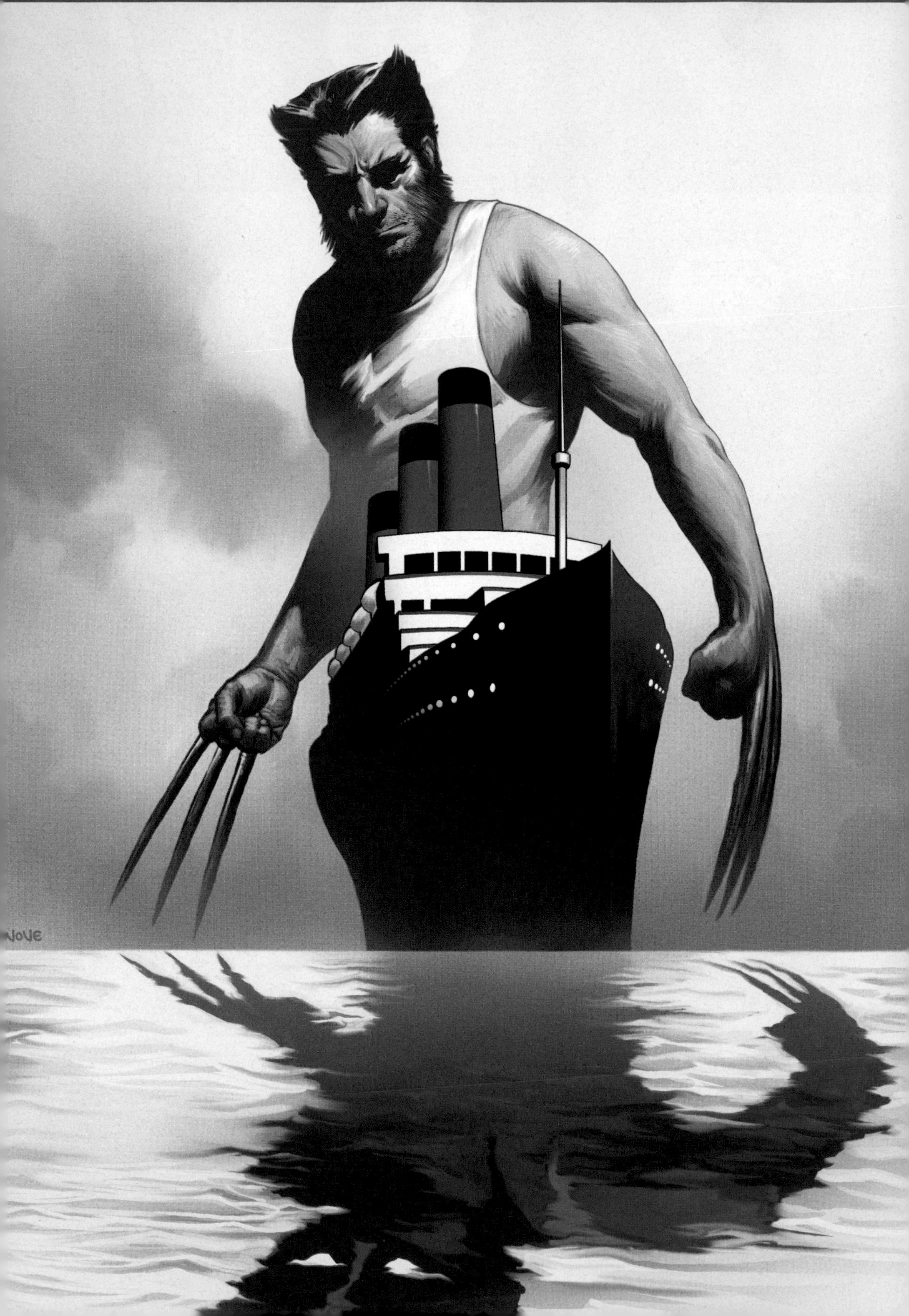
NOVE

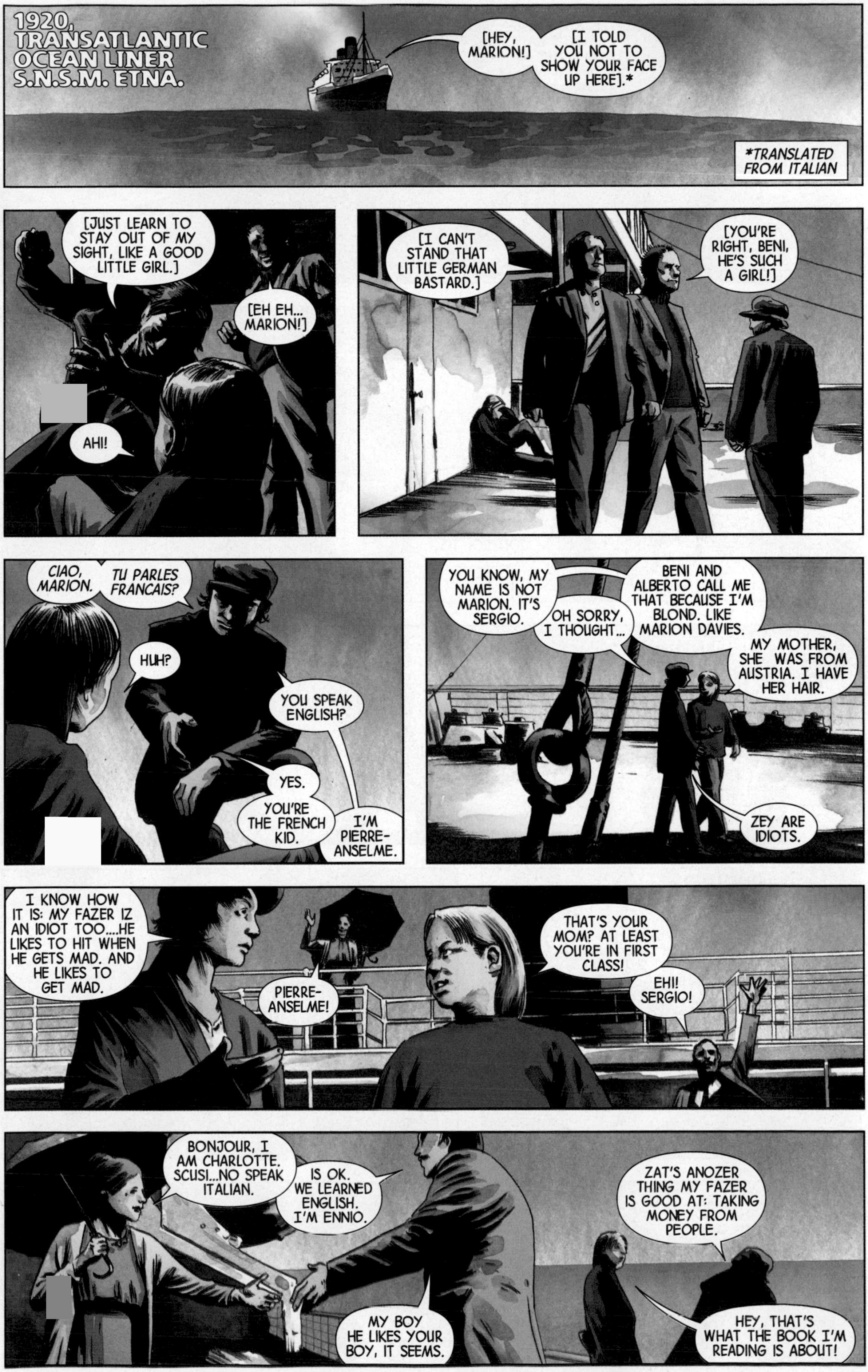
1920, TRANSATLANTIC OCEAN LINER S.N.S.M. ETNA.
[HEY, MARION!]
[I TOLD YOU NOT TO SHOW YOUR FACE UP HERE].*
*TRANSLATED FROM ITALIAN
[JUST LEARN TO STAY OUT OF MY SIGHT, LIKE A GOOD LITTLE GIRL.]
[EH EH... MARION!]
AHI!
[I CAN'T STAND THAT LITTLE GERMAN BASTARD.]
[YOU'RE RIGHT, BENI, HE'S SUCH A GIRL!]
CIAO, MARION.
TU PARLES FRANCAIS?
HUH?
YOU SPEAK ENGLISH?
YES.
YOU'RE THE FRENCH KID.
I'M PIERRE-ANSELME.
YOU KNOW, MY NAME IS NOT MARION. IT'S SERGIO.
OH SORRY, I THOUGHT...
BENI AND ALBERTO CALL ME THAT BECAUSE I'M BLOND. LIKE MARION DAVIES.
MY MOTHER, SHE WAS FROM AUSTRIA. I HAVE HER HAIR.
ZEY ARE IDIOTS.
I KNOW HOW IT IS: MY FAZER IZ AN IDIOT TOO....HE LIKES TO HIT WHEN HE GETS MAD. AND HE LIKES TO GET MAD.
PIERRE-ANSELME!
THAT'S YOUR MOM? AT LEAST YOU'RE IN FIRST CLASS!
EHI! SERGIO!
BONJOUR, I AM CHARLOTTE. SCUSI...NO SPEAK ITALIAN.
IS OK. WE LEARNED ENGLISH. I'M ENNIO.
MY BOY HE LIKES YOUR BOY, IT SEEMS.
ZAT'S ANOZER THING MY FAZER IS GOOD AT: TAKING MONEY FROM PEOPLE.
HEY, THAT'S WHAT THE BOOK I'M READING IS ABOUT!

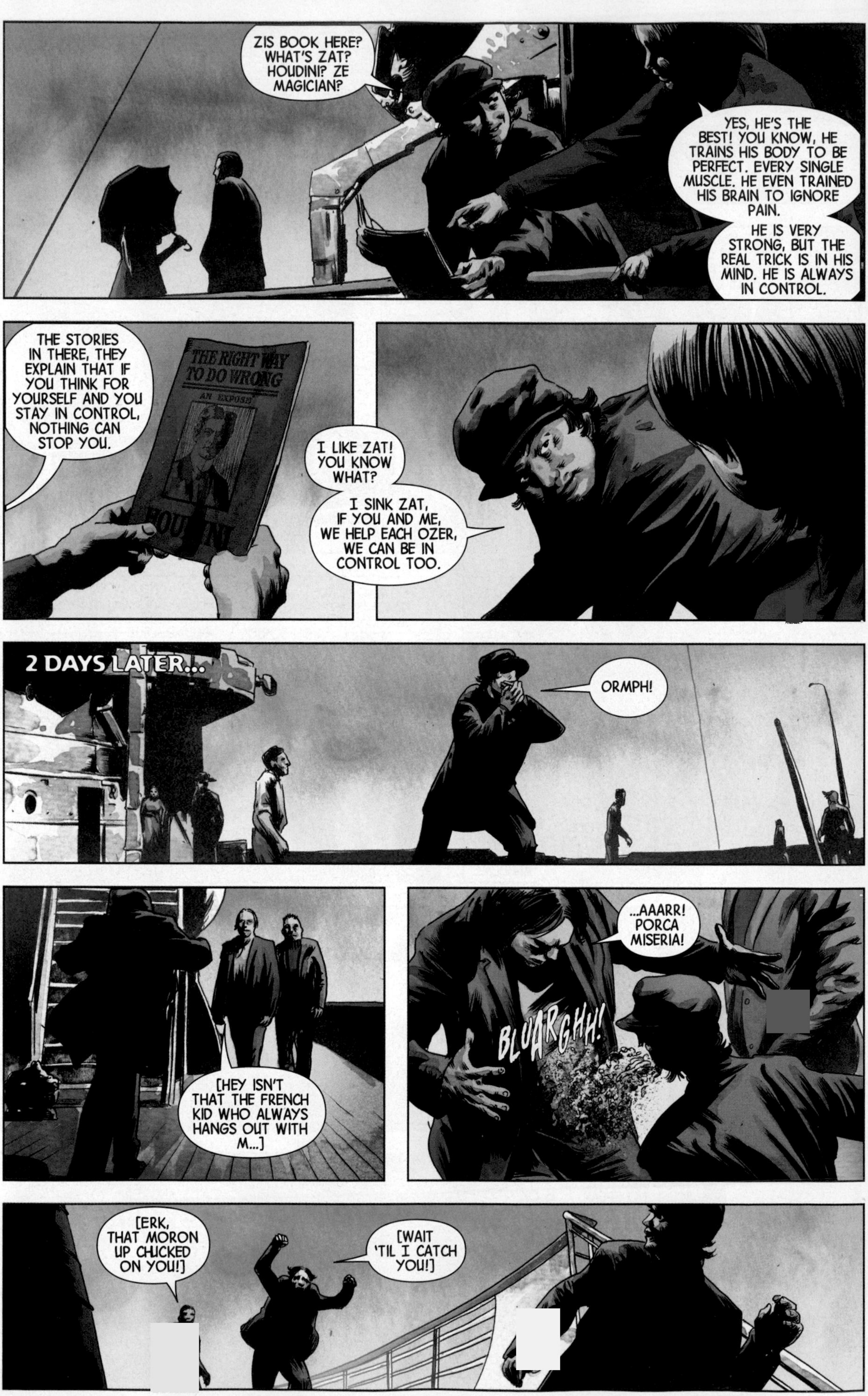
ZIS BOOK HERE? WHAT'S ZAT? HOUDINI? ZE MAGICIAN?
YES, HE'S THE BEST! YOU KNOW, HE TRAINS HIS BODY TO BE PERFECT. EVERY SINGLE MUSCLE. HE EVEN TRAINED HIS BRAIN TO IGNORE PAIN.
HE IS VERY STRONG, BUT THE REAL TRICK IS IN HIS MIND. HE IS ALWAYS IN CONTROL.
THE STORIES IN THERE, THEY EXPLAIN THAT IF YOU THINK FOR YOURSELF AND YOU STAY IN CONTROL, NOTHING CAN STOP YOU.
THE RIGHT WAY TO DO WRONG
AN EXPOSÉ
HOUDINI
I LIKE ZAT! YOU KNOW WHAT?
I SINK ZAT, IF YOU AND ME, WE HELP EACH OZER, WE CAN BE IN CONTROL TOO.
2 DAYS LATER...
ORMPH!
[HEY ISN'T THAT THE FRENCH KID WHO ALWAYS HANGS OUT WITH M...]
...AAARR! PORCA MISERIA!
BLUARGHH!
[ERK, THAT MORON UP CHUCKED ON YOU!]
[WAIT 'TIL I CATCH YOU!]

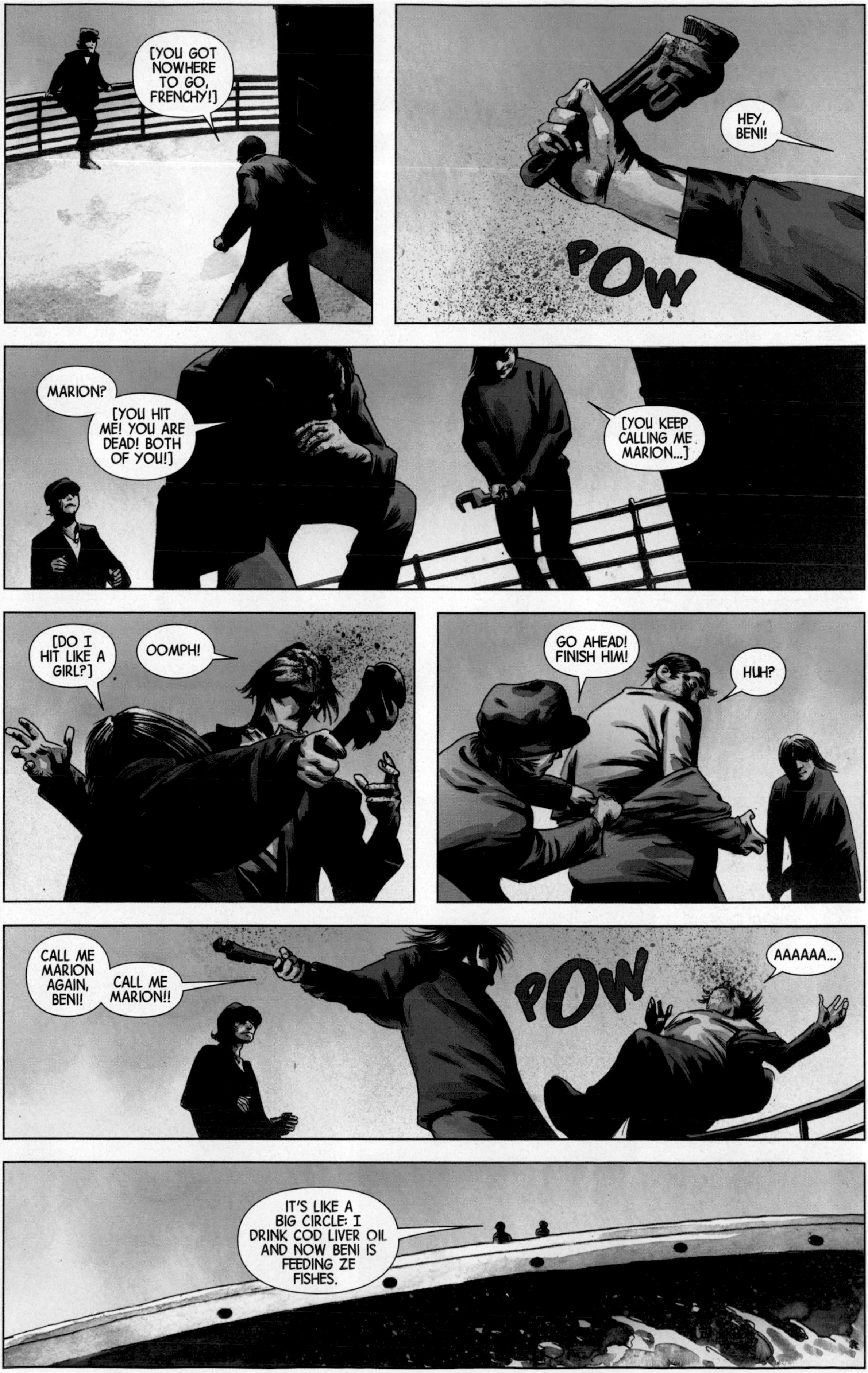
[YOU GOT NOWHERE TO GO, FRENCHY!]
HEY, BENI!
POW
MARION?
[YOU HIT ME! YOU ARE DEAD! BOTH OF YOU!]
[YOU KEEP CALLING ME MARION...]
[DO I HIT LIKE A GIRL?]
OOMPH!
GO AHEAD! FINISH HIM!
HUH?
CALL ME MARION AGAIN, BENI!
CALL ME MARION!!
POW
AAAAAA...
IT'S LIKE A BIG CIRCLE: I DRINK COD LIVER OIL AND NOW BENI IS FEEDING ZE FISHES.

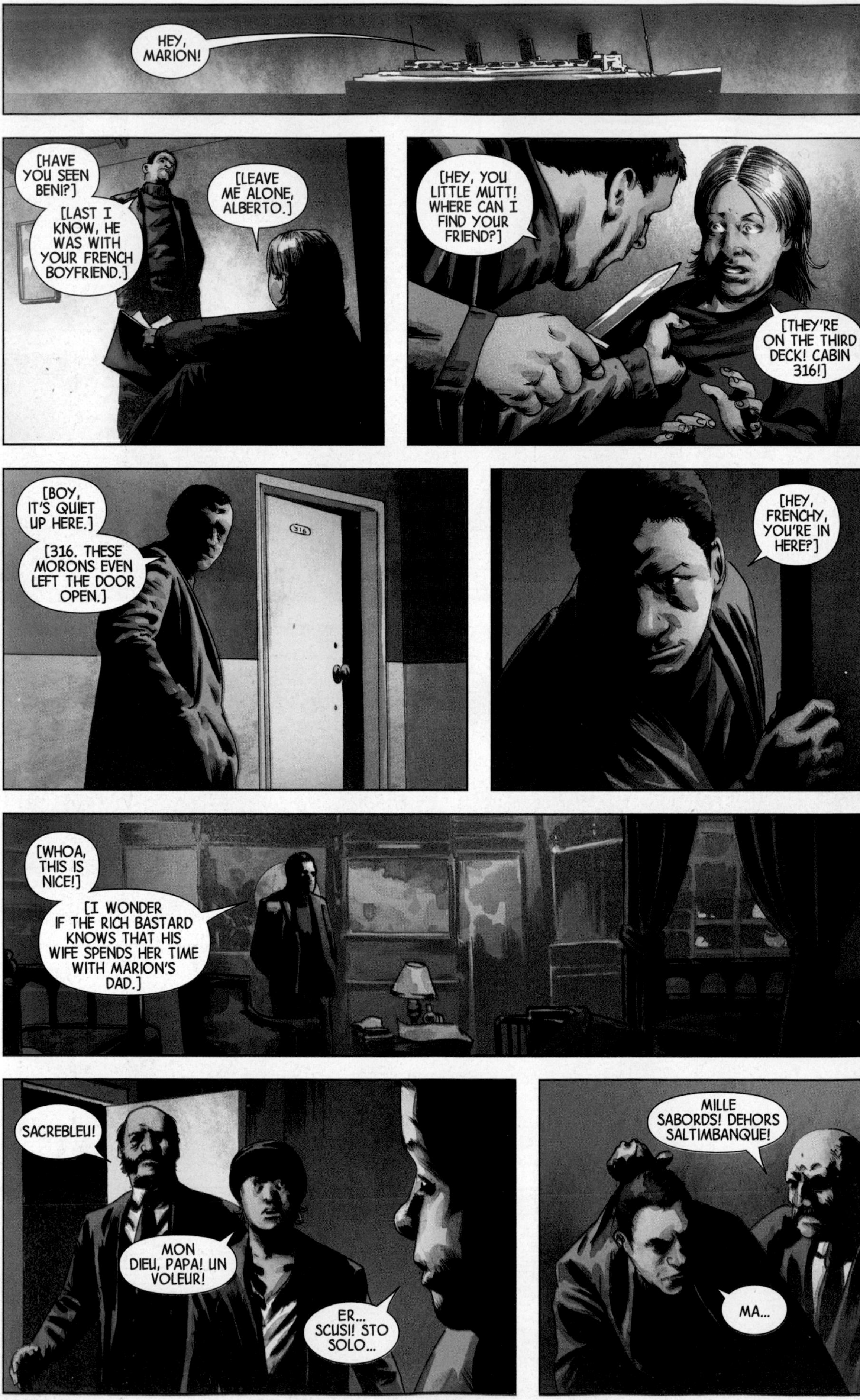
HEY, MARION!
[HAVE YOU SEEN BENI?]
[LAST I KNOW, HE WAS WITH YOUR FRENCH BOYFRIEND.]
[LEAVE ME ALONE, ALBERTO.]
[HEY, YOU LITTLE MUTT! WHERE CAN I FIND YOUR FRIEND?]
[THEY'RE ON THE THIRD DECK! CABIN 316!]
[BOY, IT'S QUIET UP HERE.]
[316. THESE MORONS EVEN LEFT THE DOOR OPEN.]
[HEY, FRENCHY, YOU'RE IN HERE?]
[WHOA, THIS IS NICE!]
[I WONDER IF THE RICH BASTARD KNOWS THAT HIS WIFE SPENDS HER TIME WITH MARION'S DAD.]
SACREBLEU!
MON DIEU, PAPA! UN VOLEUR!
ER... SCUSI! STO SOLO...
MILLE SABORDS! DEHORS SALTIMBANQUE!
MA...

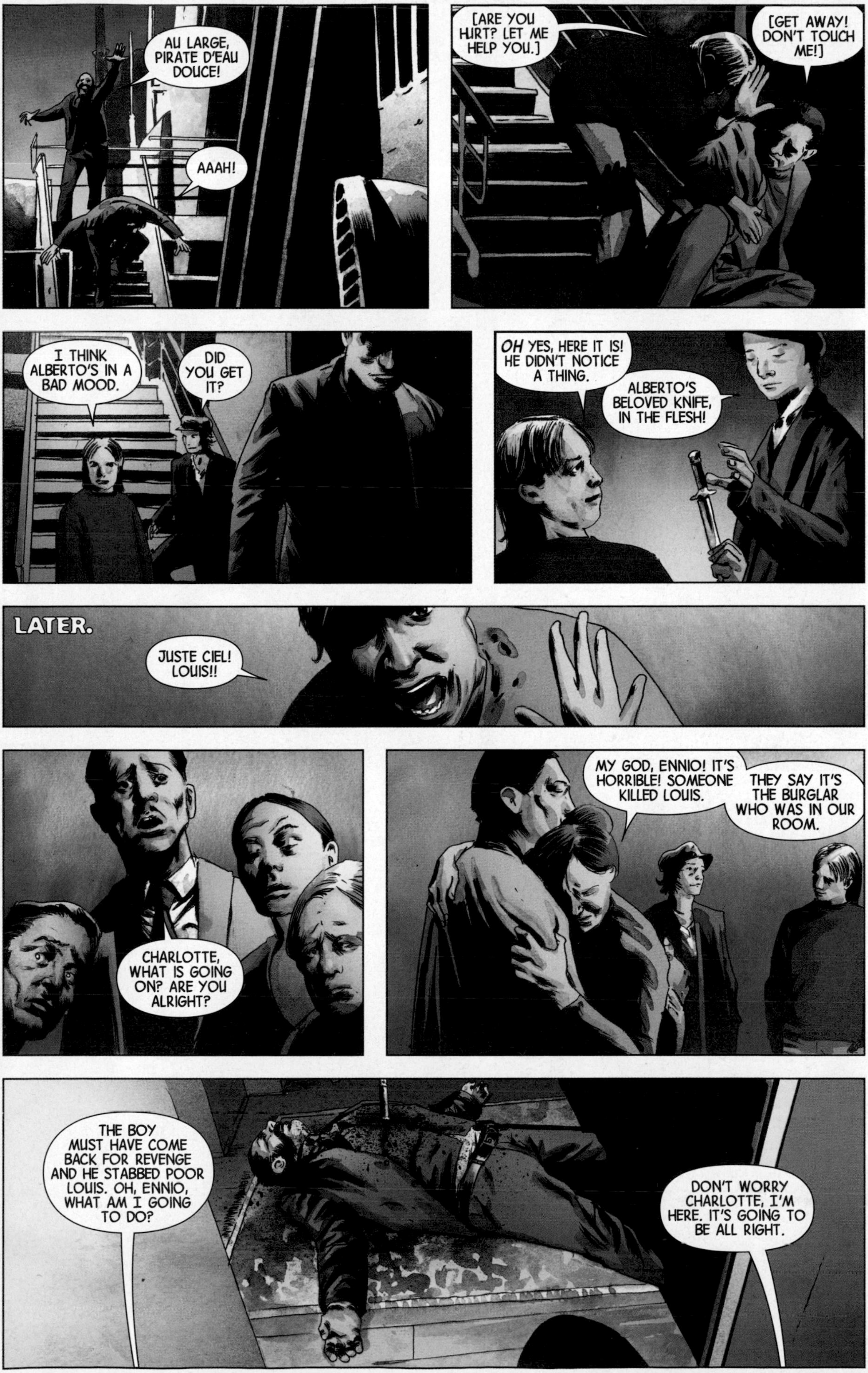
AU LARGE, PIRATE D'EAU DOUCE!
AAAH!
[ARE YOU HURT? LET ME HELP YOU.]
[GET AWAY! DON'T TOUCH ME!]
I THINK ALBERTO'S IN A BAD MOOD.
DID YOU GET IT?
OH YES, HERE IT IS! HE DIDN'T NOTICE A THING.
ALBERTO'S BELOVED KNIFE, IN THE FLESH!
LATER.
JUSTE CIEL! LOUIS!!
CHARLOTTE, WHAT IS GOING ON? ARE YOU ALRIGHT?
MY GOD, ENNIO! IT'S HORRIBLE! SOMEONE KILLED LOUIS.
THEY SAY IT'S THE BURGLAR WHO WAS IN OUR ROOM.
THE BOY MUST HAVE COME BACK FOR REVENGE AND HE STABBED POOR LOUIS. OH, ENNIO, WHAT AM I GOING TO DO?
DON'T WORRY CHARLOTTE, I'M HERE. IT'S GOING TO BE ALL RIGHT.

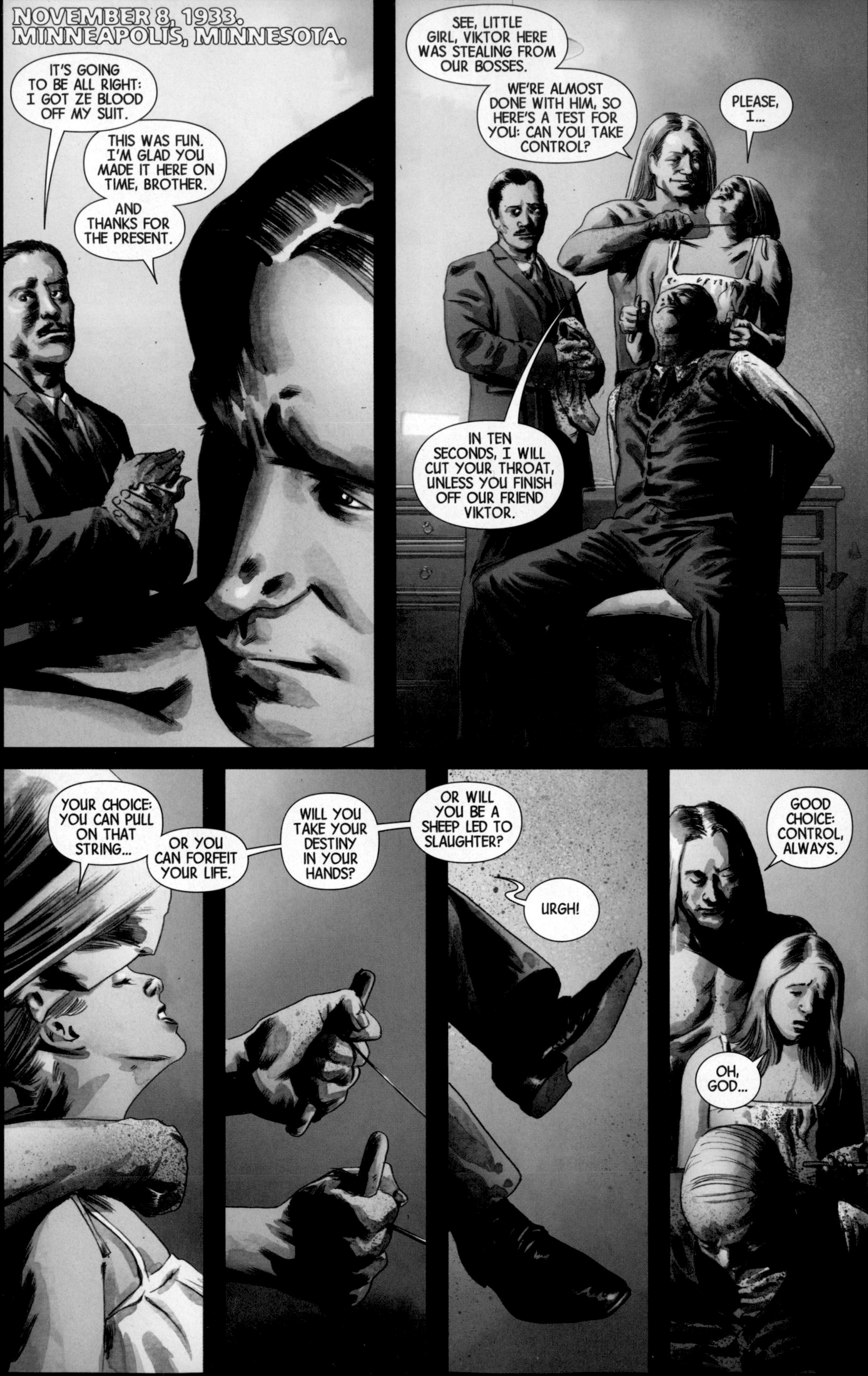
NOVEMBER 8, 1933.
MINNEAPOLIS, MINNESOTA.
IT'S GOING TO BE ALL RIGHT: I GOT ZE BLOOD OFF MY SUIT.
THIS WAS FUN. I'M GLAD YOU MADE IT HERE ON TIME, BROTHER.
AND THANKS FOR THE PRESENT.
SEE, LITTLE GIRL, VIKTOR HERE WAS STEALING FROM OUR BOSSES.
WE'RE ALMOST DONE WITH HIM, SO HERE'S A TEST FOR YOU: CAN YOU TAKE CONTROL?
PLEASE, I...
IN TEN SECONDS, I WILL CUT YOUR THROAT, UNLESS YOU FINISH OFF OUR FRIEND VIKTOR.
YOUR CHOICE: YOU CAN PULL ON THAT STRING...
OR YOU CAN FORFEIT YOUR LIFE.
WILL YOU TAKE YOUR DESTINY IN YOUR HANDS?
OR WILL YOU BE A SHEEP LED TO SLAUGHTER?
URGH!
GOOD CHOICE: CONTROL, ALWAYS.
OH, GOD...

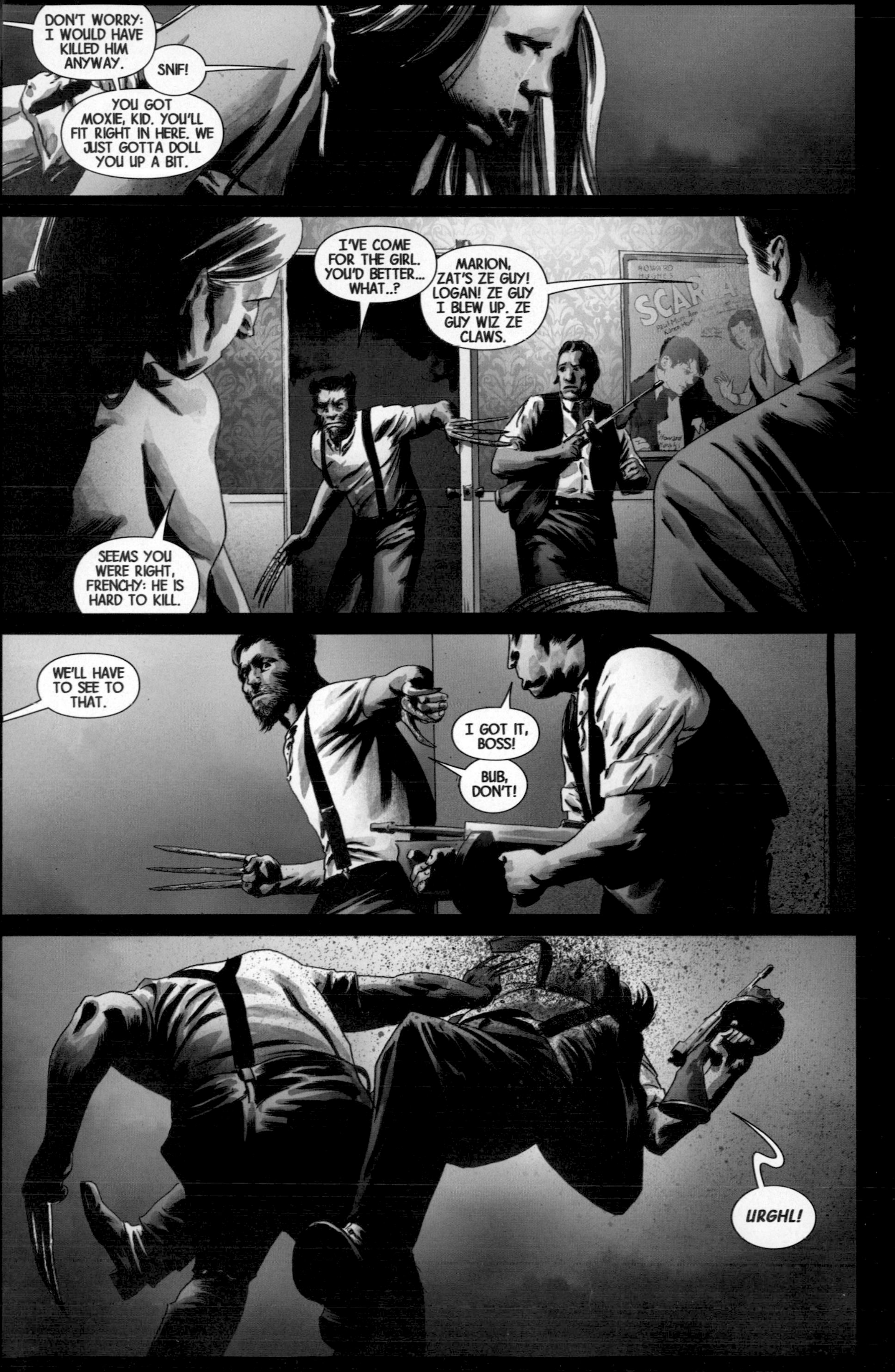
DON'T WORRY: I WOULD HAVE KILLED HIM ANYWAY.
SNIF!
YOU GOT MOXIE, KID. YOU'LL FIT RIGHT IN HERE. WE JUST GOTTA DOLL YOU UP A BIT.
I'VE COME FOR THE GIRL. YOU'D BETTER... WHAT..?
MARION, ZAT'S ZE GUY! LOGAN! ZE GUY I BLEW UP. ZE GUY WIZ ZE CLAWS.
SEEMS YOU WERE RIGHT, FRENCHY: HE IS HARD TO KILL.
WE'LL HAVE TO SEE TO THAT.
I GOT IT, BOSS!
BUB, DON'T!
URGHL!

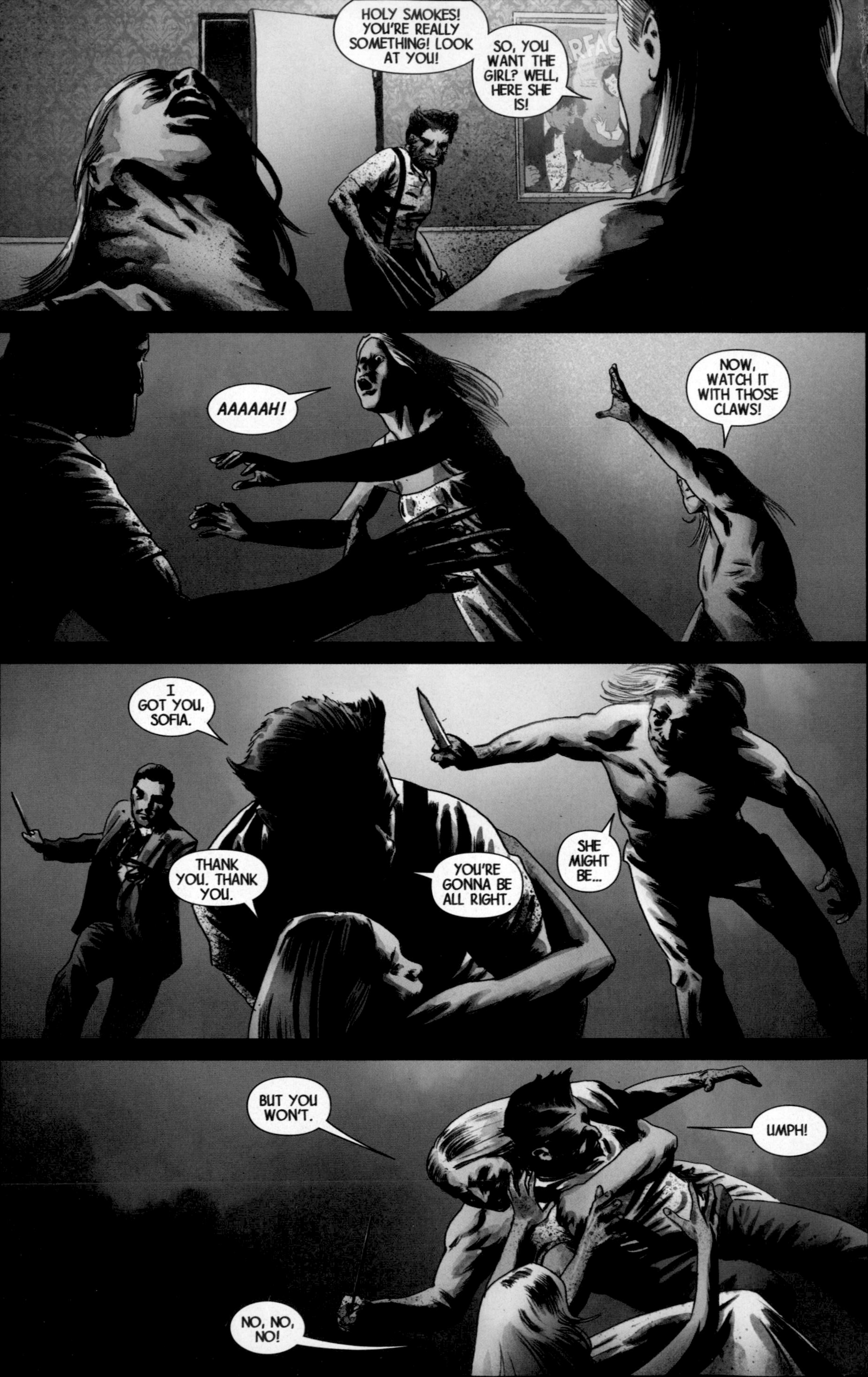
HOLY SMOKES! YOU'RE REALLY SOMETHING! LOOK AT YOU!
SO, YOU WANT THE GIRL? WELL, HERE SHE IS!
AAAAAH!
NOW, WATCH IT WITH THOSE CLAWS!
I GOT YOU, SOFIA.
THANK YOU. THANK YOU.
YOU'RE GONNA BE ALL RIGHT.
SHE MIGHT BE...
BUT YOU WON'T.
UMPH!
NO, NO, NO!

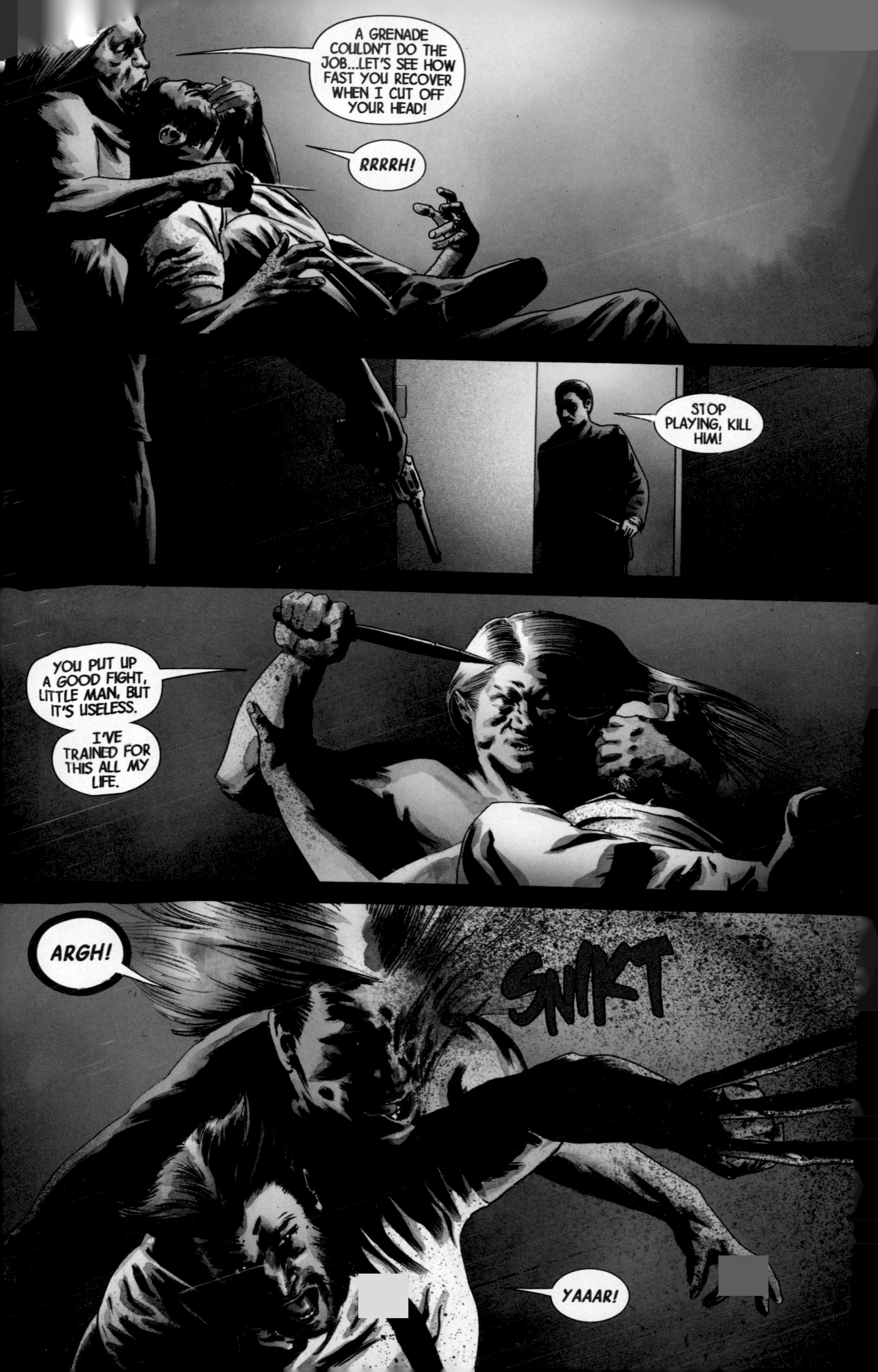
A GRENADE COULDN'T DO THE JOB...LET'S SEE HOW FAST YOU RECOVER WHEN I CUT OFF YOUR HEAD!
RRRRH!
STOP PLAYING, KILL HIM!
YOU PUT UP A GOOD FIGHT, LITTLE MAN, BUT IT'S USELESS.
I'VE TRAINED FOR THIS ALL MY LIFE.
ARGH!
SNIKT
YAAAR!

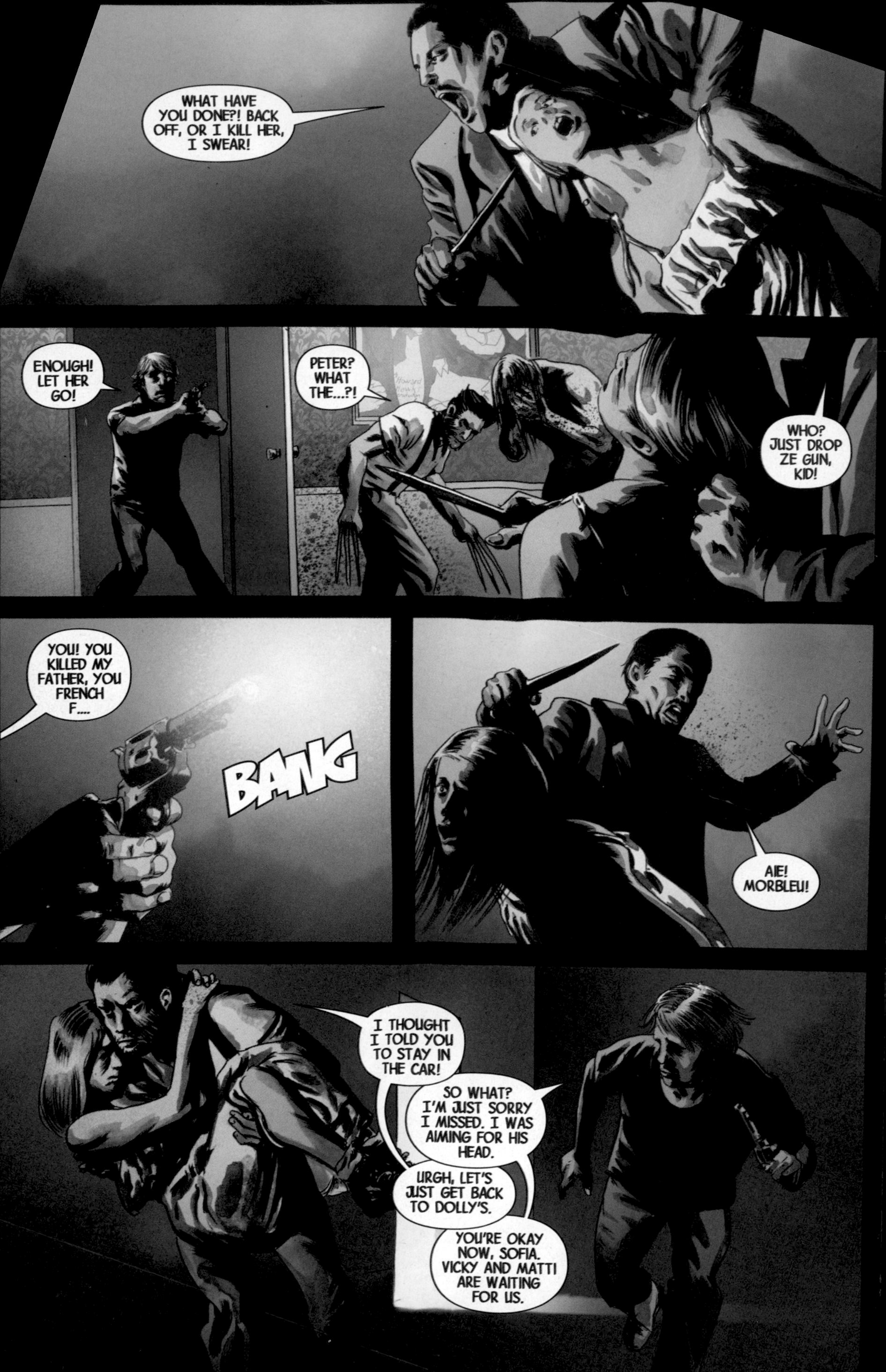
WHAT HAVE YOU DONE?! BACK OFF, OR I KILL HER, I SWEAR!
ENOUGH! LET HER GO!
PETER? WHAT THE...?!
WHO? JUST DROP ZE GUN, KID!
YOU! YOU KILLED MY FATHER, YOU FRENCH F....
BANG
AIE! MORBLEU!
I THOUGHT I TOLD YOU TO STAY IN THE CAR!
SO WHAT? I'M JUST SORRY I MISSED. I WAS AIMING FOR HIS HEAD.
URGH, LET'S JUST GET BACK TO DOLLY'S.
YOU'RE OKAY NOW, SOFIA. VICKY AND MATTI ARE WAITING FOR US.

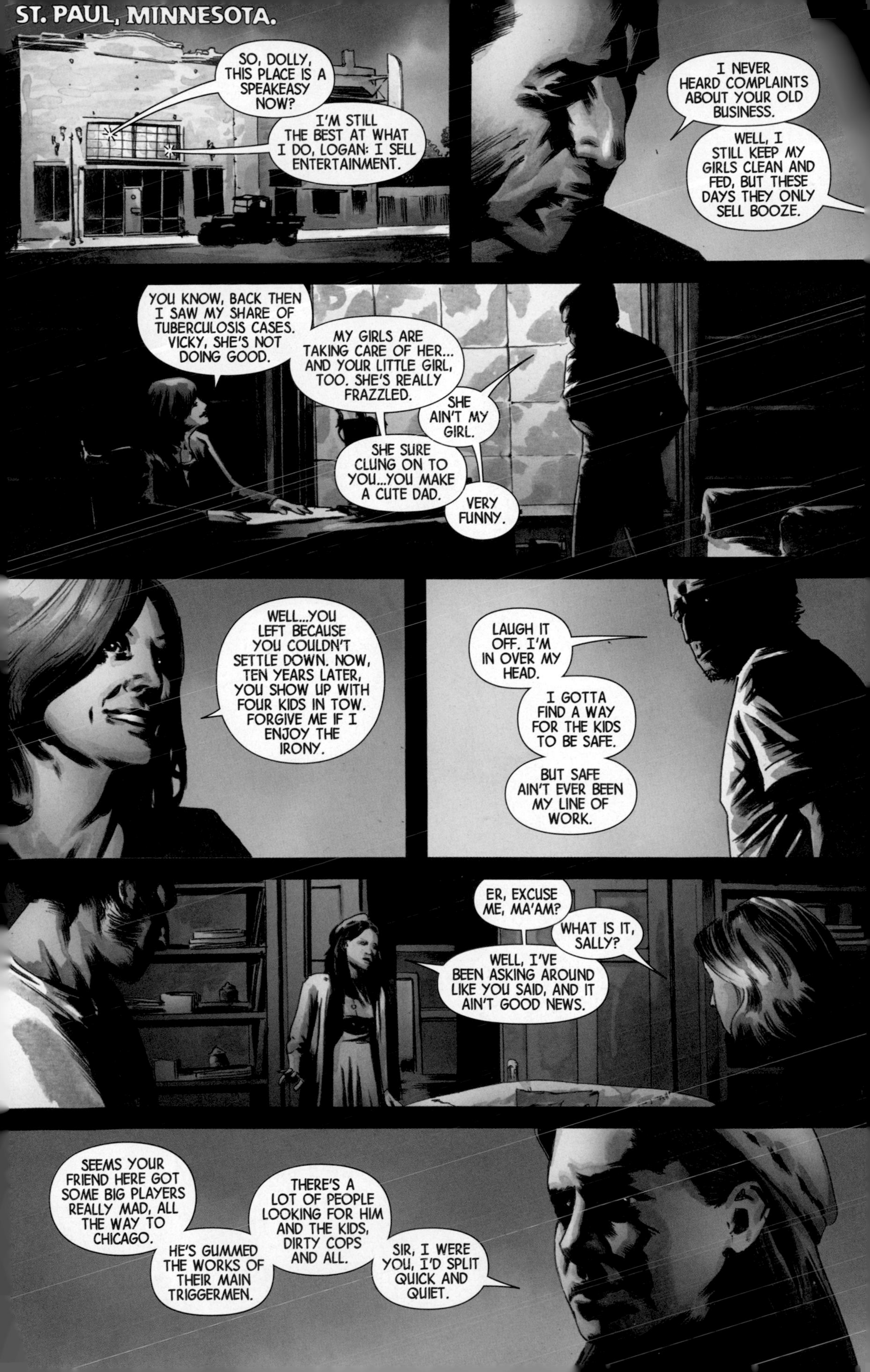
ST. PAUL, MINNESOTA.
SO, DOLLY, THIS PLACE IS A SPEAKEASY NOW?
I'M STILL THE BEST AT WHAT I DO, LOGAN: I SELL ENTERTAINMENT.
I NEVER HEARD COMPLAINTS ABOUT YOUR OLD BUSINESS.
WELL, I STILL KEEP MY GIRLS CLEAN AND FED, BUT THESE DAYS THEY ONLY SELL BOOZE.
YOU KNOW, BACK THEN I SAW MY SHARE OF TUBERCULOSIS CASES. VICKY, SHE'S NOT DOING GOOD.
MY GIRLS ARE TAKING CARE OF HER... AND YOUR LITTLE GIRL, TOO. SHE'S REALLY FRAZZLED.
SHE AIN'T MY GIRL.
SHE SURE CLUNG ON TO YOU...YOU MAKE A CUTE DAD.
VERY FUNNY.
WELL...YOU LEFT BECAUSE YOU COULDN'T SETTLE DOWN. NOW, TEN YEARS LATER, YOU SHOW UP WITH FOUR KIDS IN TOW. FORGIVE ME IF I ENJOY THE IRONY.
LAUGH IT OFF. I'M IN OVER MY HEAD.
I GOTTA FIND A WAY FOR THE KIDS TO BE SAFE.
BUT SAFE AIN'T EVER BEEN MY LINE OF WORK.
ER, EXCUSE ME, MA'AM?
WHAT IS IT, SALLY?
WELL, I'VE BEEN ASKING AROUND LIKE YOU SAID, AND IT AIN'T GOOD NEWS.
SEEMS YOUR FRIEND HERE GOT SOME BIG PLAYERS REALLY MAD, ALL THE WAY TO CHICAGO.
HE'S GUMMED THE WORKS OF THEIR MAIN TRIGGERMEN.
THERE'S A LOT OF PEOPLE LOOKING FOR HIM AND THE KIDS, DIRTY COPS AND ALL.
SIR, I WERE YOU, I'D SPLIT QUICK AND QUIET.

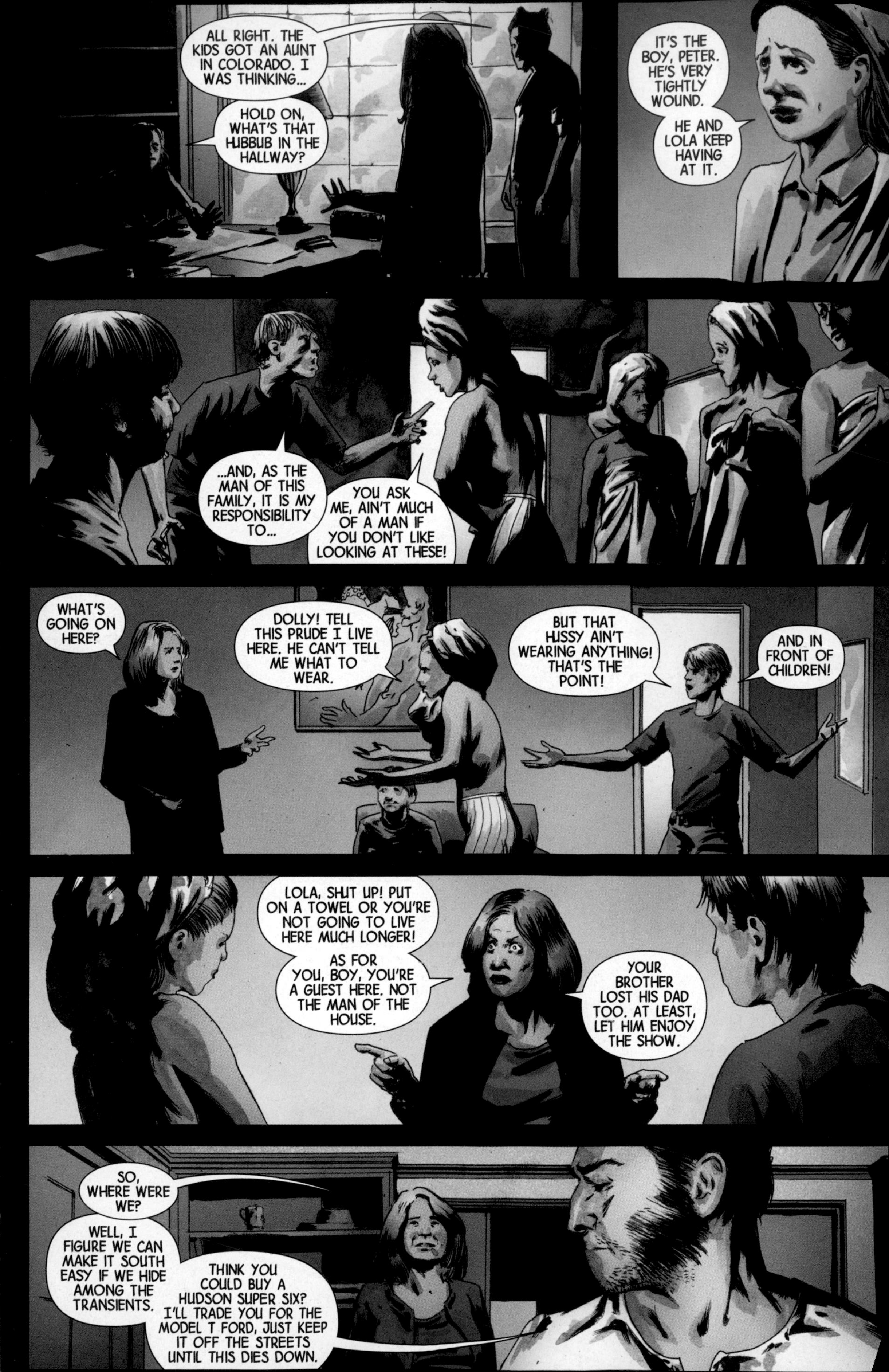
ALL RIGHT. THE KIDS GOT AN AUNT IN COLORADO. I WAS THINKING...
HOLD ON, WHAT'S THAT HUBBUB IN THE HALLWAY?
IT'S THE BOY, PETER. HE'S VERY TIGHTLY WOUND.
HE AND LOLA KEEP HAVING AT IT.
...AND, AS THE MAN OF THIS FAMILY, IT IS MY RESPONSIBILITY TO...
YOU ASK ME, AIN'T MUCH OF A MAN IF YOU DON'T LIKE LOOKING AT THESE!
WHAT'S GOING ON HERE?
DOLLY! TELL THIS PRUDE I LIVE HERE. HE CAN'T TELL ME WHAT TO WEAR.
BUT THAT HUSSY AIN'T WEARING ANYTHING! THAT'S THE POINT!
AND IN FRONT OF CHILDREN!
LOLA, SHUT UP! PUT ON A TOWEL OR YOU'RE NOT GOING TO LIVE HERE MUCH LONGER!
AS FOR YOU, BOY, YOU'RE A GUEST HERE. NOT THE MAN OF THE HOUSE.
YOUR BROTHER LOST HIS DAD TOO. AT LEAST, LET HIM ENJOY THE SHOW.
SO, WHERE WERE WE?
WELL, I FIGURE WE CAN MAKE IT SOUTH EASY IF WE HIDE AMONG THE TRANSIENTS.
THINK YOU COULD BUY A HUDSON SUPER SIX? I'LL TRADE YOU FOR THE MODEL T FORD, JUST KEEP IT OFF THE STREETS UNTIL THIS DIES DOWN.

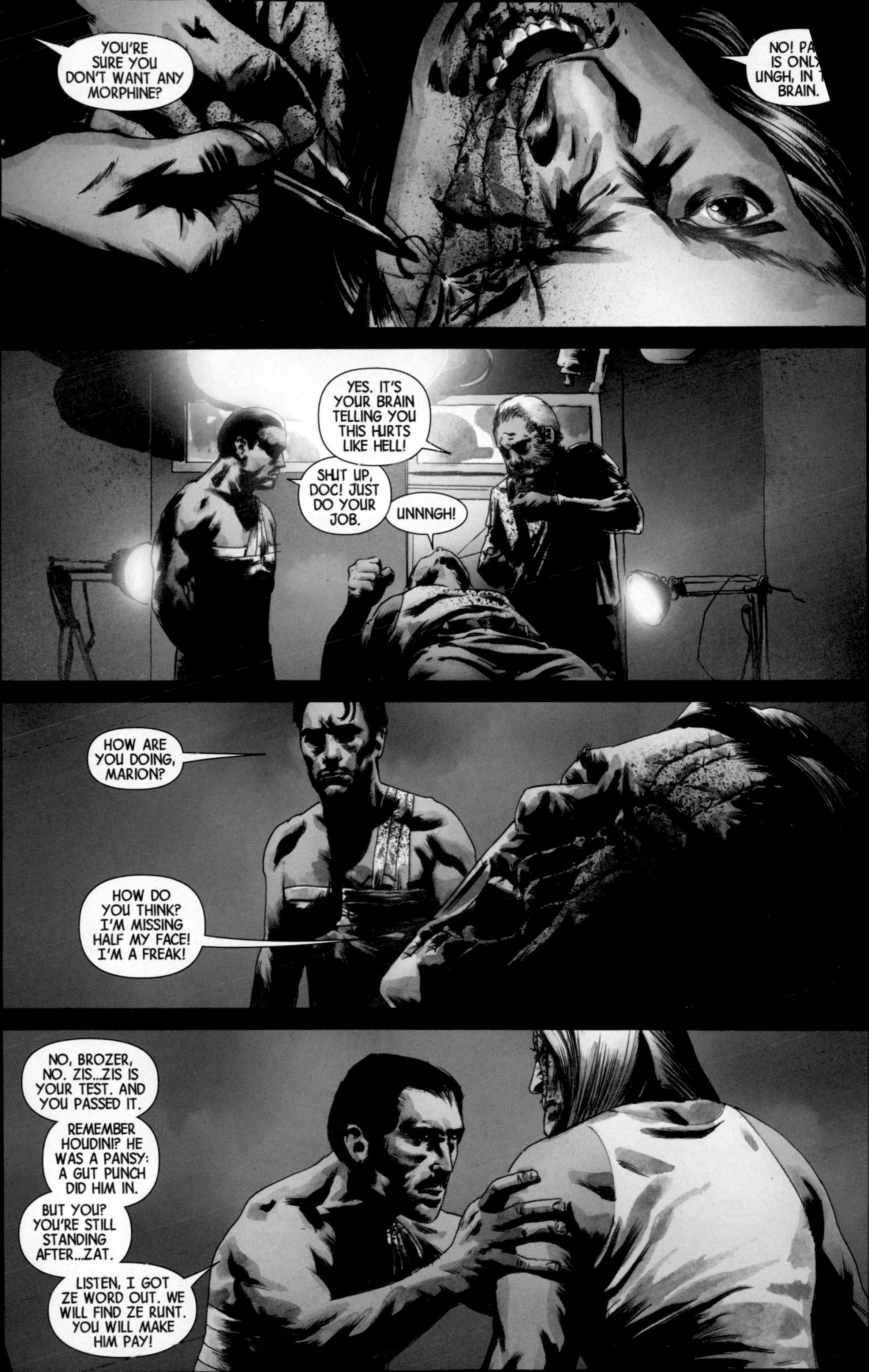
YOU'RE SURE YOU DON'T WANT ANY MORPHINE?
NO! PA IS ONLY UNGH, IN T BRAIN.
YES. IT'S YOUR BRAIN TELLING YOU THIS HURTS LIKE HELL!
SHUT UP, DOC! JUST DO YOUR JOB.
UNNNGH!
HOW ARE YOU DOING, MARION?
HOW DO YOU THINK? I'M MISSING HALF MY FACE! I'M A FREAK!
NO, BROZER, NO. ZIS...ZIS IS YOUR TEST. AND YOU PASSED IT.
REMEMBER HOUDINI? HE WAS A PANSY: A GUT PUNCH DID HIM IN.
BUT YOU? YOU'RE STILL STANDING AFTER...ZAT.
LISTEN, I GOT ZE WORD OUT. WE WILL FIND ZE RUNT. YOU WILL MAKE HIM PAY!

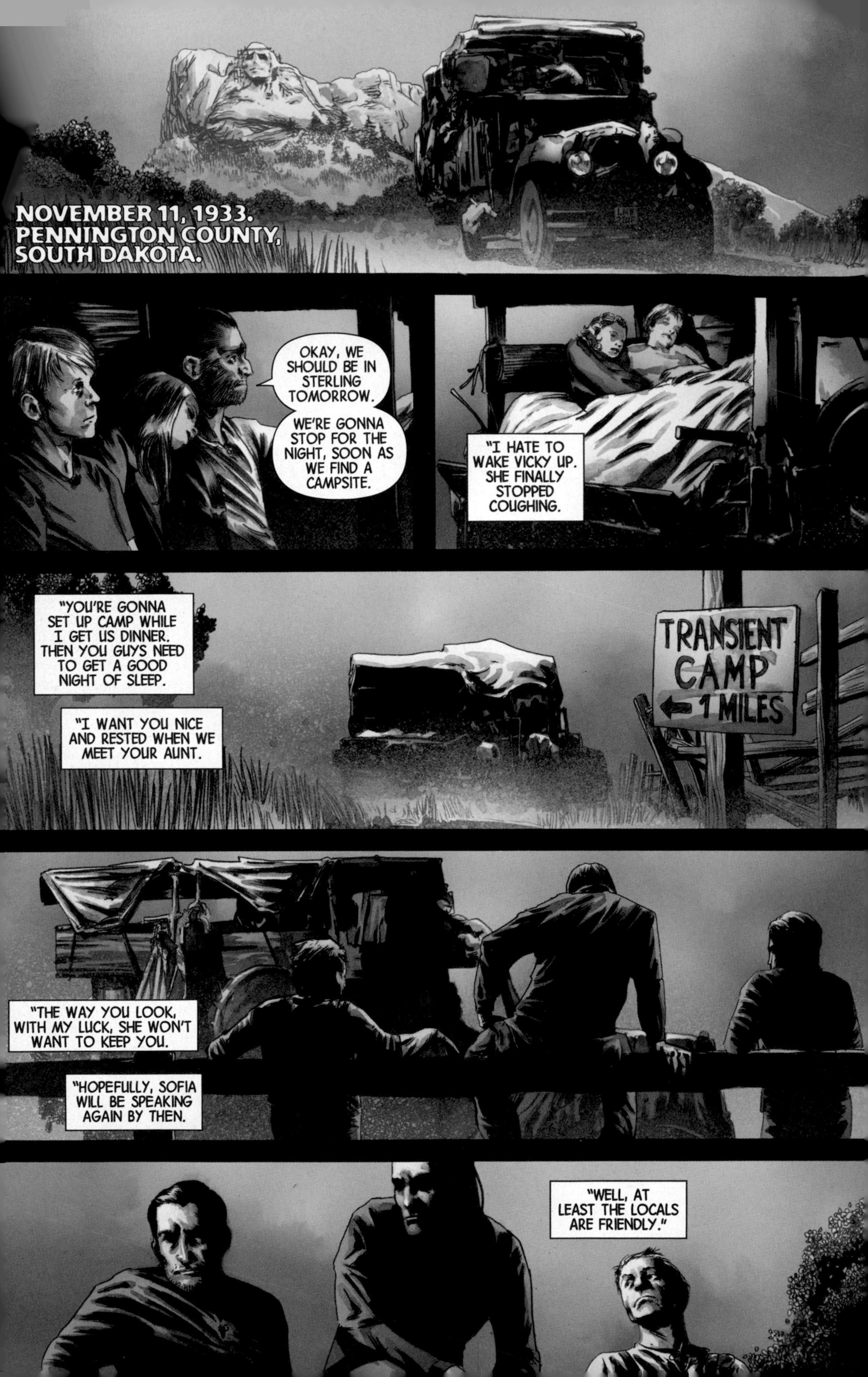
NOVEMBER 11, 1933. PENNINGTON COUNTY, SOUTH DAKOTA.
OKAY, WE SHOULD BE IN STERLING TOMORROW.
WE'RE GONNA STOP FOR THE NIGHT, SOON AS WE FIND A CAMPSITE.
"I HATE TO WAKE VICKY UP. SHE FINALLY STOPPED COUGHING.
"YOU'RE GONNA SET UP CAMP WHILE I GET US DINNER. THEN YOU GUYS NEED TO GET A GOOD NIGHT OF SLEEP.
"I WANT YOU NICE AND RESTED WHEN WE MEET YOUR AUNT.
TRANSIENT CAMP 1 MILES
"THE WAY YOU LOOK, WITH MY LUCK, SHE WON'T WANT TO KEEP YOU.
"HOPEFULLY, SOFIA WILL BE SPEAKING AGAIN BY THEN.
"WELL, AT LEAST THE LOCALS ARE FRIENDLY."

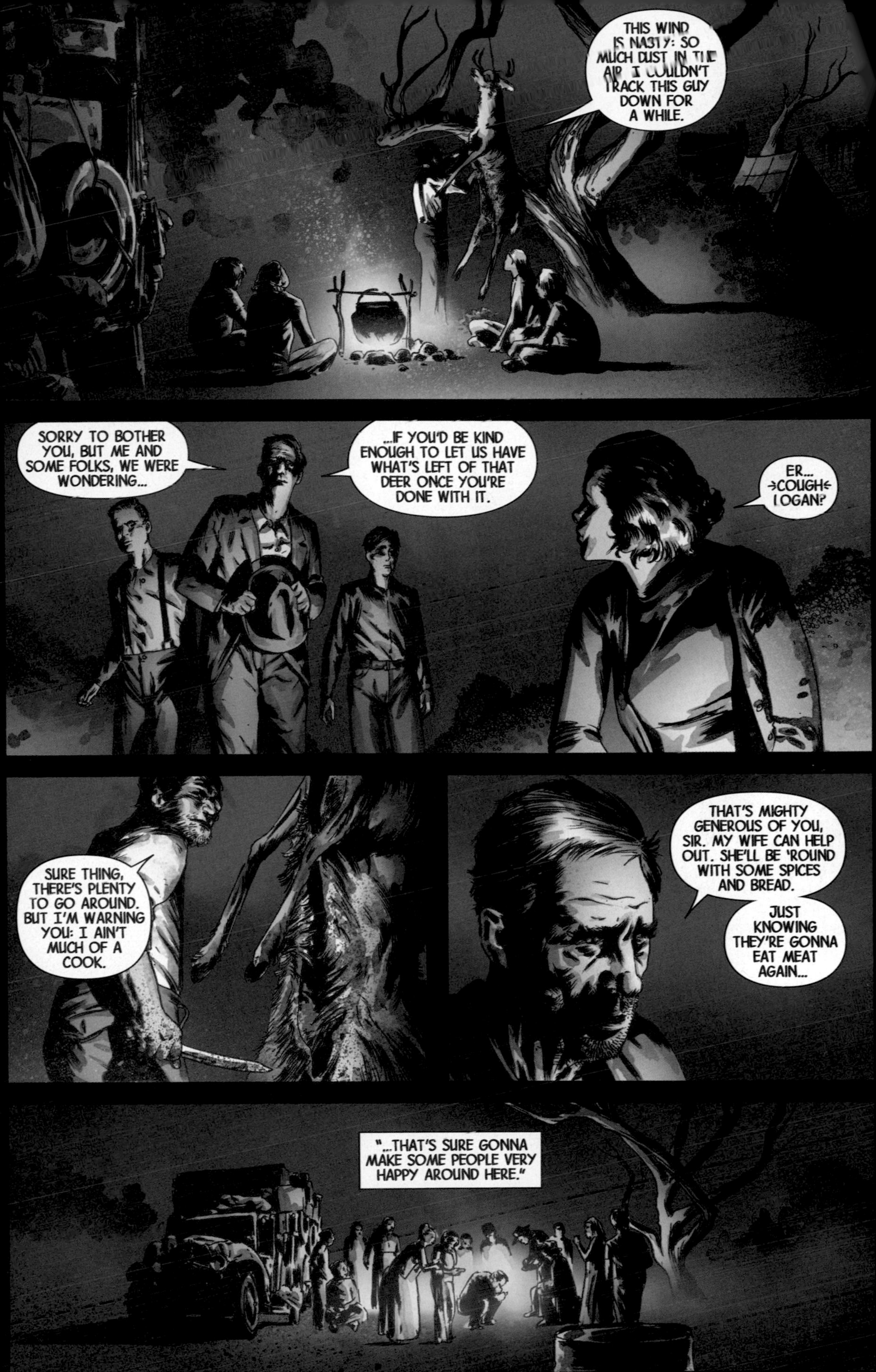

THIS WIND IS NASTY: SO MUCH DUST IN THE AIR I COULDN'T TRACK THIS GUY DOWN FOR A WHILE.
SORRY TO BOTHER YOU, BUT ME AND SOME FOLKS, WE WERE WONDERING...
...IF YOU'D BE KIND ENOUGH TO LET US HAVE WHAT'S LEFT OF THAT DEER ONCE YOU'RE DONE WITH IT.
ER... COUGH LOGAN?
SURE THING, THERE'S PLENTY TO GO AROUND. BUT I'M WARNING YOU: I AIN'T MUCH OF A COOK.
THAT'S MIGHTY GENEROUS OF YOU, SIR. MY WIFE CAN HELP OUT. SHE'LL BE 'ROUND WITH SOME SPICES AND BREAD.
JUST KNOWING THEY'RE GONNA EAT MEAT AGAIN...
"...THAT'S SURE GONNA MAKE SOME PEOPLE VERY HAPPY AROUND HERE."

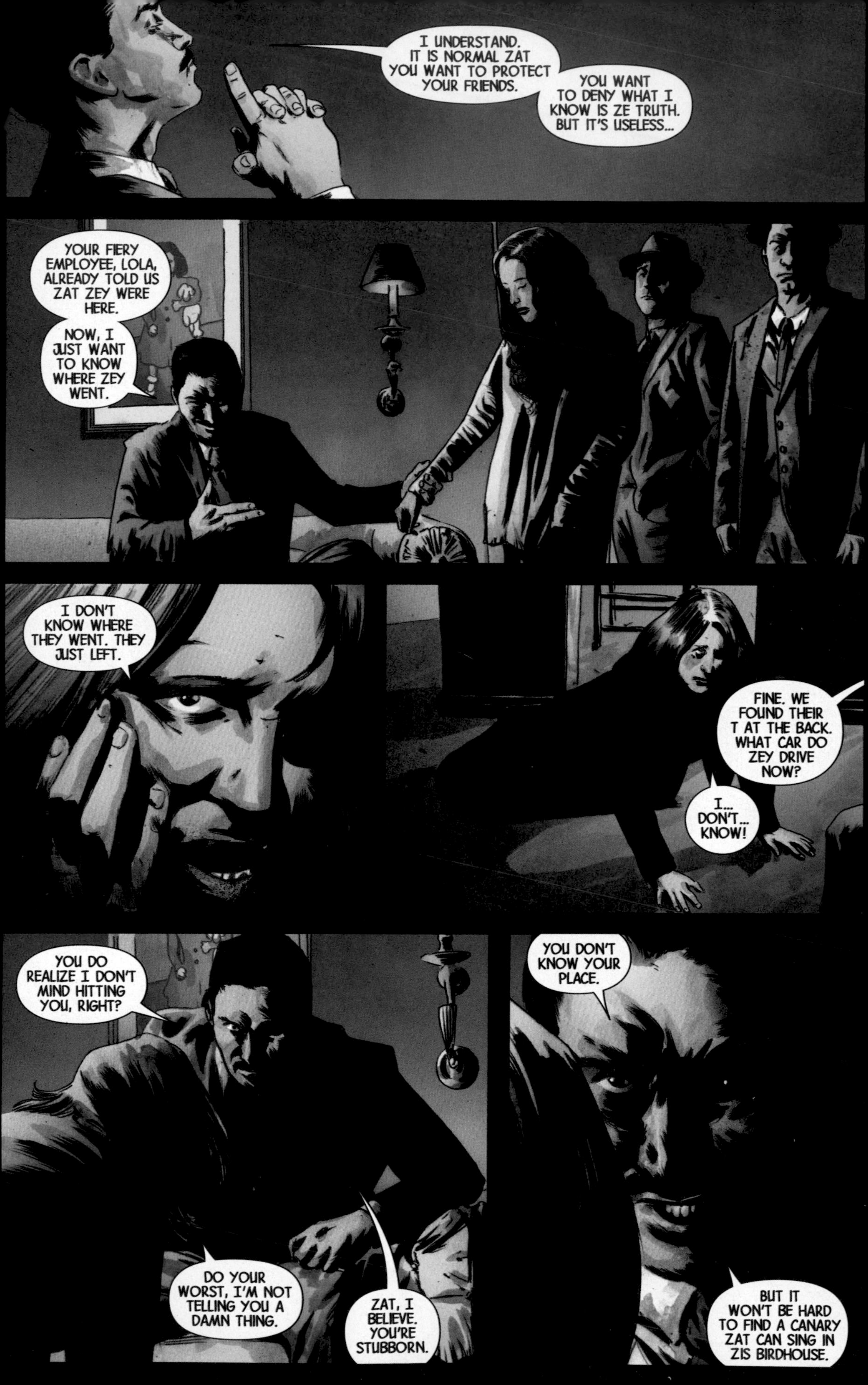
I UNDERSTAND. IT IS NORMAL ZAT YOU WANT TO PROTECT YOUR FRIENDS.
YOU WANT TO DENY WHAT I KNOW IS ZE TRUTH. BUT IT'S USELESS...
YOUR FIERY EMPLOYEE, LOLA, ALREADY TOLD US ZAT ZEY WERE HERE.
NOW, I JUST WANT TO KNOW WHERE ZEY WENT.
I DON'T KNOW WHERE THEY WENT. THEY JUST LEFT.
FINE. WE FOUND THEIR T AT THE BACK. WHAT CAR DO ZEY DRIVE NOW?
I... DON'T... KNOW!
YOU DO REALIZE I DON'T MIND HITTING YOU, RIGHT?
DO YOUR WORST, I'M NOT TELLING YOU A DAMN THING.
ZAT, I BELIEVE. YOU'RE STUBBORN.
YOU DON'T KNOW YOUR PLACE.
BUT IT WON'T BE HARD TO FIND A CANARY ZAT CAN SING IN ZIS BIRDHOUSE.

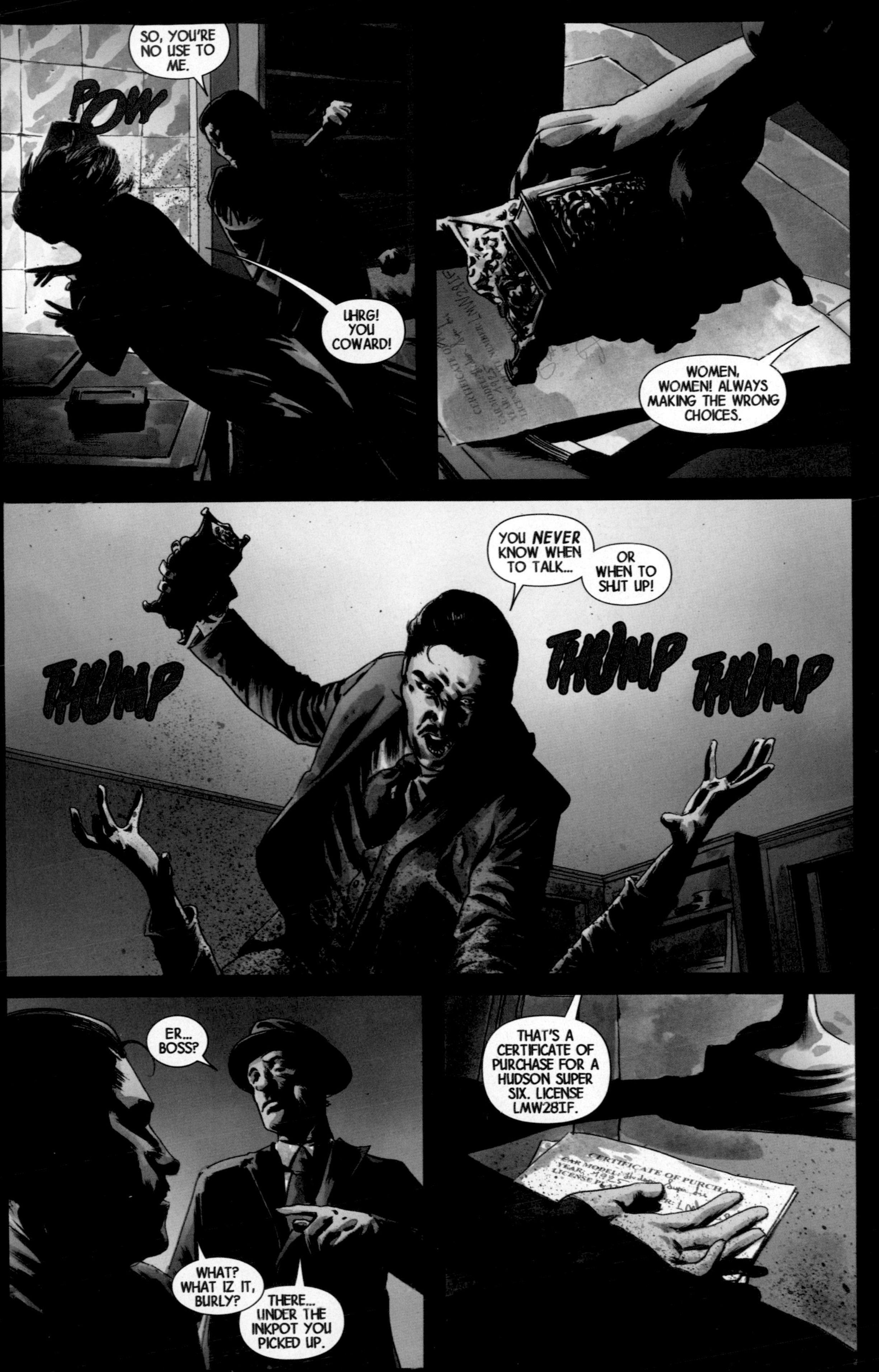

SO, YOU'RE NO USE TO ME.
POW
UHRG! YOU COWARD!
WOMEN, WOMEN! ALWAYS MAKING THE WRONG CHOICES.
YOU *NEVER* KNOW WHEN TO TALK...
OR WHEN TO SHUT UP!
THUMP
THUMP
THUMP
ER... BOSS?
WHAT? WHAT IZ IT, BURLY?
THERE... UNDER THE INKPOT YOU PICKED UP.
THAT'S A CERTIFICATE OF PURCHASE FOR A HUDSON SUPER SIX. LICENSE LMW28IF.

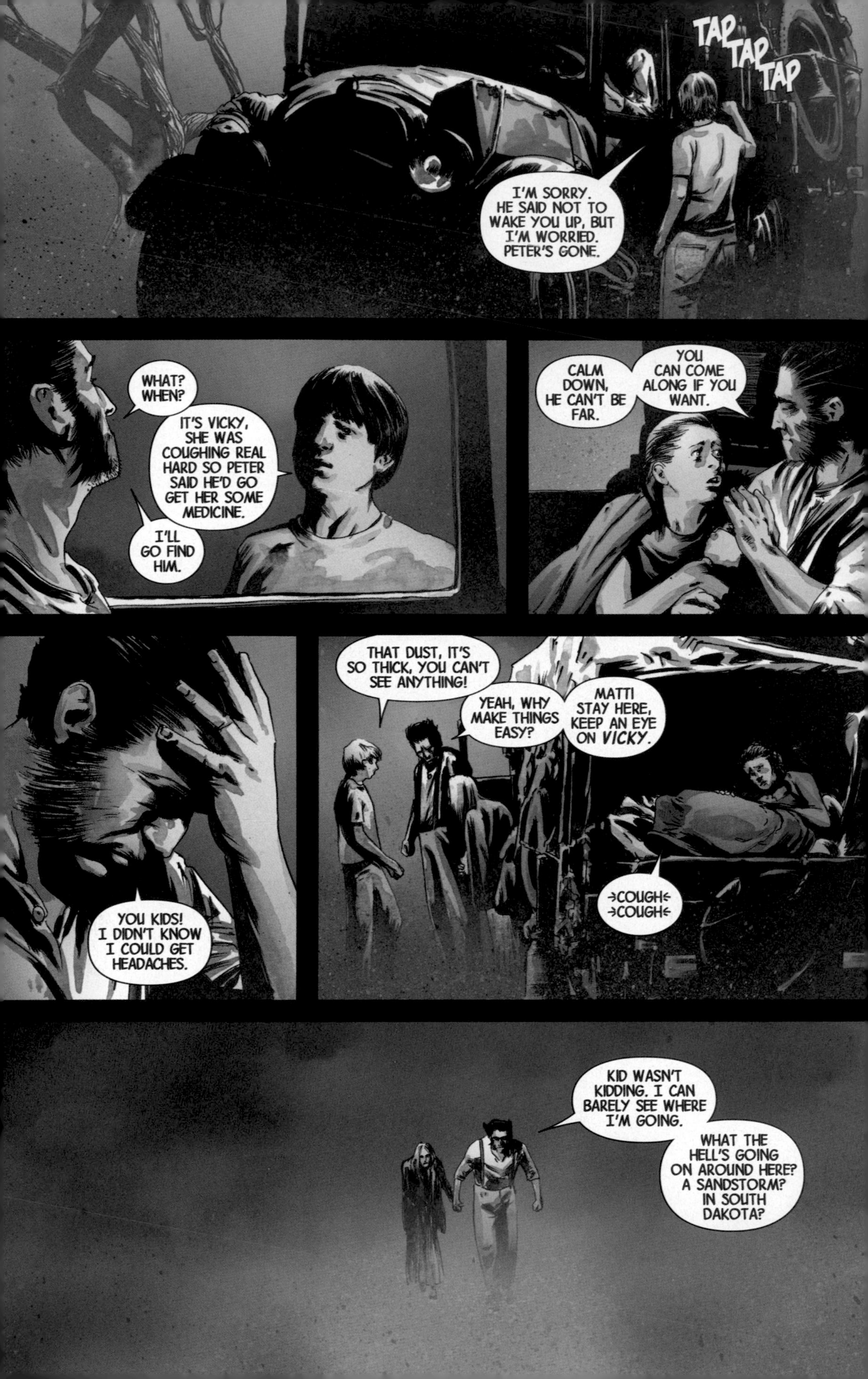
TAP TAP TAP
I'M SORRY. HE SAID NOT TO WAKE YOU UP, BUT I'M WORRIED. PETER'S GONE.
WHAT? WHEN?
IT'S VICKY, SHE WAS COUGHING REAL HARD SO PETER SAID HE'D GO GET HER SOME MEDICINE.
I'LL GO FIND HIM.
CALM DOWN, HE CAN'T BE FAR.
YOU CAN COME ALONG IF YOU WANT.
YOU KIDS! I DIDN'T KNOW I COULD GET HEADACHES.
THAT DUST, IT'S SO THICK, YOU CAN'T SEE ANYTHING!
YEAH, WHY MAKE THINGS EASY?
MATTI STAY HERE, KEEP AN EYE ON VICKY.
COUGH
COUGH
KID WASN'T KIDDING. I CAN BARELY SEE WHERE I'M GOING.
WHAT THE HELL'S GOING ON AROUND HERE? A SANDSTORM? IN SOUTH DAKOTA?

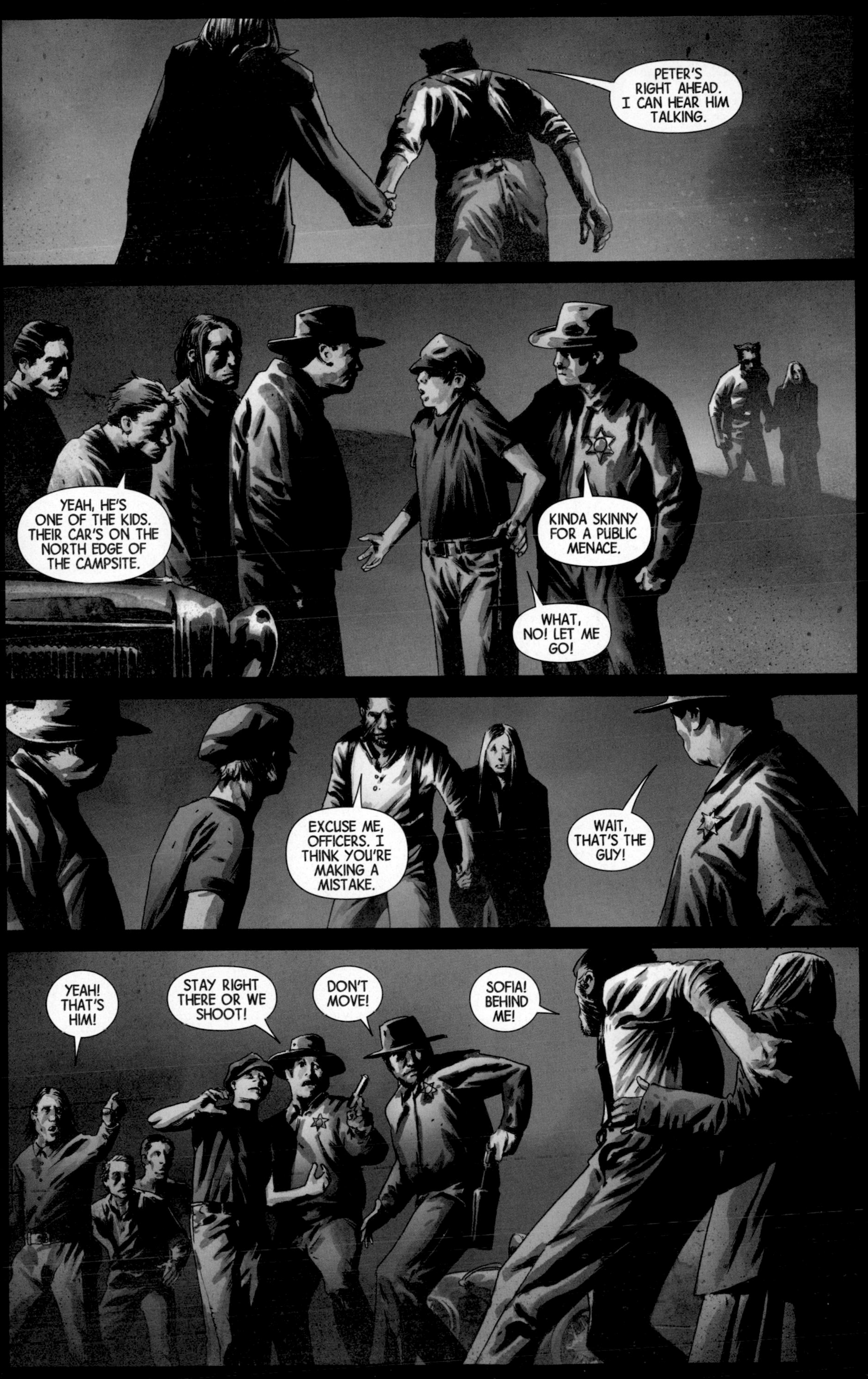
PETER'S RIGHT AHEAD. I CAN HEAR HIM TALKING.
YEAH, HE'S ONE OF THE KIDS. THEIR CAR'S ON THE NORTH EDGE OF THE CAMPSITE.
KINDA SKINNY FOR A PUBLIC MENACE.
WHAT, NO! LET ME GO!
EXCUSE ME, OFFICERS. I THINK YOU'RE MAKING A MISTAKE.
WAIT, THAT'S THE GUY!
YEAH! THAT'S HIM!
STAY RIGHT THERE OR WE SHOOT!
DON'T MOVE!
SOFIA! BEHIND ME!

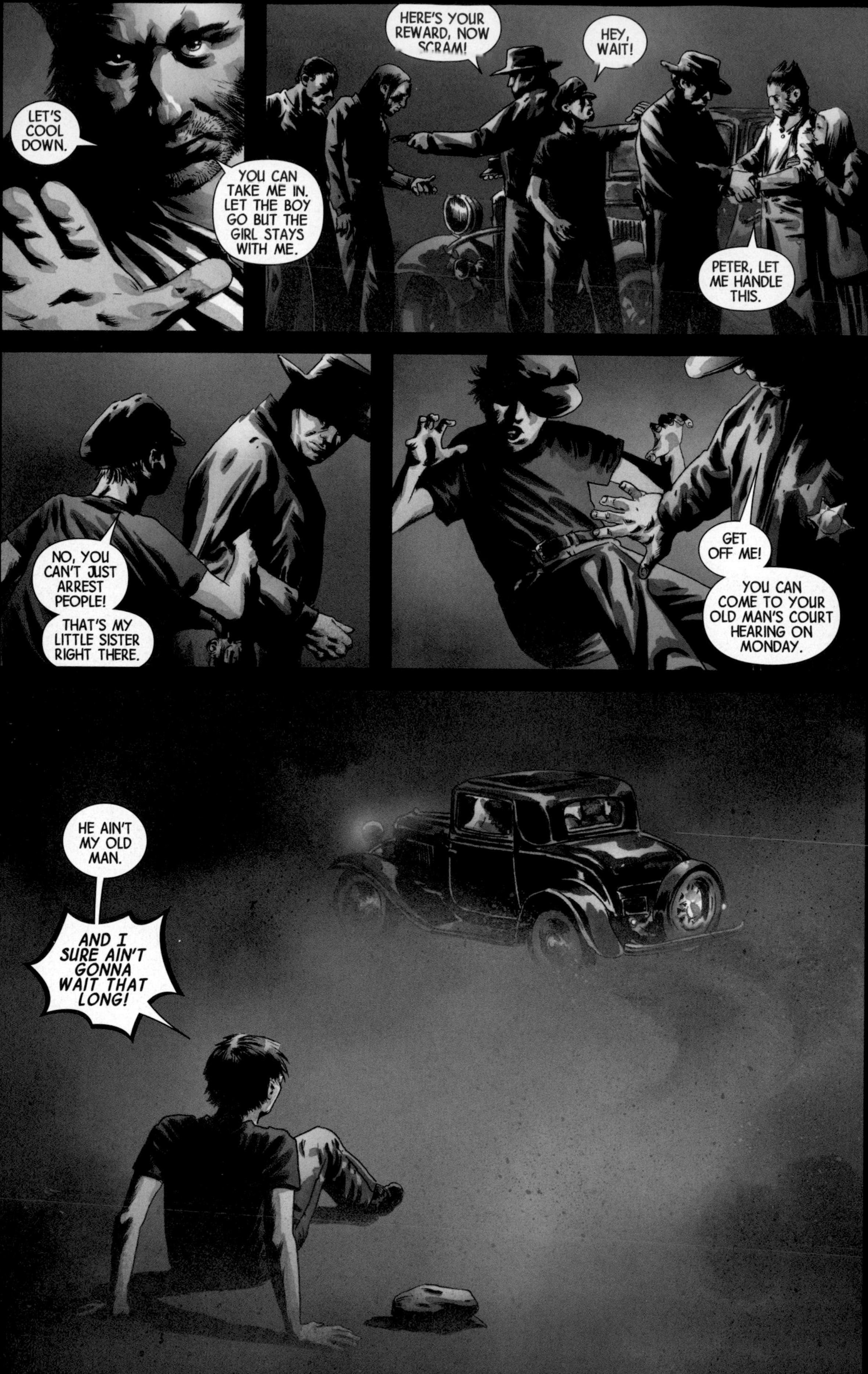
LET'S COOL DOWN.
YOU CAN TAKE ME IN. LET THE BOY GO BUT THE GIRL STAYS WITH ME.
HERE'S YOUR REWARD, NOW SCRAM!
HEY, WAIT!
PETER, LET ME HANDLE THIS.
NO, YOU CAN'T JUST ARREST PEOPLE!
THAT'S MY LITTLE SISTER RIGHT THERE.
GET OFF ME!
YOU CAN COME TO YOUR OLD MAN'S COURT HEARING ON MONDAY.
HE AIN'T MY OLD MAN.
AND I SURE AIN'T GONNA WAIT THAT LONG!

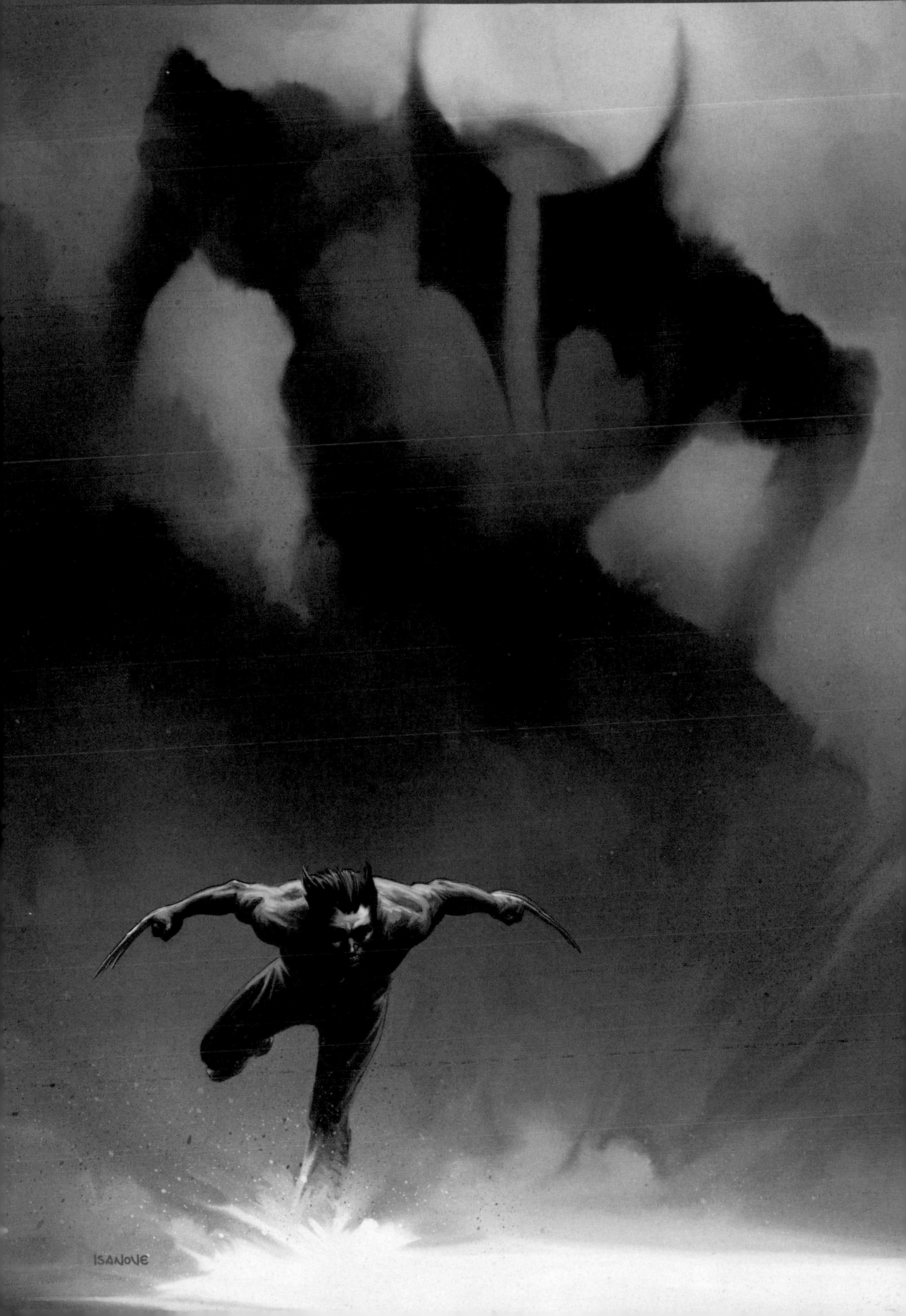
ISANOVE

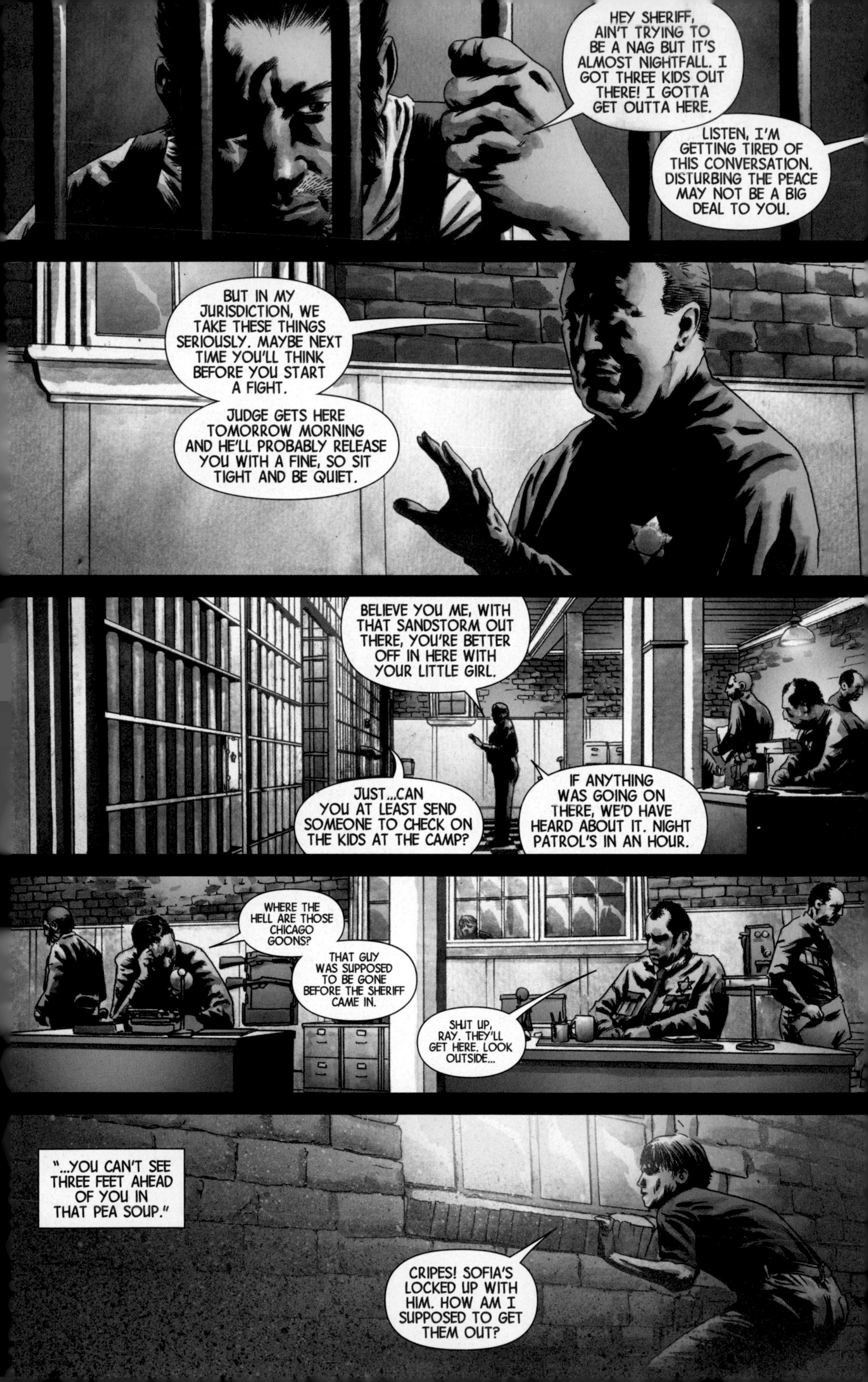
HEY SHERIFF, AIN'T TRYING TO BE A NAG BUT IT'S ALMOST NIGHTFALL. I GOT THREE KIDS OUT THERE! I GOTTA GET OUTTA HERE.
LISTEN, I'M GETTING TIRED OF THIS CONVERSATION. DISTURBING THE PEACE MAY NOT BE A BIG DEAL TO YOU.
BUT IN MY JURISDICTION, WE TAKE THESE THINGS SERIOUSLY. MAYBE NEXT TIME YOU'LL THINK BEFORE YOU START A FIGHT.
JUDGE GETS HERE TOMORROW MORNING AND HE'LL PROBABLY RELEASE YOU WITH A FINE, SO SIT TIGHT AND BE QUIET.
BELIEVE YOU ME, WITH THAT SANDSTORM OUT THERE, YOU'RE BETTER OFF IN HERE WITH YOUR LITTLE GIRL.
JUST...CAN YOU AT LEAST SEND SOMEONE TO CHECK ON THE KIDS AT THE CAMP?
IF ANYTHING WAS GOING ON THERE, WE'D HAVE HEARD ABOUT IT. NIGHT PATROL'S IN AN HOUR.
WHERE THE HELL ARE THOSE CHICAGO GOONS?
THAT GUY WAS SUPPOSED TO BE GONE BEFORE THE SHERIFF CAME IN.
SHUT UP, RAY. THEY'LL GET HERE. LOOK OUTSIDE...
"...YOU CAN'T SEE THREE FEET AHEAD OF YOU IN THAT PEA SOUP."
CRIPES! SOFIA'S LOCKED UP WITH HIM. HOW AM I SUPPOSED TO GET THEM OUT?

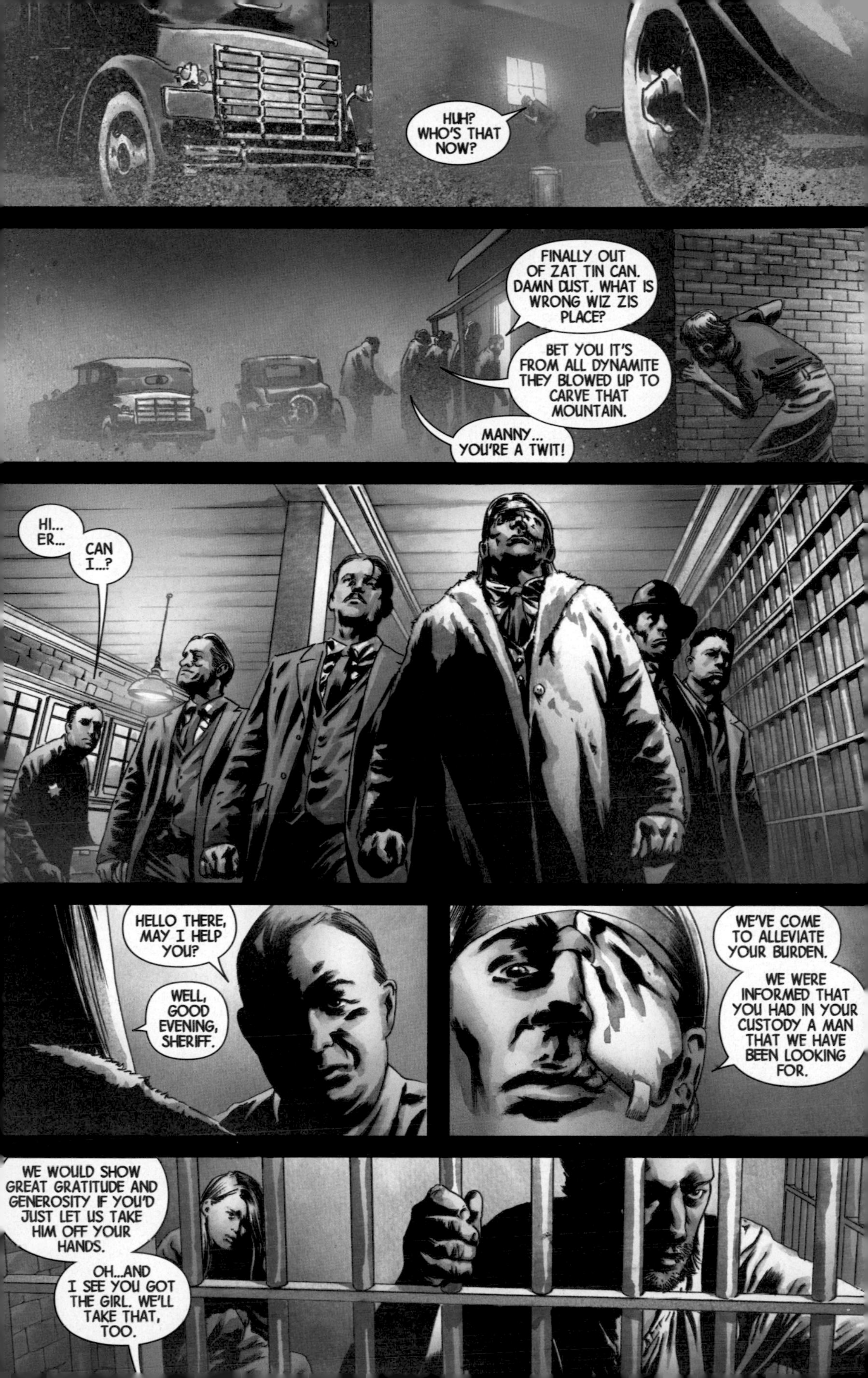
HUH? WHO'S THAT NOW?
FINALLY OUT OF ZAT TIN CAN. DAMN DUST. WHAT IS WRONG WIZ ZIS PLACE?
BET YOU IT'S FROM ALL DYNAMITE THEY BLOWED UP TO CARVE THAT MOUNTAIN.
MANNY... YOU'RE A TWIT!
HI... ER...
CAN I...?
HELLO THERE, MAY I HELP YOU?
WELL, GOOD EVENING, SHERIFF.
WE'VE COME TO ALLEVIATE YOUR BURDEN.
WE WERE INFORMED THAT YOU HAD IN YOUR CUSTODY A MAN THAT WE HAVE BEEN LOOKING FOR.
WE WOULD SHOW GREAT GRATITUDE AND GENEROSITY IF YOU'D JUST LET US TAKE HIM OFF YOUR HANDS.
OH...AND I SEE YOU GOT THE GIRL. WE'LL TAKE THAT, TOO.

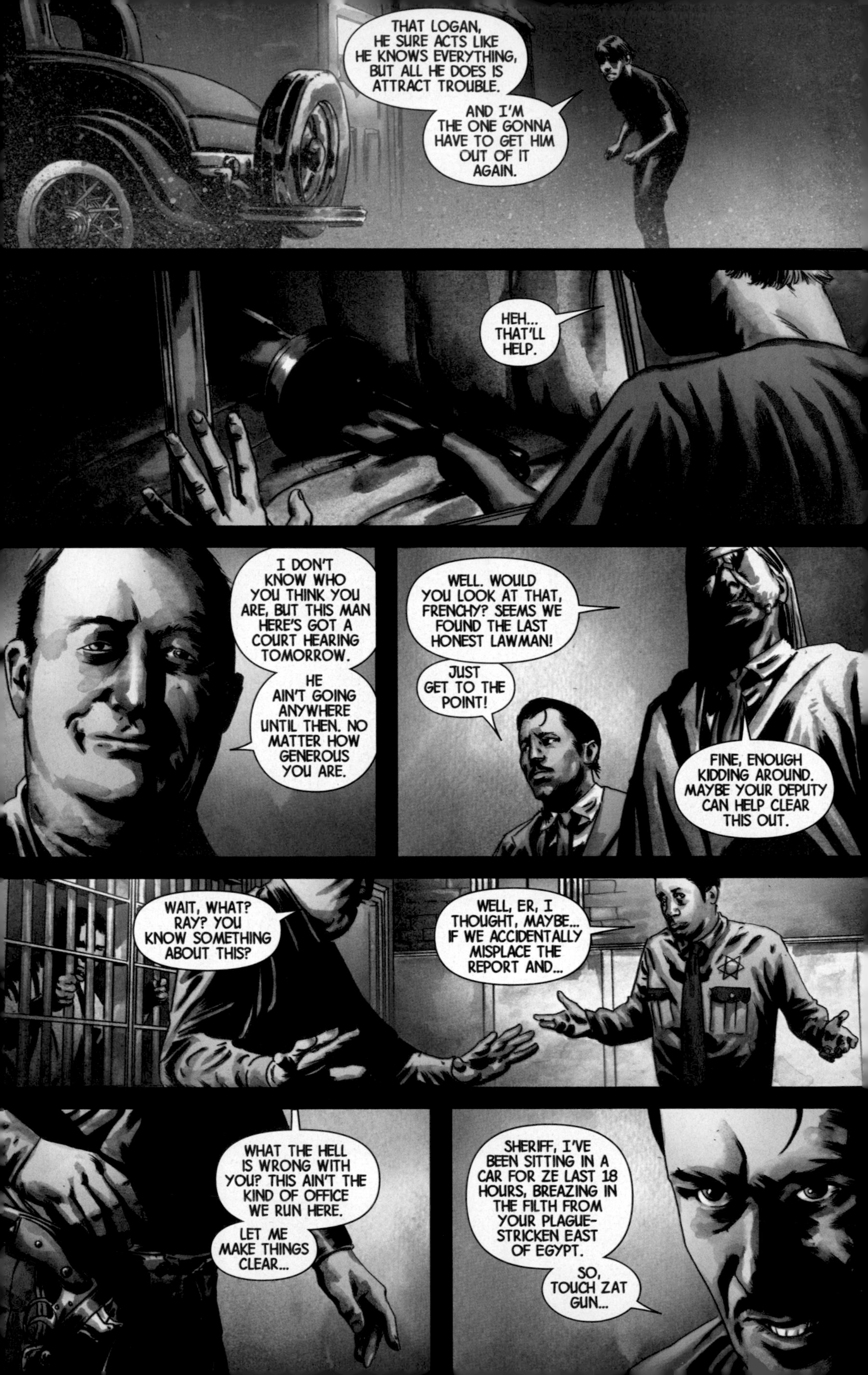
THAT LOGAN, HE SURE ACTS LIKE HE KNOWS EVERYTHING, BUT ALL HE DOES IS ATTRACT TROUBLE.
AND I'M THE ONE GONNA HAVE TO GET HIM OUT OF IT AGAIN.
HEH... THAT'LL HELP.
I DON'T KNOW WHO YOU THINK YOU ARE, BUT THIS MAN HERE'S GOT A COURT HEARING TOMORROW.
HE AIN'T GOING ANYWHERE UNTIL THEN. NO MATTER HOW GENEROUS YOU ARE.
WELL. WOULD YOU LOOK AT THAT, FRENCHY? SEEMS WE FOUND THE LAST HONEST LAWMAN!
JUST GET TO THE POINT!
FINE, ENOUGH KIDDING AROUND. MAYBE YOUR DEPUTY CAN HELP CLEAR THIS OUT.
WAIT, WHAT? RAY? YOU KNOW SOMETHING ABOUT THIS?
WELL, ER, I THOUGHT, MAYBE... IF WE ACCIDENTALLY MISPLACE THE REPORT AND...
WHAT THE HELL IS WRONG WITH YOU? THIS AIN'T THE KIND OF OFFICE WE RUN HERE.
LET ME MAKE THINGS CLEAR...
SHERIFF, I'VE BEEN SITTING IN A CAR FOR ZE LAST 18 HOURS, BREAZING IN THE FILTH FROM YOUR PLAGUE-STRICKEN EAST OF EGYPT.
SO, TOUCH ZAT GUN...

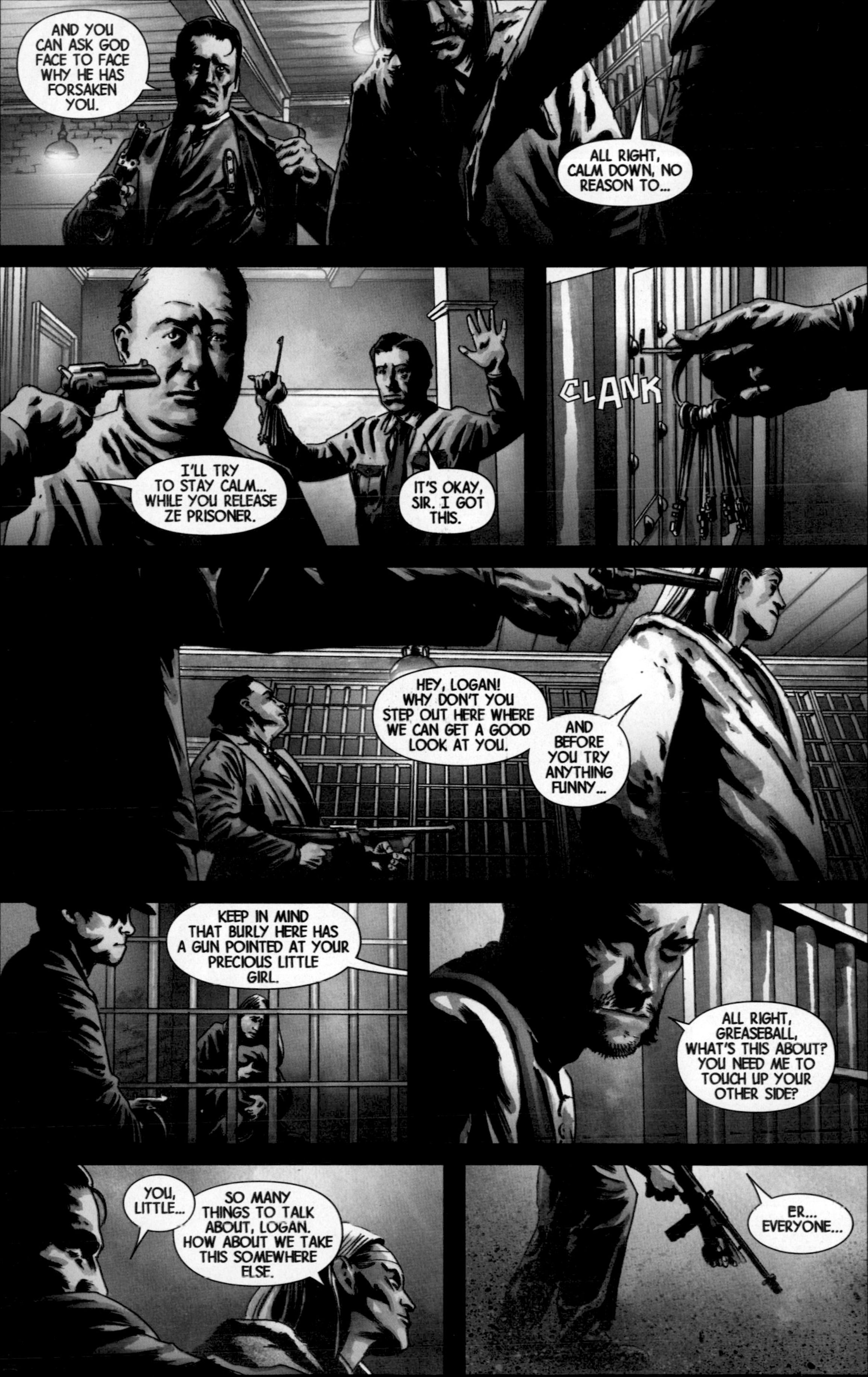
AND YOU CAN ASK GOD FACE TO FACE WHY HE HAS FORSAKEN YOU.
ALL RIGHT, CALM DOWN, NO REASON TO...
I'LL TRY TO STAY CALM... WHILE YOU RELEASE ZE PRISONER.
IT'S OKAY, SIR. I GOT THIS.
CLANK
HEY, LOGAN! WHY DON'T YOU STEP OUT HERE WHERE WE CAN GET A GOOD LOOK AT YOU.
AND BEFORE YOU TRY ANYTHING FUNNY...
KEEP IN MIND THAT BURLY HERE HAS A GUN POINTED AT YOUR PRECIOUS LITTLE GIRL.
ALL RIGHT, GREASEBALL, WHAT'S THIS ABOUT? YOU NEED ME TO TOUCH UP YOUR OTHER SIDE?
YOU, LITTLE...
SO MANY THINGS TO TALK ABOUT, LOGAN. HOW ABOUT WE TAKE THIS SOMEWHERE ELSE.
ER... EVERYONE...

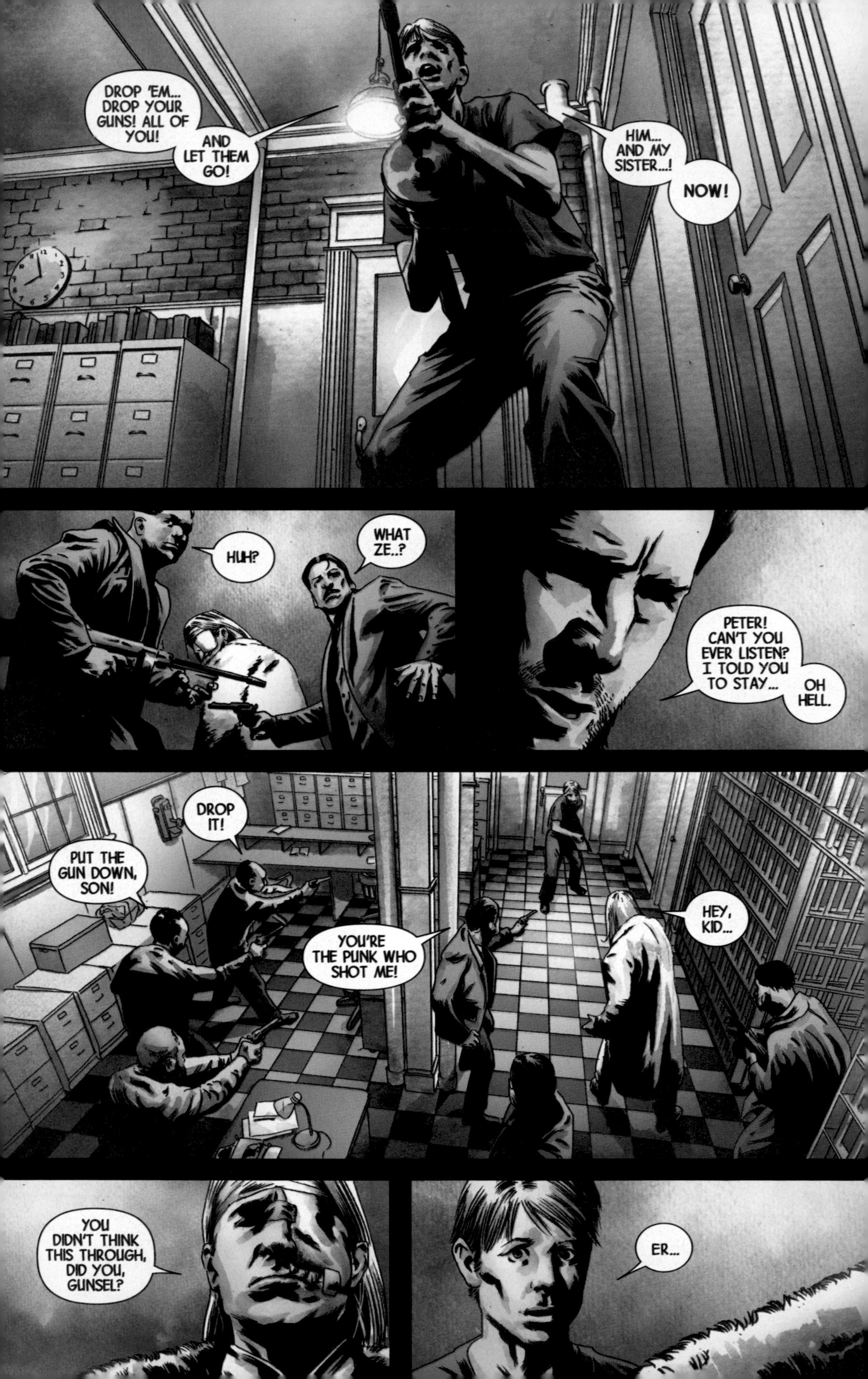
DROP 'EM... DROP YOUR GUNS! ALL OF YOU!
AND LET THEM GO!
HIM... AND MY SISTER...!
NOW!
HUH?
WHAT ZE..?
PETER! CAN'T YOU EVER LISTEN? I TOLD YOU TO STAY...
OH HELL.
DROP IT!
PUT THE GUN DOWN, SON!
YOU'RE THE PUNK WHO SHOT ME!
HEY, KID...
YOU DIDN'T THINK THIS THROUGH, DID YOU, GUNSEL?
ER...

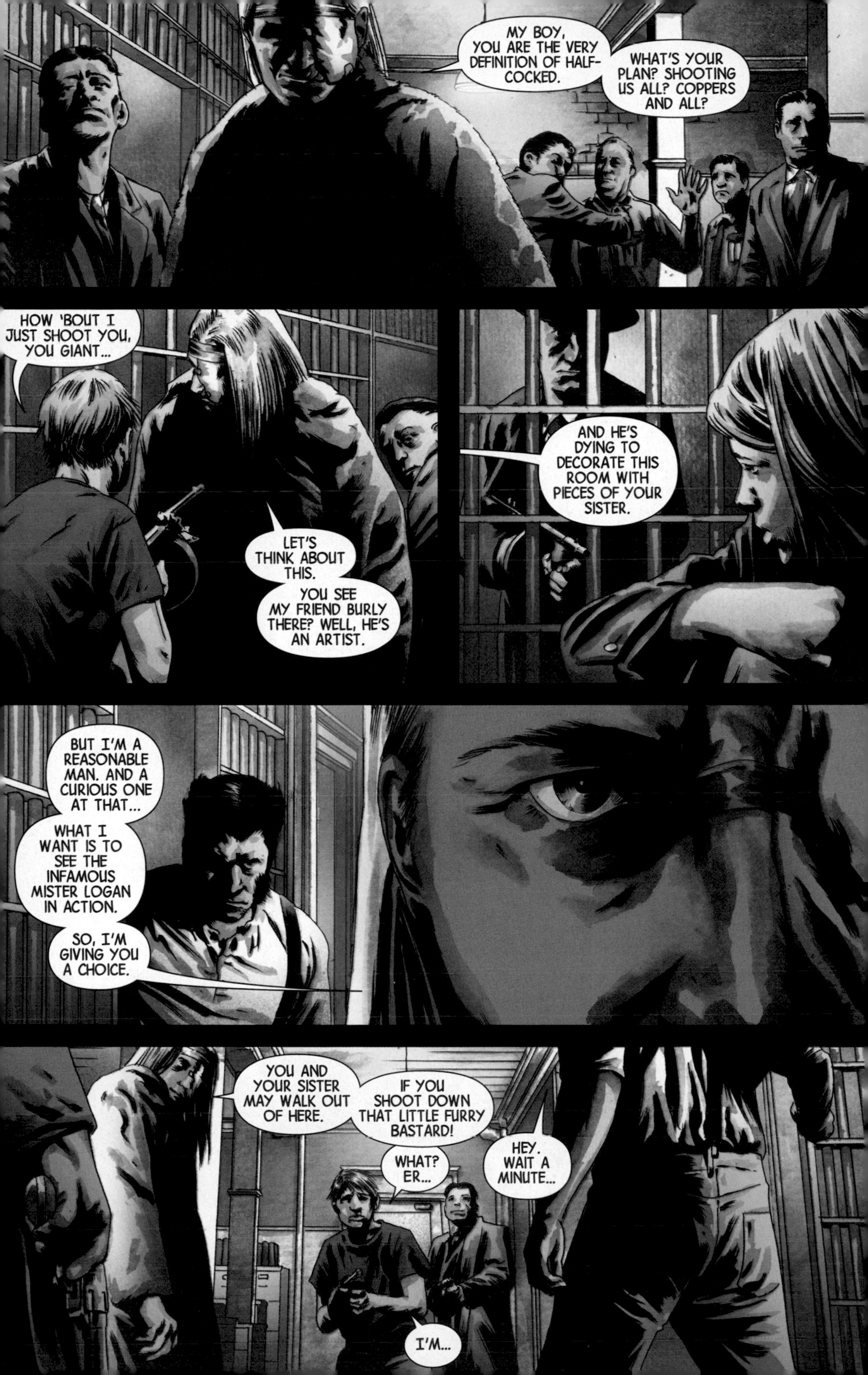
MY BOY, YOU ARE THE VERY DEFINITION OF HALF-COCKED.
WHAT'S YOUR PLAN? SHOOTING US ALL? COPPERS AND ALL?
HOW 'BOUT I JUST SHOOT YOU, YOU GIANT...
LET'S THINK ABOUT THIS.
YOU SEE MY FRIEND BURLY THERE? WELL, HE'S AN ARTIST.
AND HE'S DYING TO DECORATE THIS ROOM WITH PIECES OF YOUR SISTER.
BUT I'M A REASONABLE MAN. AND A CURIOUS ONE AT THAT...
WHAT I WANT IS TO SEE THE INFAMOUS MISTER LOGAN IN ACTION.
SO, I'M GIVING YOU A CHOICE.
YOU AND YOUR SISTER MAY WALK OUT OF HERE.
IF YOU SHOOT DOWN THAT LITTLE FURRY BASTARD!
WHAT? ER...
HEY. WAIT A MINUTE...
I'M...

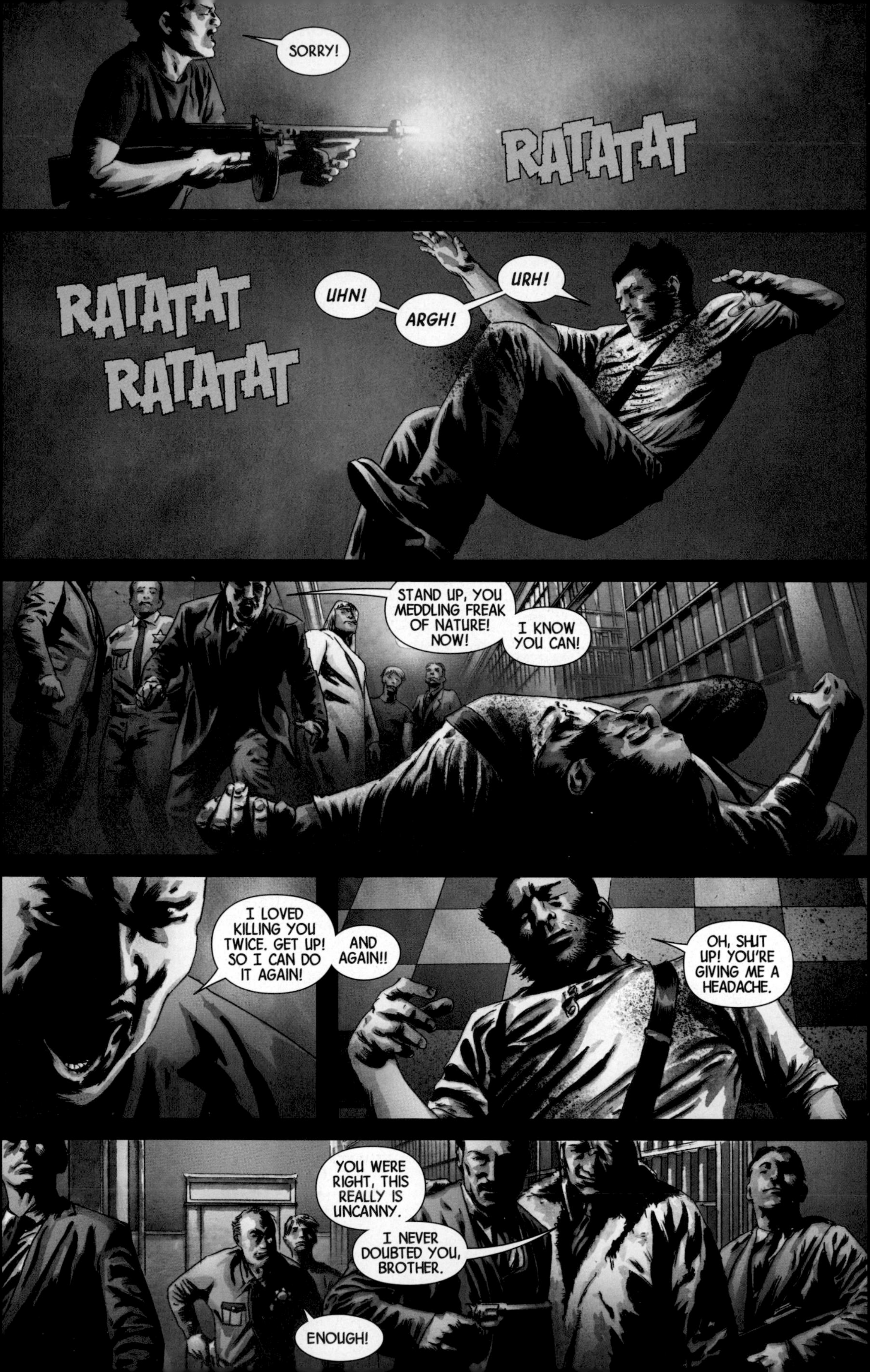
SORRY!
RATATAT
RATATAT
RATATAT
UHN!
ARGH!
URH!
STAND UP, YOU MEDDLING FREAK OF NATURE! NOW!
I KNOW YOU CAN!
I LOVED KILLING YOU TWICE. GET UP! SO I CAN DO IT AGAIN!
AND AGAIN!!
OH, SHUT UP! YOU'RE GIVING ME A HEADACHE.
YOU WERE RIGHT, THIS REALLY IS UNCANNY.
I NEVER DOUBTED YOU, BROTHER.
ENOUGH!

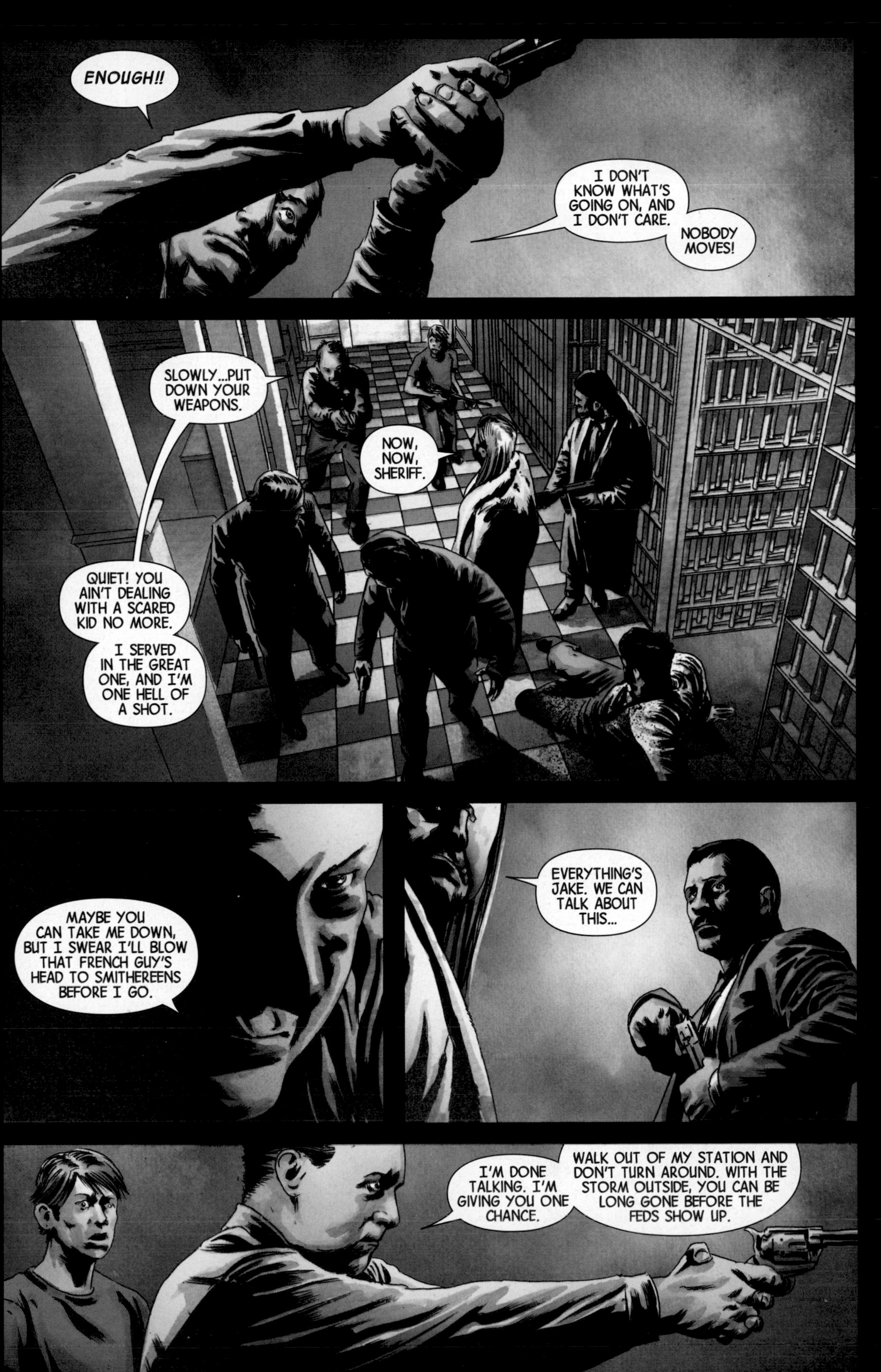
ENOUGH!!
I DON'T KNOW WHAT'S GOING ON, AND I DON'T CARE.
NOBODY MOVES!
SLOWLY...PUT DOWN YOUR WEAPONS.
NOW, NOW, SHERIFF.
QUIET! YOU AIN'T DEALING WITH A SCARED KID NO MORE.
I SERVED IN THE GREAT ONE, AND I'M ONE HELL OF A SHOT.
MAYBE YOU CAN TAKE ME DOWN, BUT I SWEAR I'LL BLOW THAT FRENCH GUY'S HEAD TO SMITHEREENS BEFORE I GO.
EVERYTHING'S JAKE. WE CAN TALK ABOUT THIS...
I'M DONE TALKING. I'M GIVING YOU ONE CHANCE.
WALK OUT OF MY STATION AND DON'T TURN AROUND. WITH THE STORM OUTSIDE, YOU CAN BE LONG GONE BEFORE THE FEDS SHOW UP.

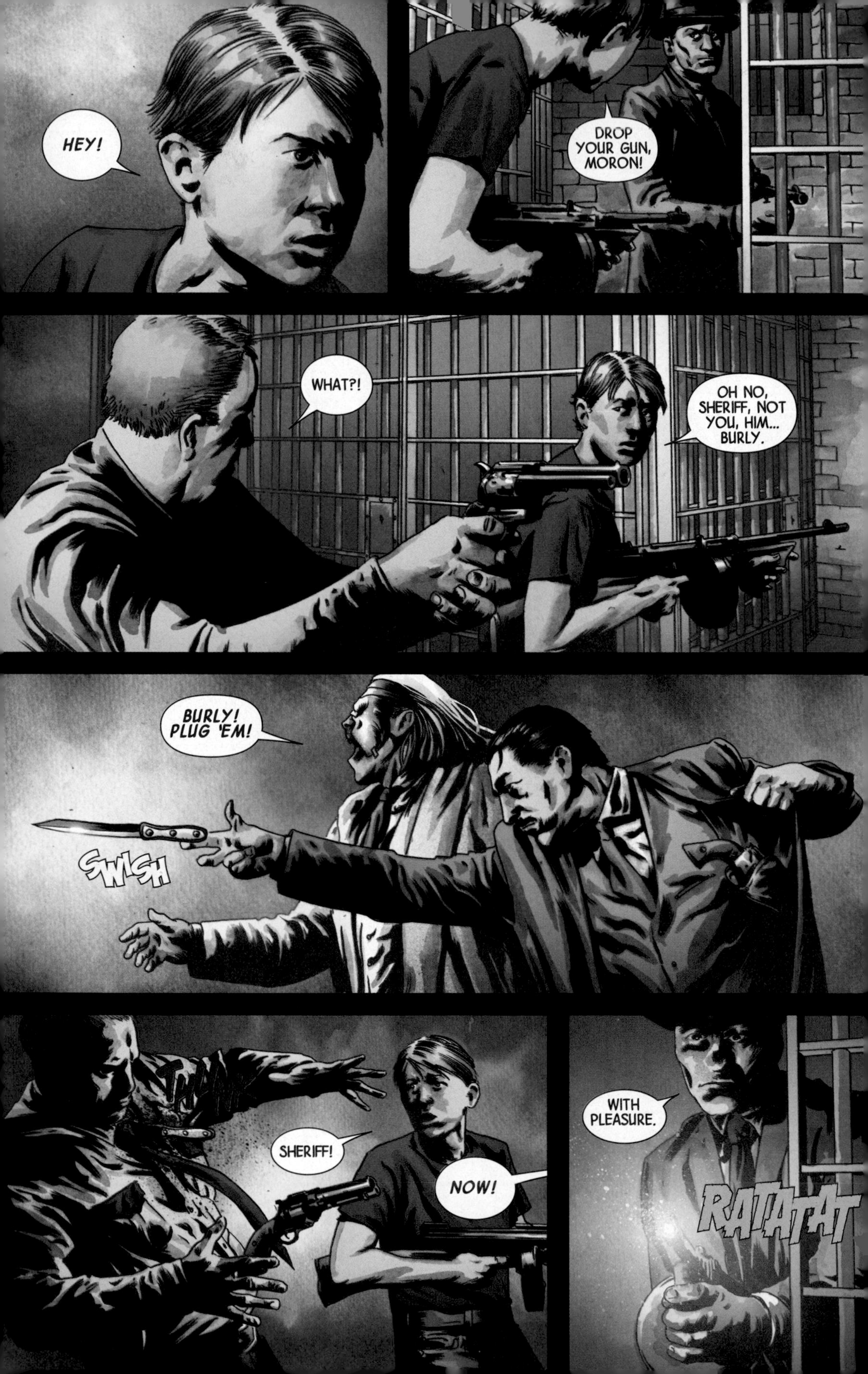
HEY!
DROP YOUR GUN, MORON!
WHAT?!
OH NO, SHERIFF, NOT YOU, HIM... BURLY.
BURLY! PLUG 'EM!
SWISH
THUMP
SHERIFF!
NOW!
WITH PLEASURE.
RATATAT

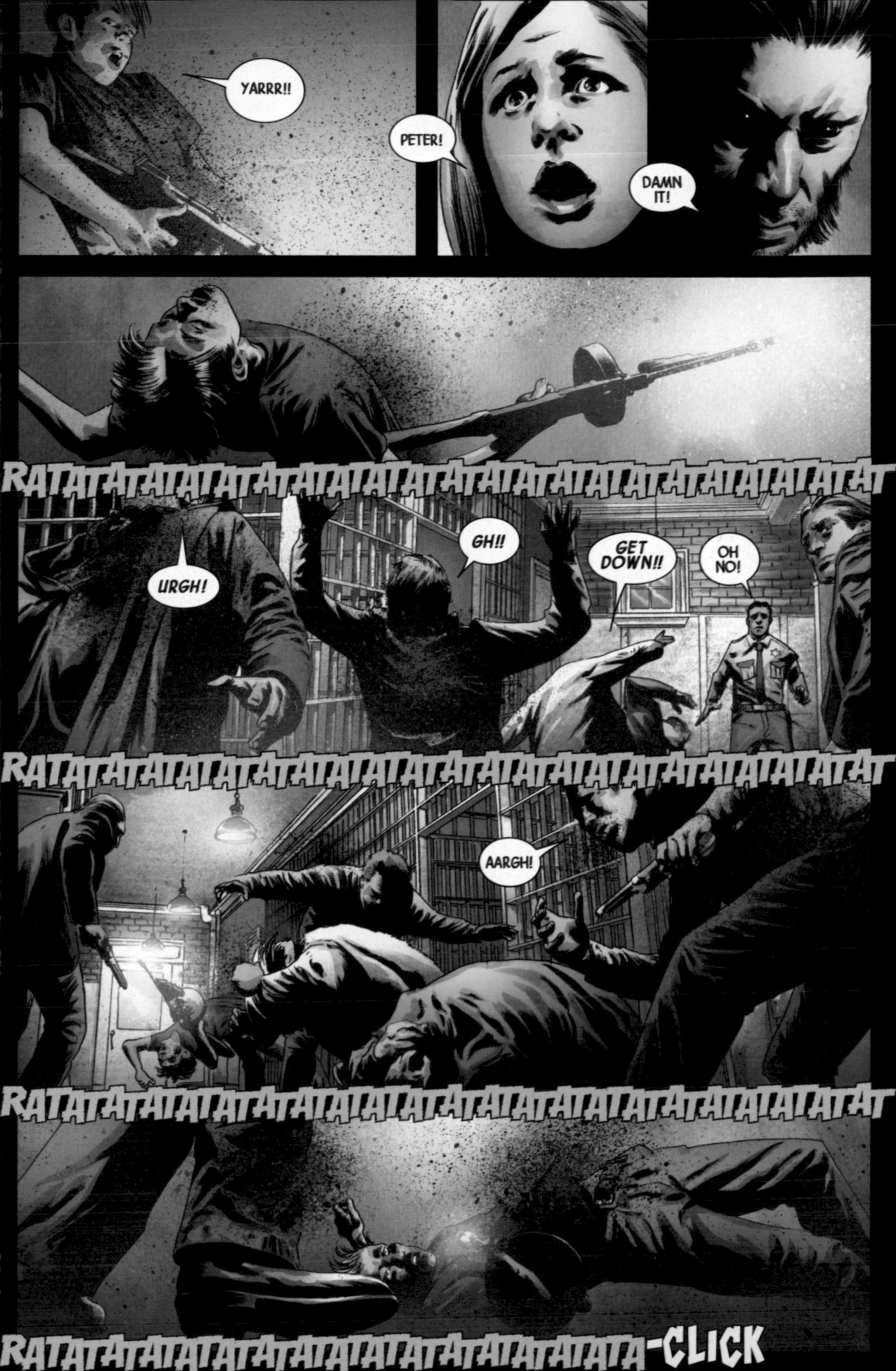
YARRR!!
PETER!
DAMN IT!
RATATATATATATATATATATATATATATATATATATATATATAT
URGH!
GH!!
GET DOWN!!
OH NO!
RATATATATATATATATATATATATATATATATATATATATATAT
AARGH!
RATATATATATATATATATATATATATATATATATATATATATAT
RATATATATATATATATATATATATATATATATATATATA-CLICK

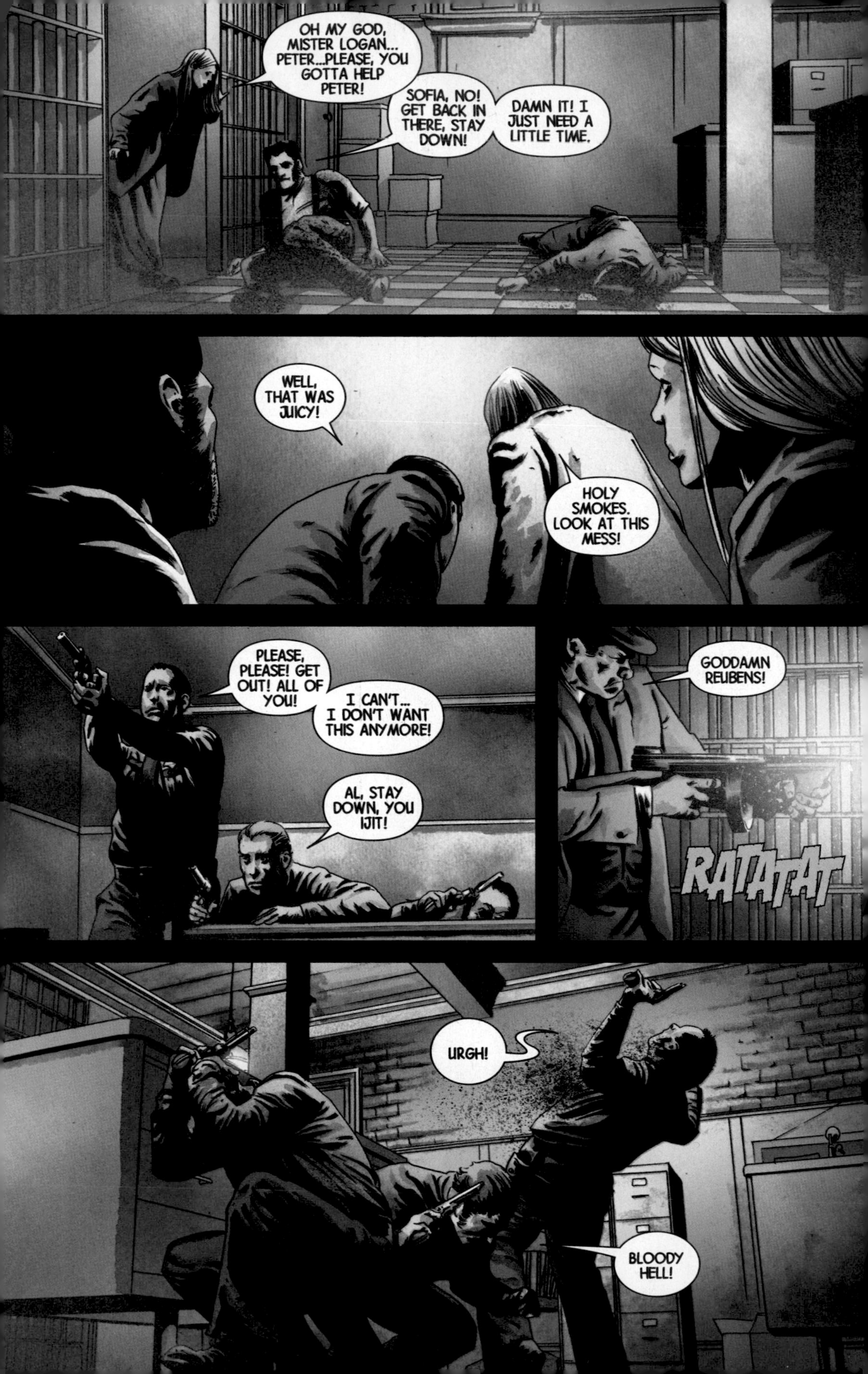
OH MY GOD, MISTER LOGAN... PETER...PLEASE, YOU GOTTA HELP PETER!
SOFIA, NO! GET BACK IN THERE, STAY DOWN!
DAMN IT! I JUST NEED A LITTLE TIME.
WELL, THAT WAS JUICY!
HOLY SMOKES. LOOK AT THIS MESS!
PLEASE, PLEASE! GET OUT! ALL OF YOU!
I CAN'T... I DON'T WANT THIS ANYMORE!
AL, STAY DOWN, YOU IJIT!
GODDAMN REUBENS!
RATATAT
URGH!
BLOODY HELL!

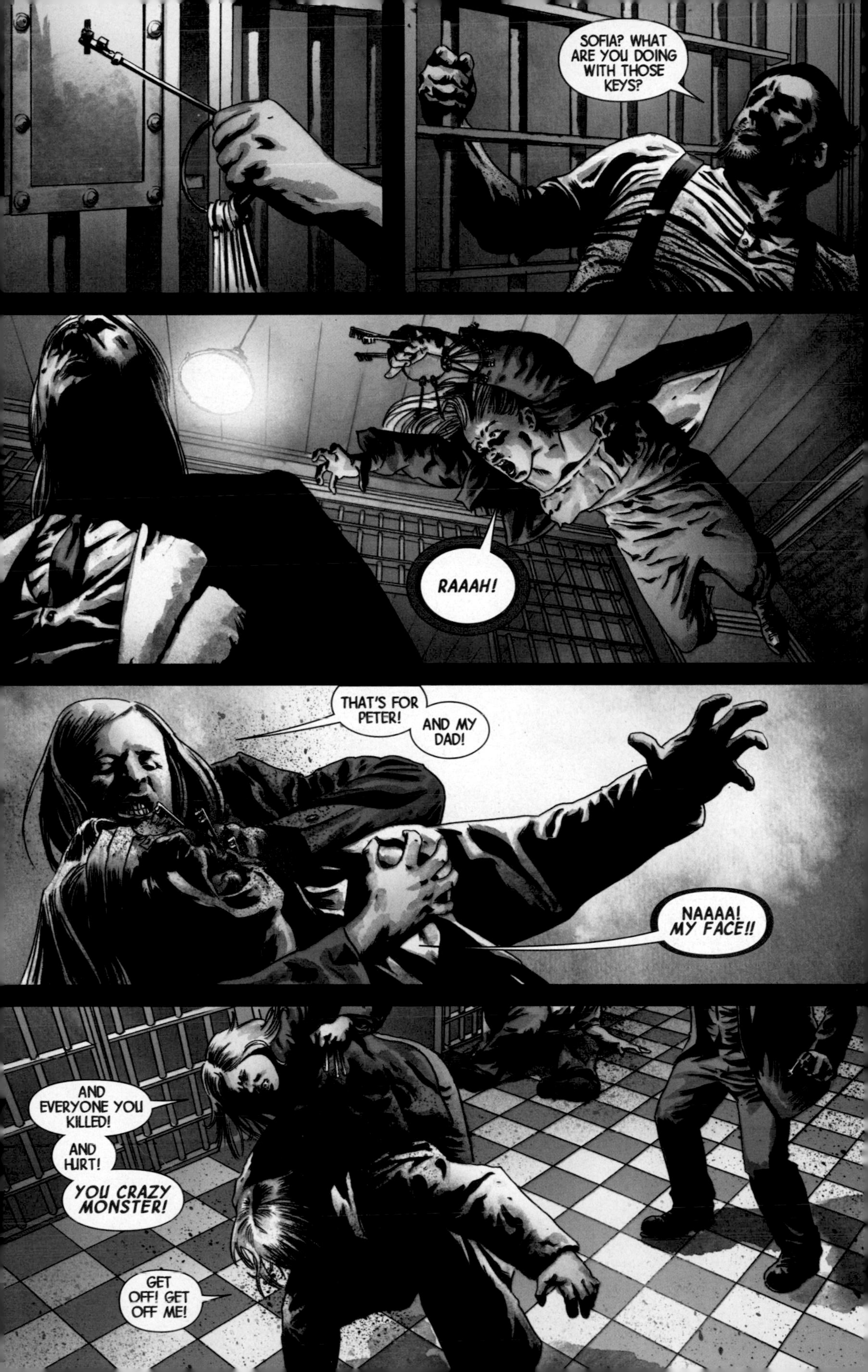
SOFIA? WHAT ARE YOU DOING WITH THOSE KEYS?
RAAAH!
THAT'S FOR PETER!
AND MY DAD!
NAAAA! MY FACE!!
AND EVERYONE YOU KILLED!
AND HURT!
YOU CRAZY MONSTER!
GET OFF! GET OFF ME!

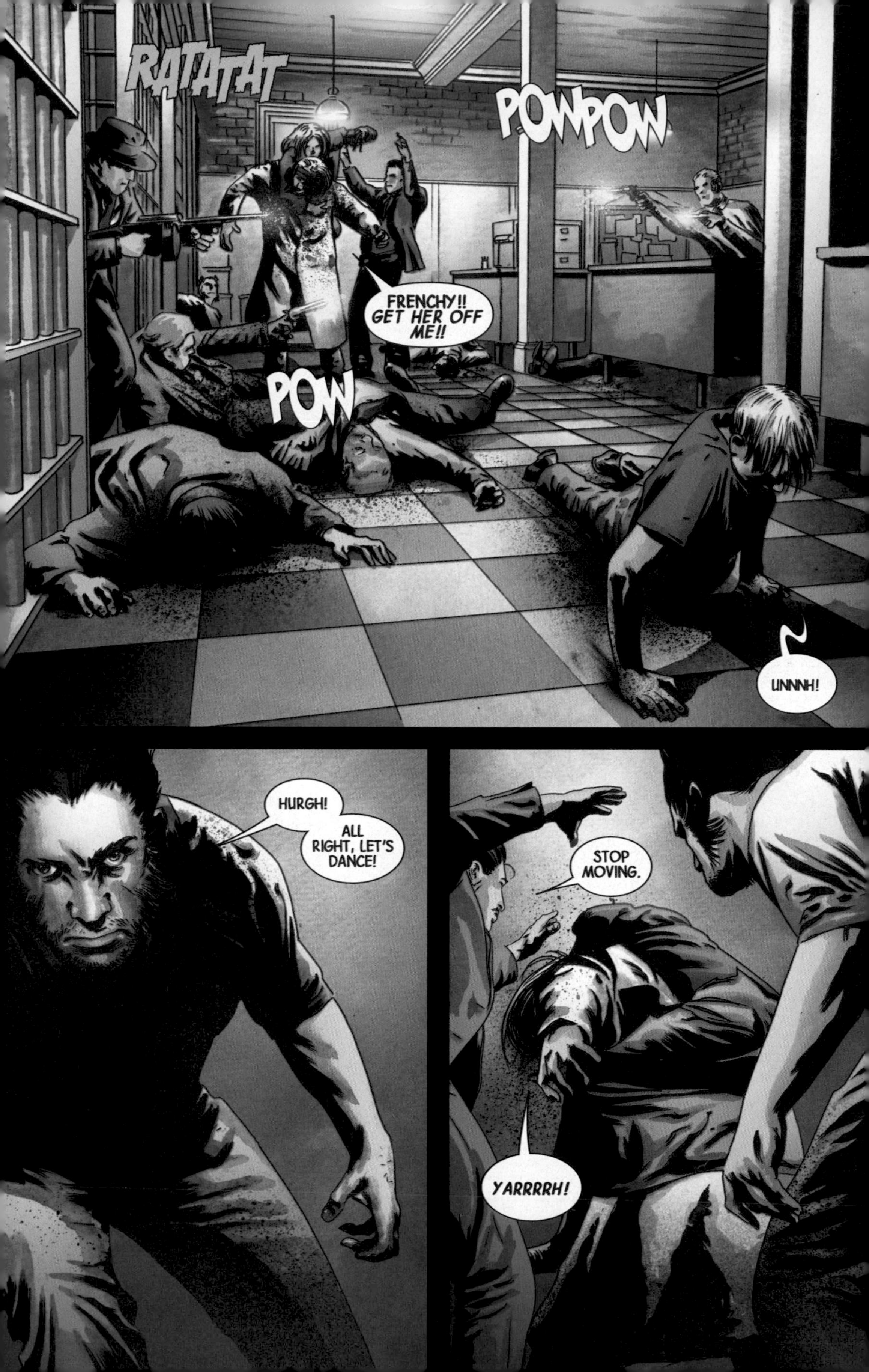
RATATAT
POWPOW
FRENCHY!! GET HER OFF ME!!
POW
UNNNH!
HURGH!
ALL RIGHT, LET'S DANCE!
STOP MOVING.
YARRRRH!

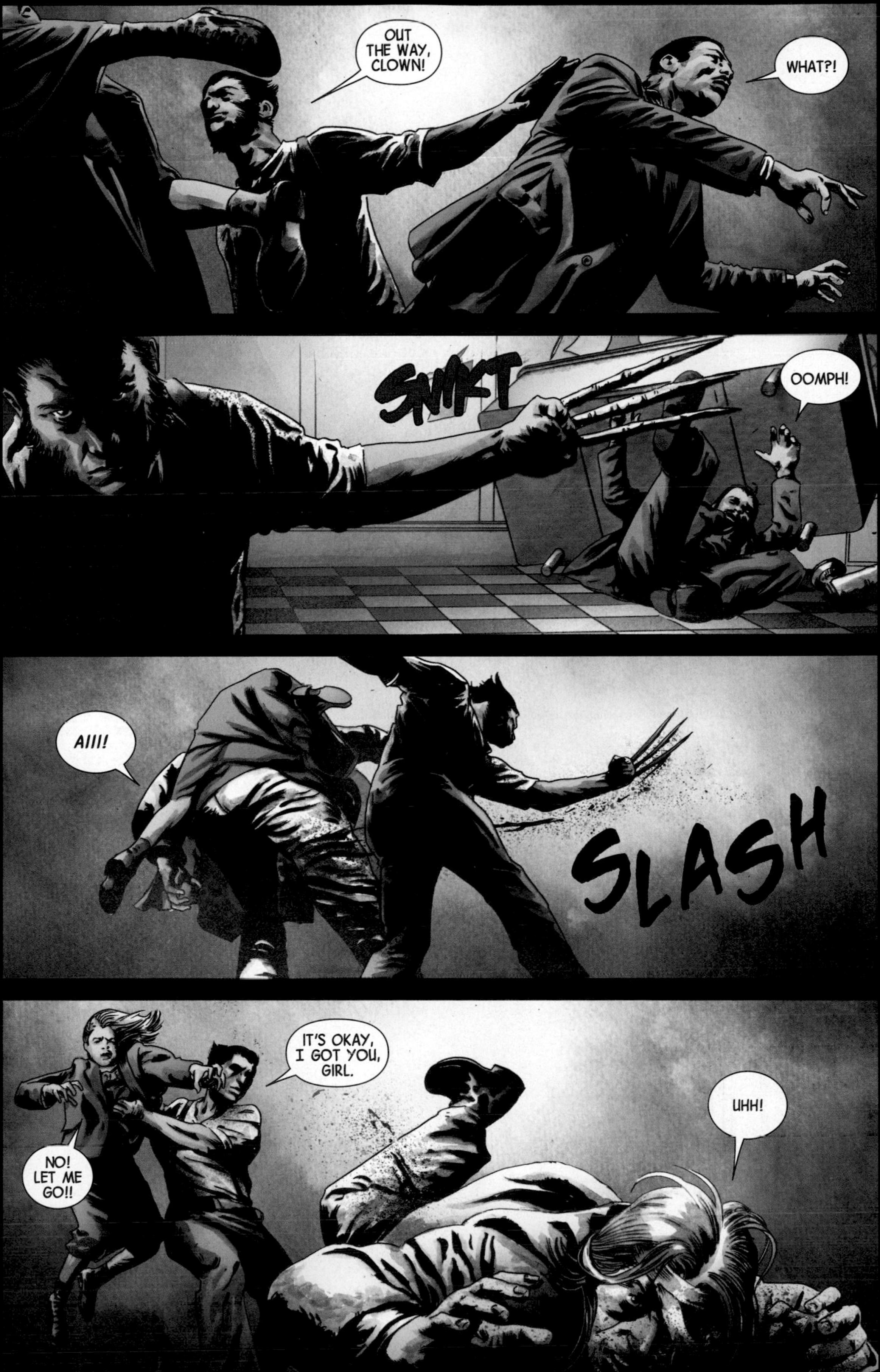
OUT THE WAY, CLOWN!
WHAT?!
SNIKT
OOMPH!
AIII!
SLASH
IT'S OKAY, I GOT YOU, GIRL.
NO! LET ME GO!!
UHH!

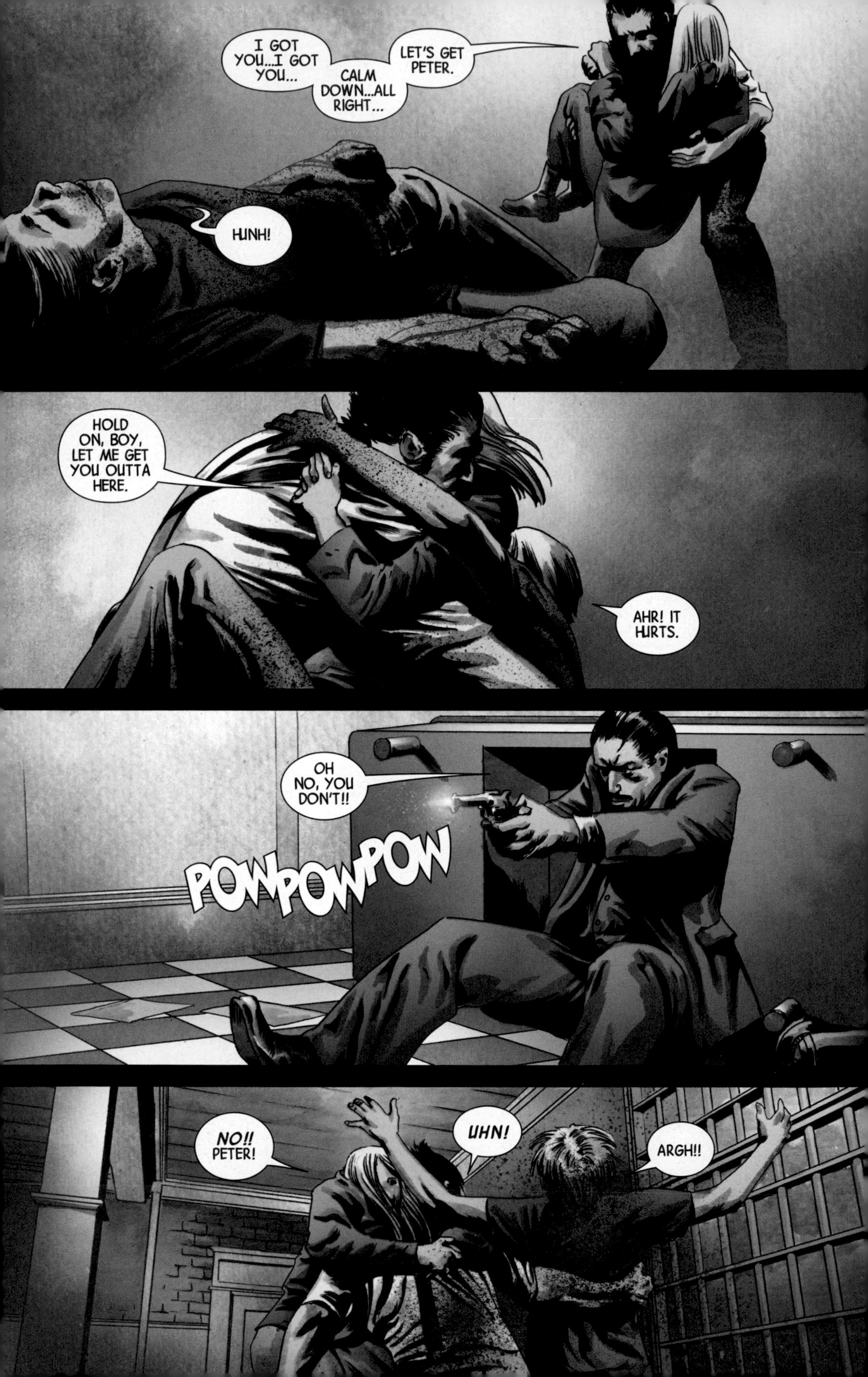
I GOT YOU...I GOT YOU...
CALM DOWN...ALL RIGHT...
LET'S GET PETER.
HUNH!
HOLD ON, BOY, LET ME GET YOU OUTTA HERE.
AHR! IT HURTS.
OH NO, YOU DON'T!!
POWPOWPOW
NO!! PETER!
UHN!
ARGH!!

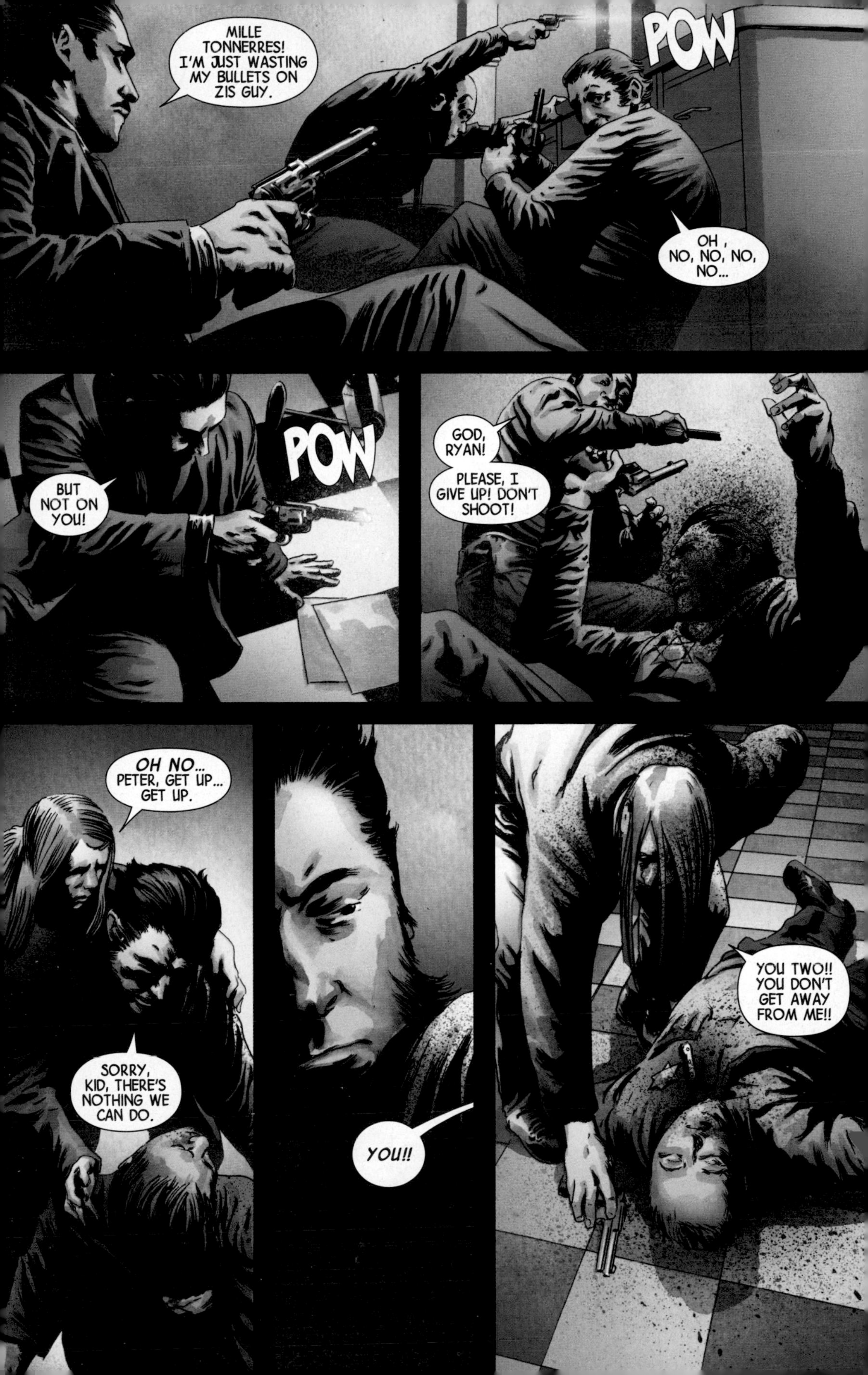
MILLE TONNERRES! I'M JUST WASTING MY BULLETS ON ZIS GUY.
POW
OH , NO, NO, NO, NO...
BUT NOT ON YOU!
POW
GOD, RYAN!
PLEASE, I GIVE UP! DON'T SHOOT!
OH NO... PETER, GET UP... GET UP.
SORRY, KID, THERE'S NOTHING WE CAN DO.
YOU!!
YOU TWO!! YOU DON'T GET AWAY FROM ME!!

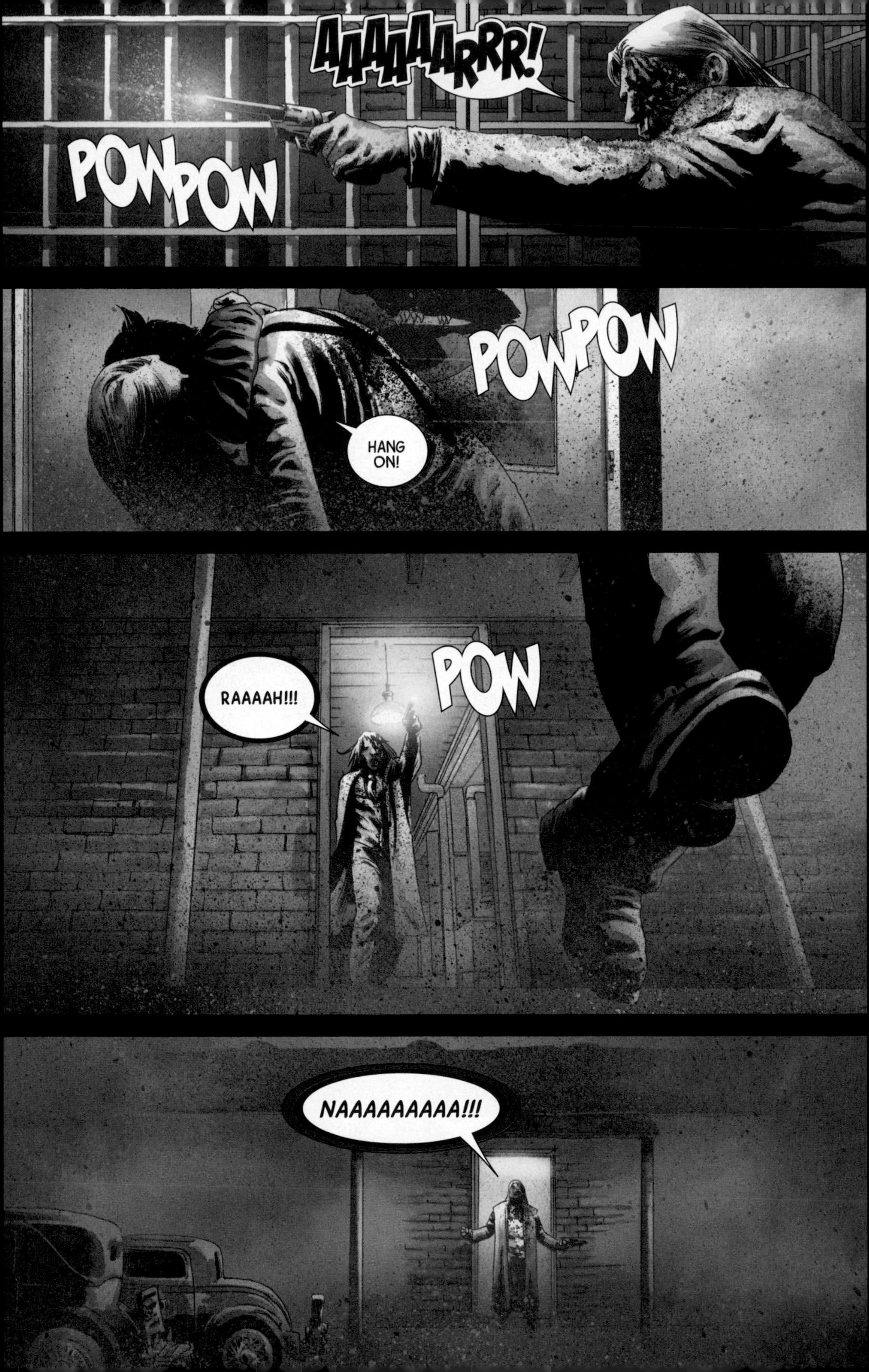
AAAAAARRR!
POW POW
POW POW
HANG ON!
POW
RAAAAH!!!
NAAAAAAAAA!!!

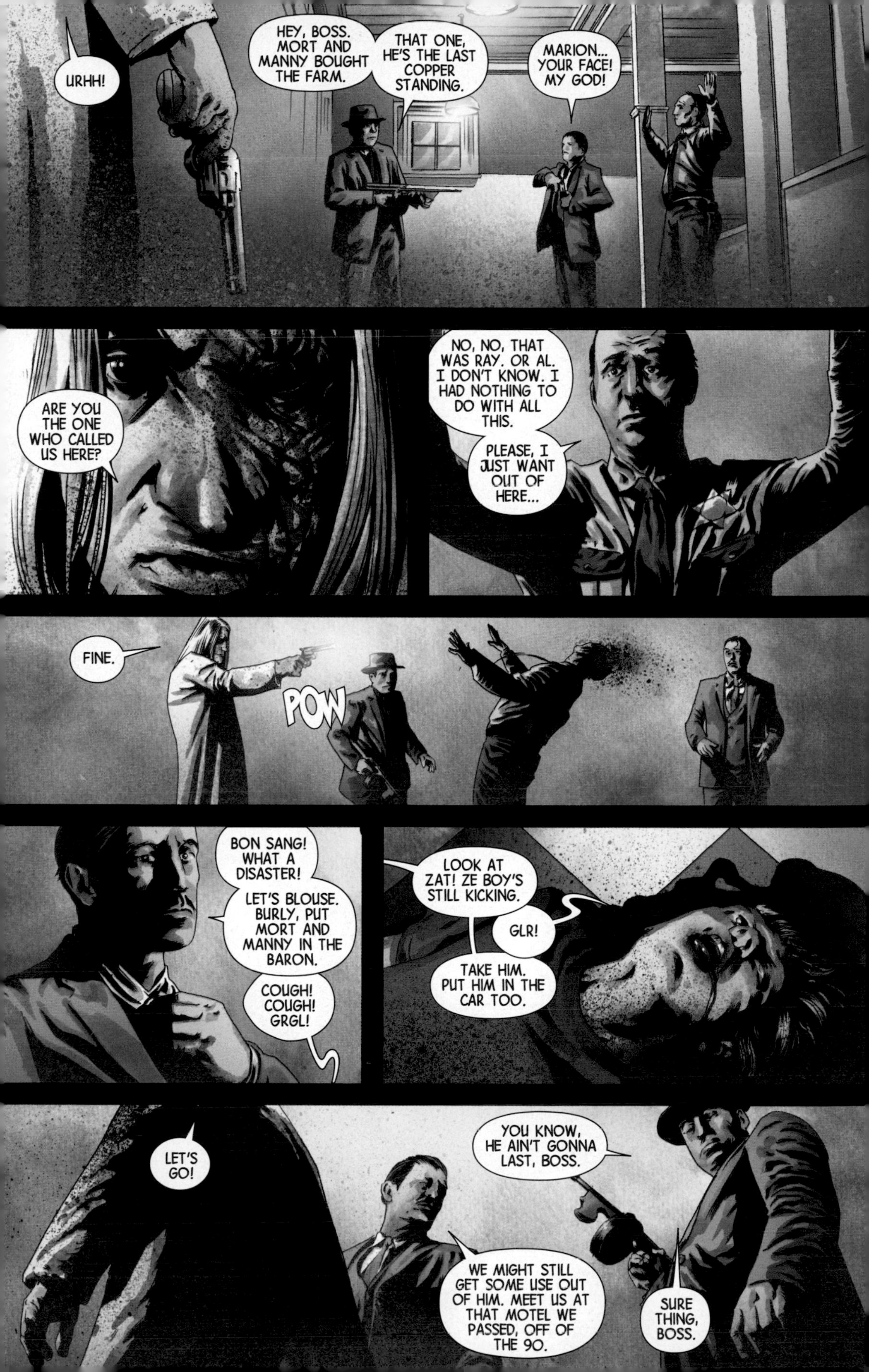
URHH!
HEY, BOSS. MORT AND MANNY BOUGHT THE FARM.
THAT ONE, HE'S THE LAST COPPER STANDING.
MARION... YOUR FACE! MY GOD!
ARE YOU THE ONE WHO CALLED US HERE?
NO, NO, THAT WAS RAY. OR AL. I DON'T KNOW. I HAD NOTHING TO DO WITH ALL THIS.
PLEASE, I JUST WANT OUT OF HERE...
FINE.
POW
BON SANG! WHAT A DISASTER!
LET'S BLOUSE. BURLY, PUT MORT AND MANNY IN THE BARON.
COUGH! COUGH! GRGL!
LOOK AT ZAT! ZE BOY'S STILL KICKING.
GLR!
TAKE HIM. PUT HIM IN THE CAR TOO.
LET'S GO!
YOU KNOW, HE AIN'T GONNA LAST, BOSS.
WE MIGHT STILL GET SOME USE OUT OF HIM. MEET US AT THAT MOTEL WE PASSED, OFF OF THE 90.
SURE THING, BOSS.

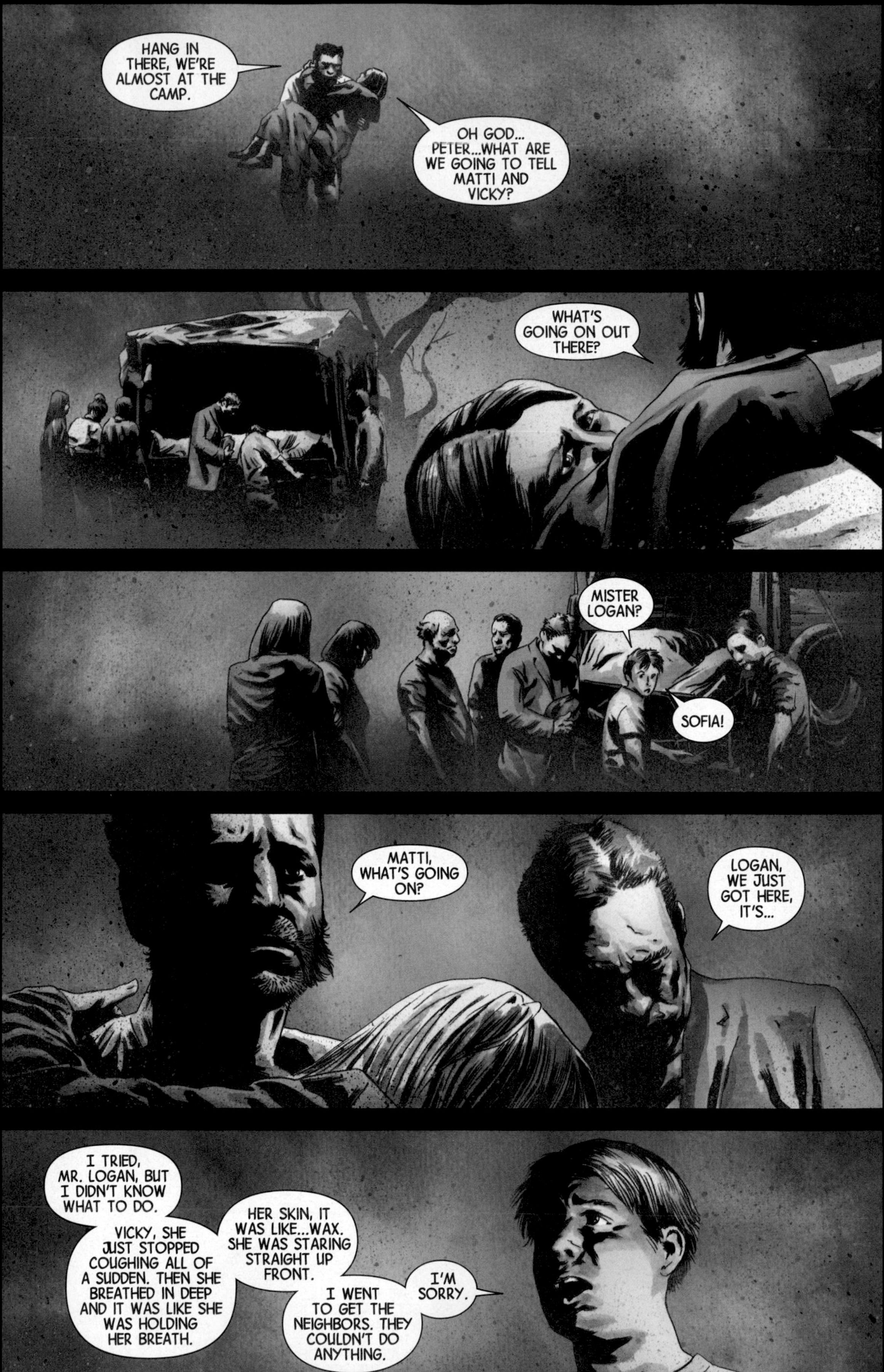
HANG IN THERE, WE'RE ALMOST AT THE CAMP.
OH GOD... PETER...WHAT ARE WE GOING TO TELL MATTI AND VICKY?
WHAT'S GOING ON OUT THERE?
MISTER LOGAN?
SOFIA!
MATTI, WHAT'S GOING ON?
LOGAN, WE JUST GOT HERE, IT'S...
I TRIED, MR. LOGAN, BUT I DIDN'T KNOW WHAT TO DO.
VICKY, SHE JUST STOPPED COUGHING ALL OF A SUDDEN. THEN SHE BREATHED IN DEEP AND IT WAS LIKE SHE WAS HOLDING HER BREATH.
HER SKIN, IT WAS LIKE...WAX. SHE WAS STARING STRAIGHT UP FRONT.
I WENT TO GET THE NEIGHBORS. THEY COULDN'T DO ANYTHING.
I'M SORRY.

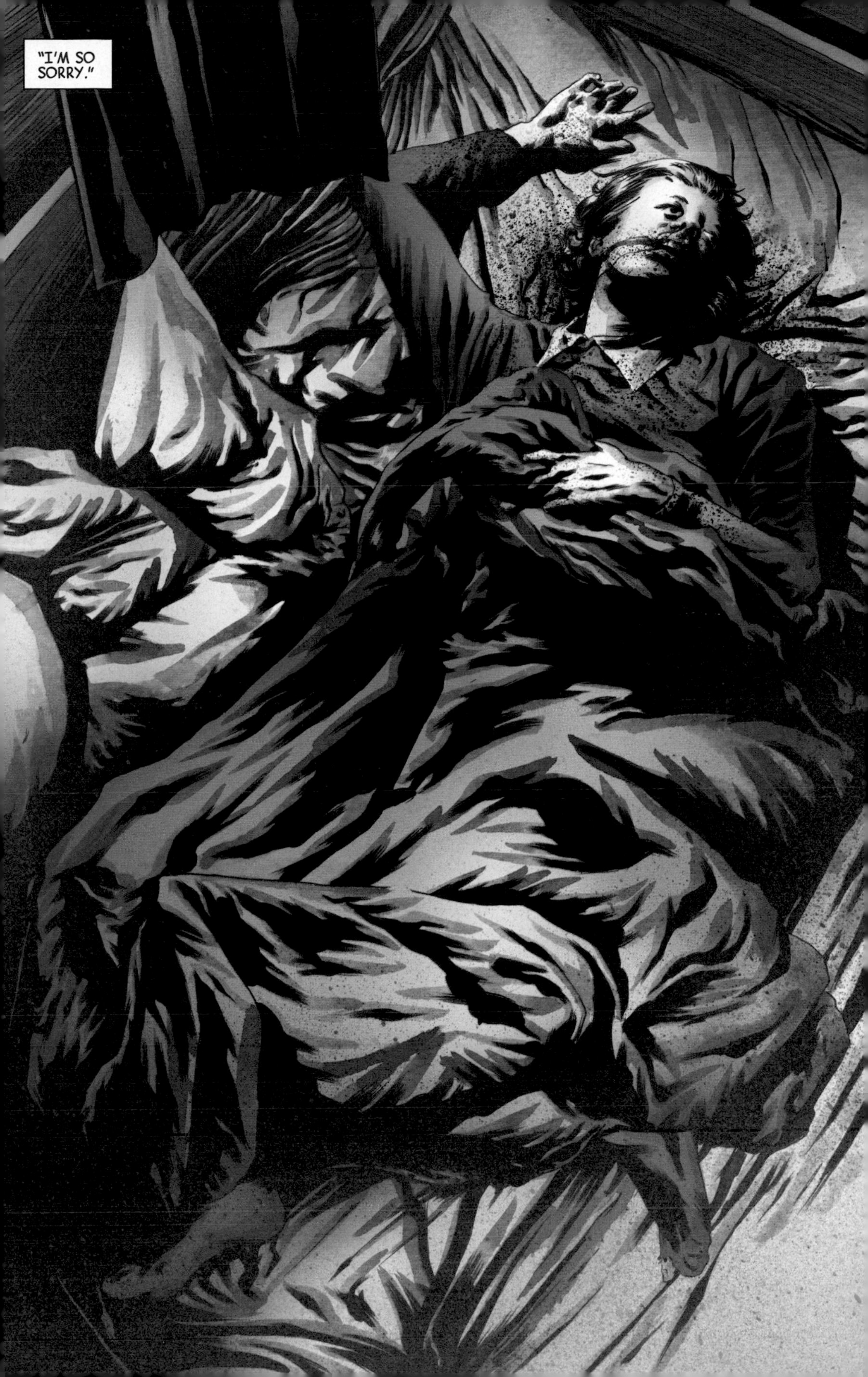
"I'M SO SORRY."

## WRATH PART 4

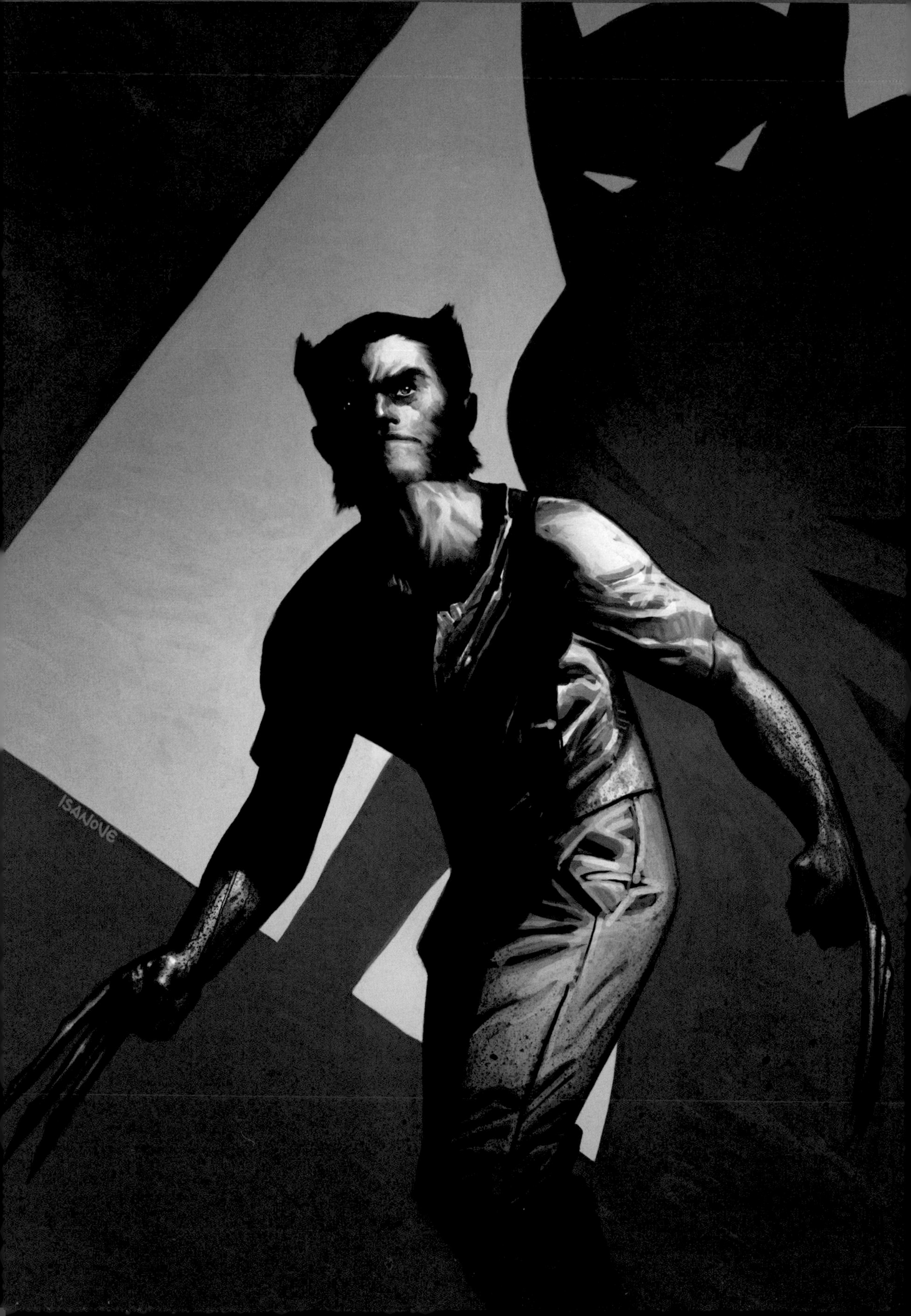
ISANOVE

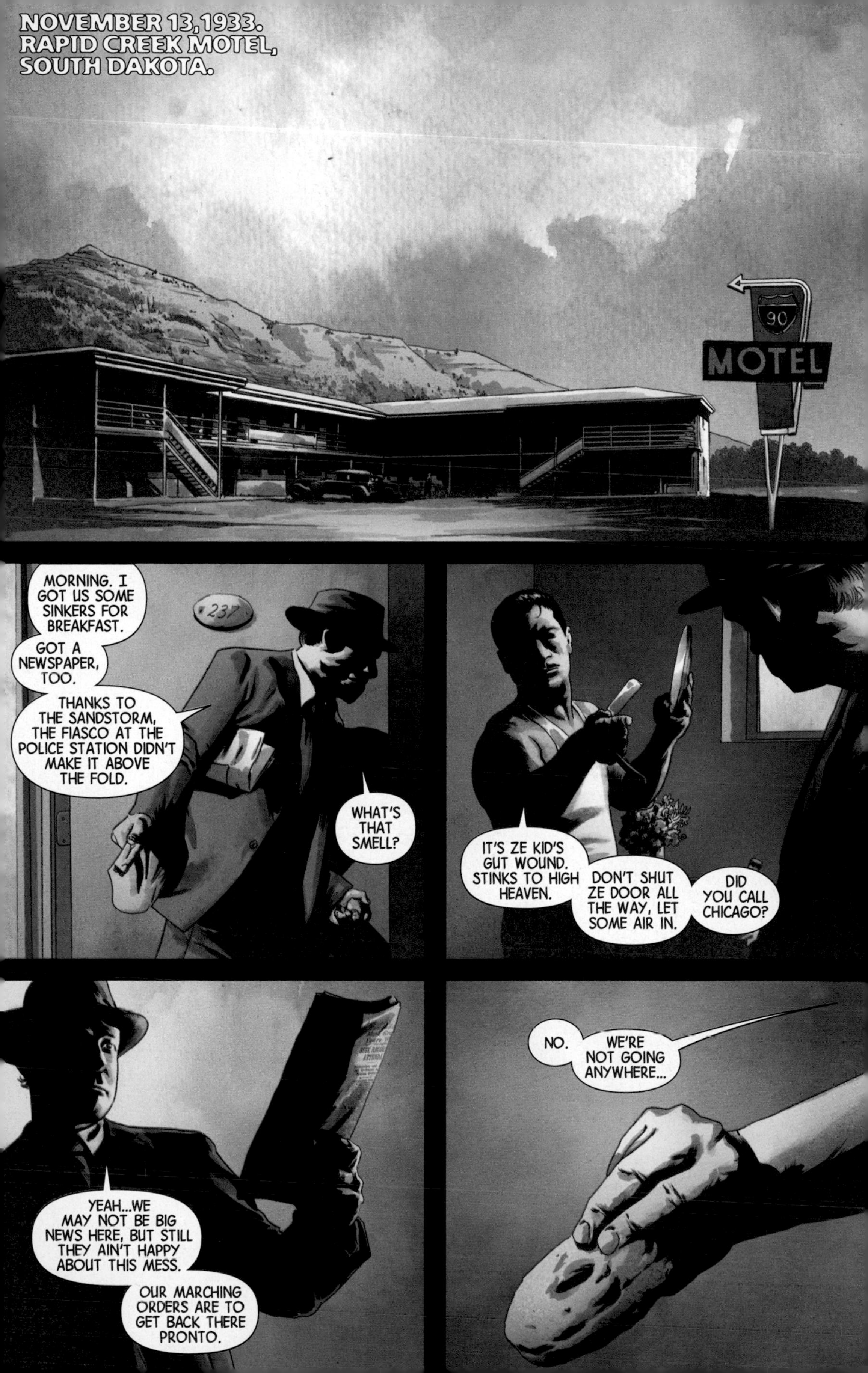
NOVEMBER 13, 1933. RAPID CREEK MOTEL, SOUTH DAKOTA.
90
MOTEL
237
MORNING. I GOT US SOME SINKERS FOR BREAKFAST.
GOT A NEWSPAPER, TOO.
THANKS TO THE SANDSTORM, THE FIASCO AT THE POLICE STATION DIDN'T MAKE IT ABOVE THE FOLD.
WHAT'S THAT SMELL?
IT'S ZE KID'S GUT WOUND. STINKS TO HIGH HEAVEN.
DON'T SHUT ZE DOOR ALL THE WAY, LET SOME AIR IN.
DID YOU CALL CHICAGO?
YEAH...WE MAY NOT BE BIG NEWS HERE, BUT STILL THEY AIN'T HAPPY ABOUT THIS MESS.
OUR MARCHING ORDERS ARE TO GET BACK THERE PRONTO.
NO.
WE'RE NOT GOING ANYWHERE...

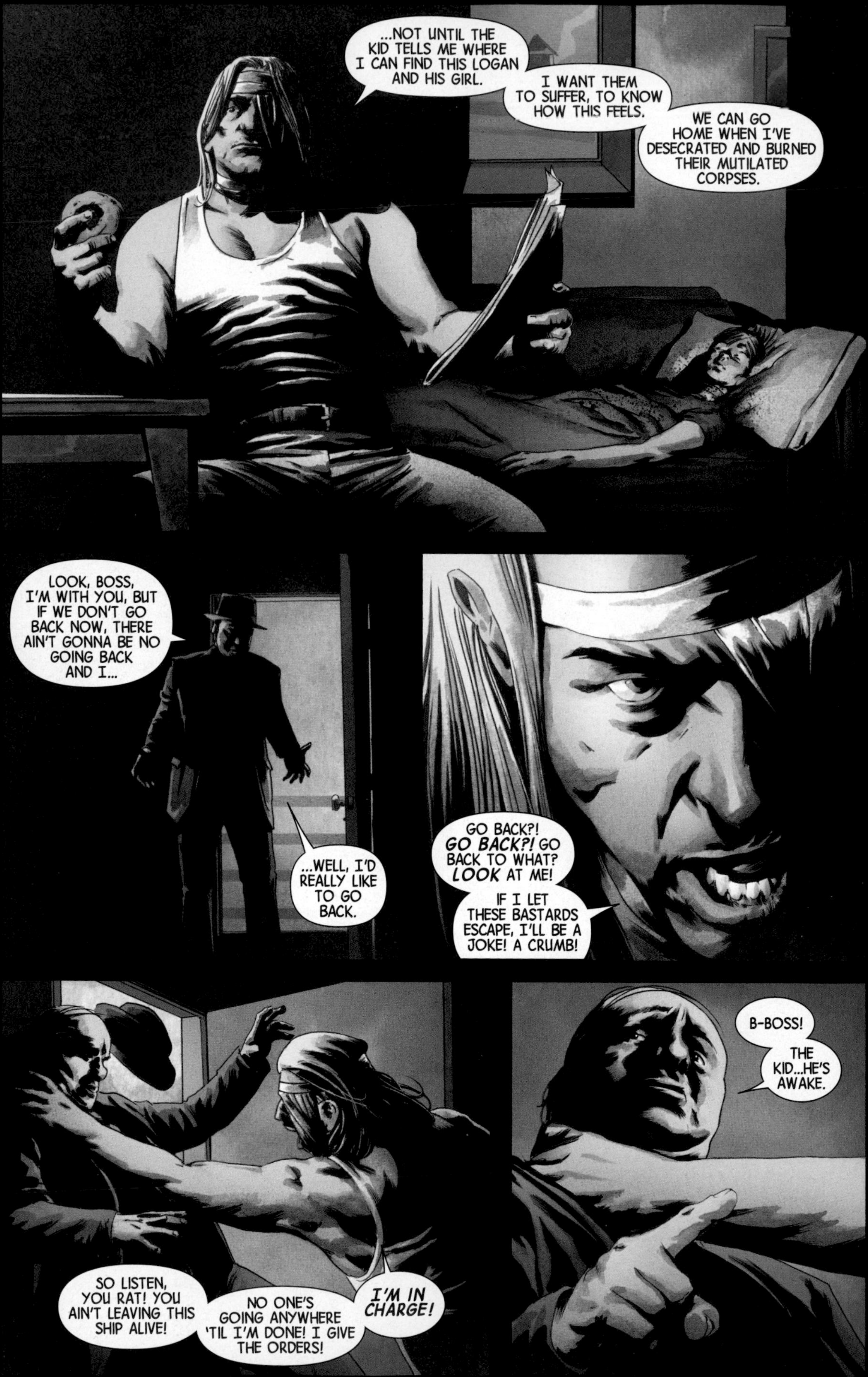
...NOT UNTIL THE KID TELLS ME WHERE I CAN FIND THIS LOGAN AND HIS GIRL.
I WANT THEM TO SUFFER, TO KNOW HOW THIS FEELS.
WE CAN GO HOME WHEN I'VE DESECRATED AND BURNED THEIR MUTILATED CORPSES.
LOOK, BOSS, I'M WITH YOU, BUT IF WE DON'T GO BACK NOW, THERE AIN'T GONNA BE NO GOING BACK AND I...
...WELL, I'D REALLY LIKE TO GO BACK.
GO BACK?! *GO BACK?!* GO BACK TO WHAT? *LOOK* AT ME!
IF I LET THESE BASTARDS ESCAPE, I'LL BE A JOKE! A CRUMB!
SO LISTEN, YOU RAT! YOU AIN'T LEAVING THIS SHIP ALIVE!
NO ONE'S GOING ANYWHERE 'TIL I'M DONE! I GIVE THE ORDERS!
*I'M IN CHARGE!*
B-BOSS!
THE KID...HE'S AWAKE.

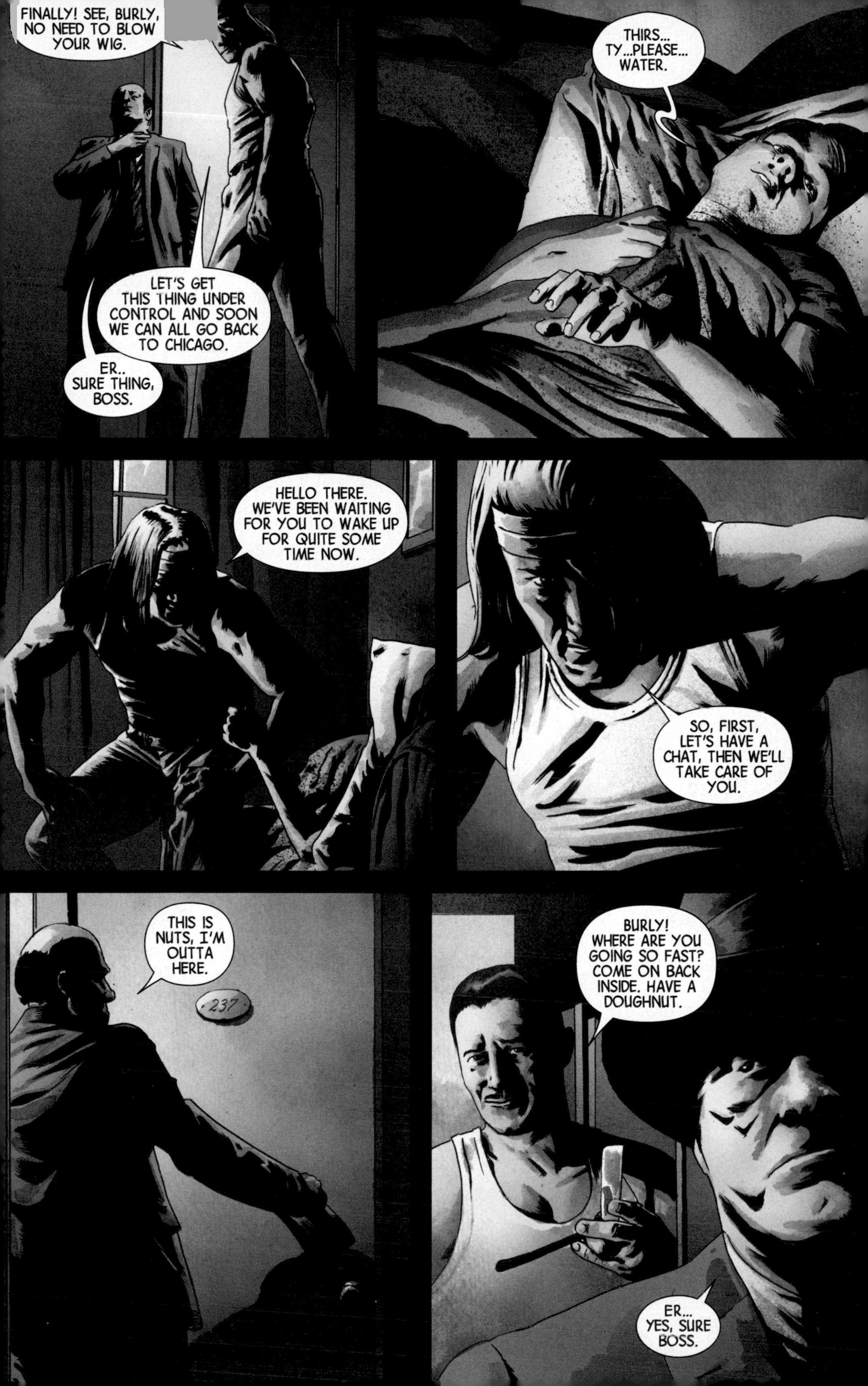
FINALLY! SEE, BURLY, NO NEED TO BLOW YOUR WIG.
LET'S GET THIS THING UNDER CONTROL AND SOON WE CAN ALL GO BACK TO CHICAGO.
ER.. SURE THING, BOSS.
THIRS... TY...PLEASE... WATER.
HELLO THERE. WE'VE BEEN WAITING FOR YOU TO WAKE UP FOR QUITE SOME TIME NOW.
SO, FIRST, LET'S HAVE A CHAT, THEN WE'LL TAKE CARE OF YOU.
THIS IS NUTS, I'M OUTTA HERE.
237
BURLY! WHERE ARE YOU GOING SO FAST? COME ON BACK INSIDE. HAVE A DOUGHNUT.
ER... YES, SURE BOSS.

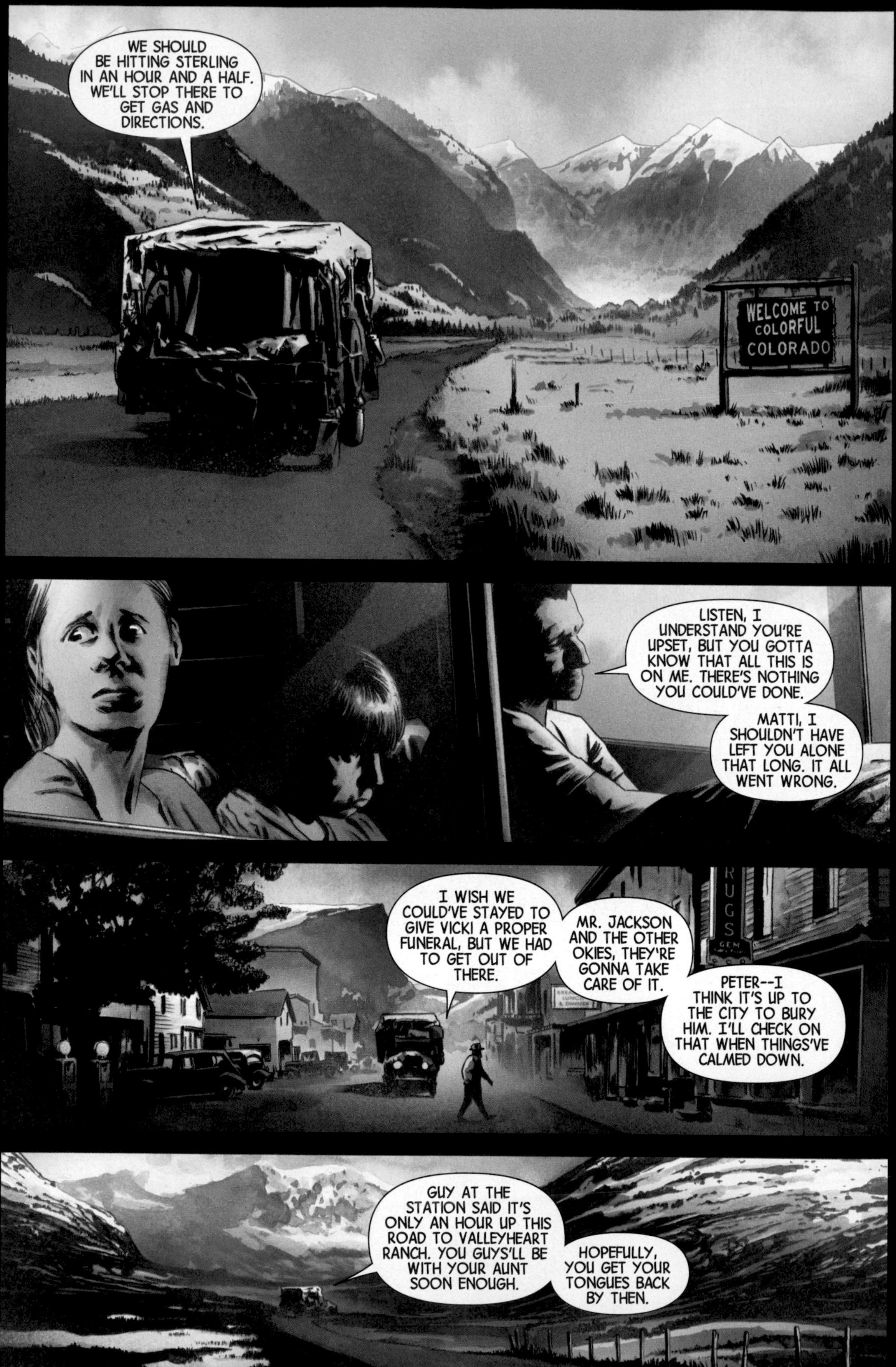
WE SHOULD BE HITTING STERLING IN AN HOUR AND A HALF. WE'LL STOP THERE TO GET GAS AND DIRECTIONS.
WELCOME TO COLORFUL COLORADO
LISTEN, I UNDERSTAND YOU'RE UPSET, BUT YOU GOTTA KNOW THAT ALL THIS IS ON ME. THERE'S NOTHING YOU COULD'VE DONE.
MATTI, I SHOULDN'T HAVE LEFT YOU ALONE THAT LONG. IT ALL WENT WRONG.
I WISH WE COULD'VE STAYED TO GIVE VICKI A PROPER FUNERAL, BUT WE HAD TO GET OUT OF THERE.
MR. JACKSON AND THE OTHER OKIES, THEY'RE GONNA TAKE CARE OF IT.
PETER--I THINK IT'S UP TO THE CITY TO BURY HIM. I'LL CHECK ON THAT WHEN THINGS'VE CALMED DOWN.
GUY AT THE STATION SAID IT'S ONLY AN HOUR UP THIS ROAD TO VALLEYHEART RANCH. YOU GUYS'LL BE WITH YOUR AUNT SOON ENOUGH.
HOPEFULLY, YOU GET YOUR TONGUES BACK BY THEN.

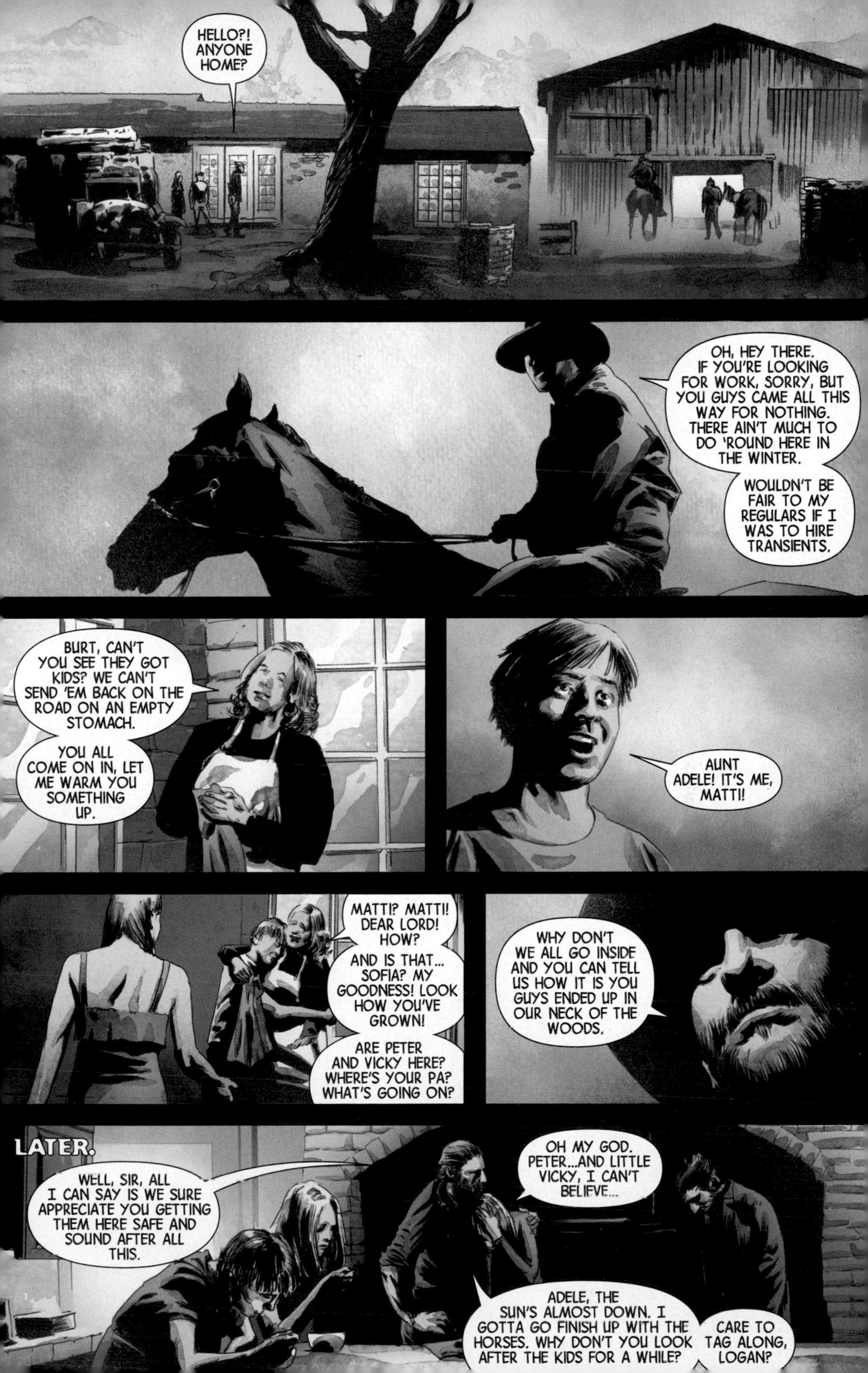
HELLO?! ANYONE HOME?
OH, HEY THERE. IF YOU'RE LOOKING FOR WORK, SORRY, BUT YOU GUYS CAME ALL THIS WAY FOR NOTHING. THERE AIN'T MUCH TO DO 'ROUND HERE IN THE WINTER.
WOULDN'T BE FAIR TO MY REGULARS IF I WAS TO HIRE TRANSIENTS.
BURT, CAN'T YOU SEE THEY GOT KIDS? WE CAN'T SEND 'EM BACK ON THE ROAD ON AN EMPTY STOMACH.
YOU ALL COME ON IN, LET ME WARM YOU SOMETHING UP.
AUNT ADELE! IT'S ME, MATT!!
MATT!? MATT!! DEAR LORD! HOW?
AND IS THAT... SOFIA? MY GOODNESS! LOOK HOW YOU'VE GROWN!
ARE PETER AND VICKY HERE? WHERE'S YOUR PA? WHAT'S GOING ON?
WHY DON'T WE ALL GO INSIDE AND YOU CAN TELL US HOW IT IS YOU GUYS ENDED UP IN OUR NECK OF THE WOODS.
LATER.
WELL, SIR, ALL I CAN SAY IS WE SURE APPRECIATE YOU GETTING THEM HERE SAFE AND SOUND AFTER ALL THIS.
OH MY GOD. PETER...AND LITTLE VICKY, I CAN'T BELIEVE...
ADELE, THE SUN'S ALMOST DOWN. I GOTTA GO FINISH UP WITH THE HORSES. WHY DON'T YOU LOOK AFTER THE KIDS FOR A WHILE?
CARE TO TAG ALONG, LOGAN?

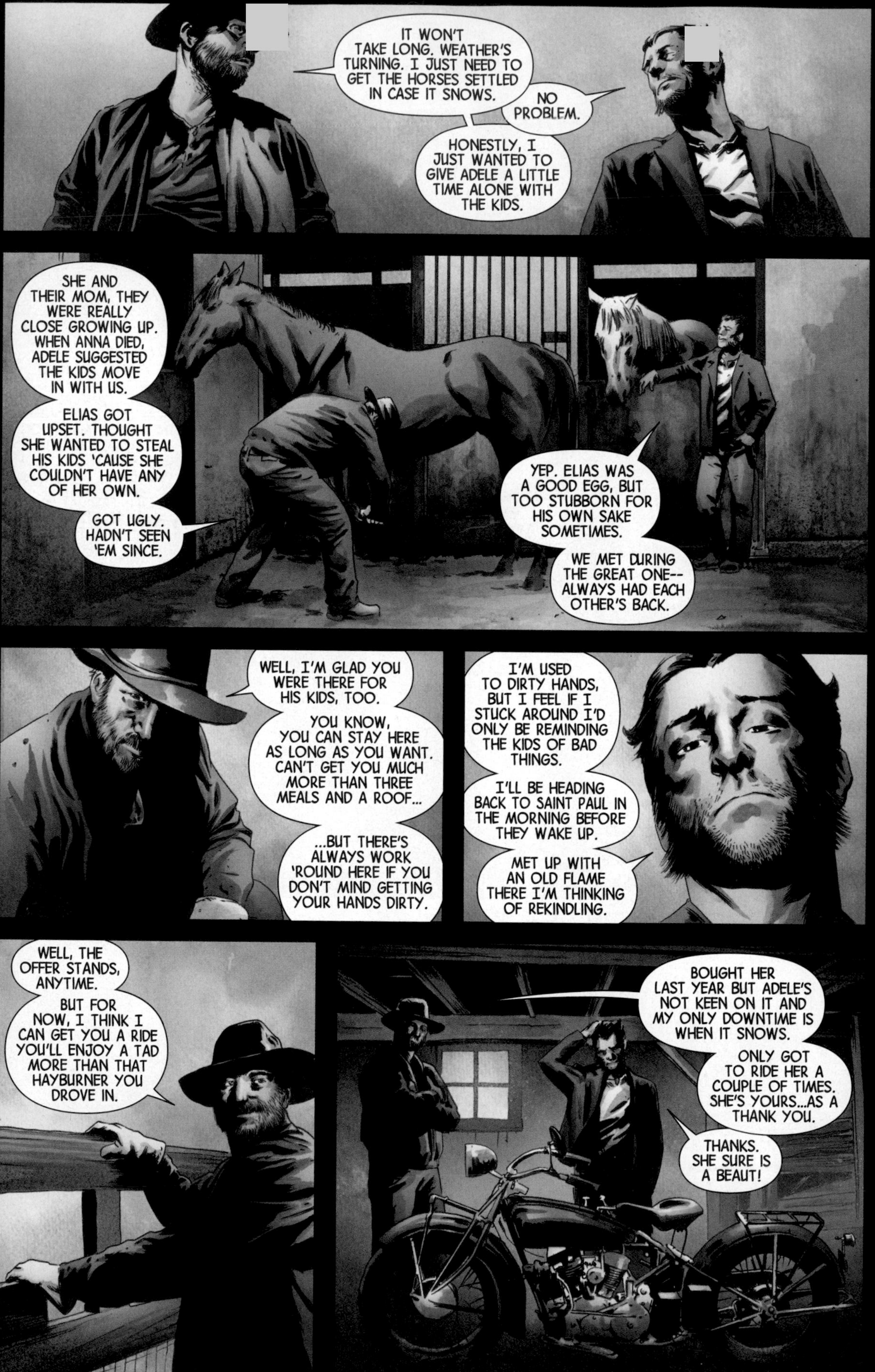
IT WON'T TAKE LONG. WEATHER'S TURNING. I JUST NEED TO GET THE HORSES SETTLED IN CASE IT SNOWS.
NO PROBLEM.
HONESTLY, I JUST WANTED TO GIVE ADELE A LITTLE TIME ALONE WITH THE KIDS.
SHE AND THEIR MOM, THEY WERE REALLY CLOSE GROWING UP. WHEN ANNA DIED, ADELE SUGGESTED THE KIDS MOVE IN WITH US.
ELIAS GOT UPSET. THOUGHT SHE WANTED TO STEAL HIS KIDS 'CAUSE SHE COULDN'T HAVE ANY OF HER OWN.
GOT UGLY. HADN'T SEEN 'EM SINCE.
YEP. ELIAS WAS A GOOD EGG, BUT TOO STUBBORN FOR HIS OWN SAKE SOMETIMES.
WE MET DURING THE GREAT ONE-- ALWAYS HAD EACH OTHER'S BACK.
WELL, I'M GLAD YOU WERE THERE FOR HIS KIDS, TOO.
YOU KNOW, YOU CAN STAY HERE AS LONG AS YOU WANT. CAN'T GET YOU MUCH MORE THAN THREE MEALS AND A ROOF...
...BUT THERE'S ALWAYS WORK 'ROUND HERE IF YOU DON'T MIND GETTING YOUR HANDS DIRTY.
I'M USED TO DIRTY HANDS, BUT I FEEL IF I STUCK AROUND I'D ONLY BE REMINDING THE KIDS OF BAD THINGS.
I'LL BE HEADING BACK TO SAINT PAUL IN THE MORNING BEFORE THEY WAKE UP.
MET UP WITH AN OLD FLAME THERE I'M THINKING OF REKINDLING.
WELL, THE OFFER STANDS, ANYTIME.
BUT FOR NOW, I THINK I CAN GET YOU A RIDE YOU'LL ENJOY A TAD MORE THAN THAT HAYBURNER YOU DROVE IN.
BOUGHT HER LAST YEAR BUT ADELE'S NOT KEEN ON IT AND MY ONLY DOWNTIME IS WHEN IT SNOWS.
ONLY GOT TO RIDE HER A COUPLE OF TIMES. SHE'S YOURS...AS A THANK YOU.
THANKS. SHE SURE IS A BEAUT!

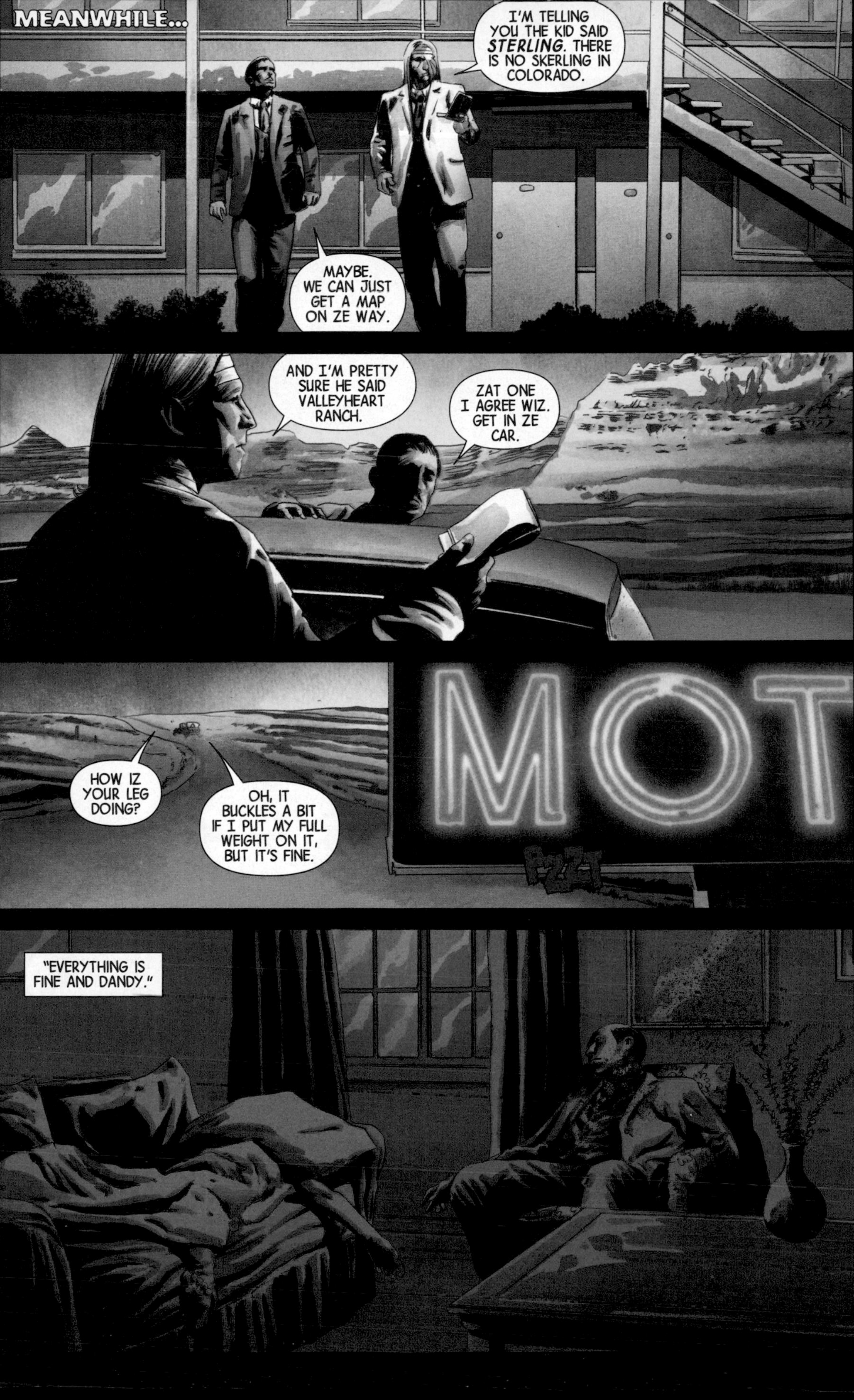
MEANWHILE...
I'M TELLING YOU THE KID SAID STERLING. THERE IS NO SKERLING IN COLORADO.
MAYBE. WE CAN JUST GET A MAP ON ZE WAY.
AND I'M PRETTY SURE HE SAID VALLEYHEART RANCH.
ZAT ONE I AGREE WIZ. GET IN ZE CAR.
MOT
HOW IZ YOUR LEG DOING?
OH, IT BUCKLES A BIT IF I PUT MY FULL WEIGHT ON IT, BUT IT'S FINE.
FZZT
"EVERYTHING IS FINE AND DANDY."

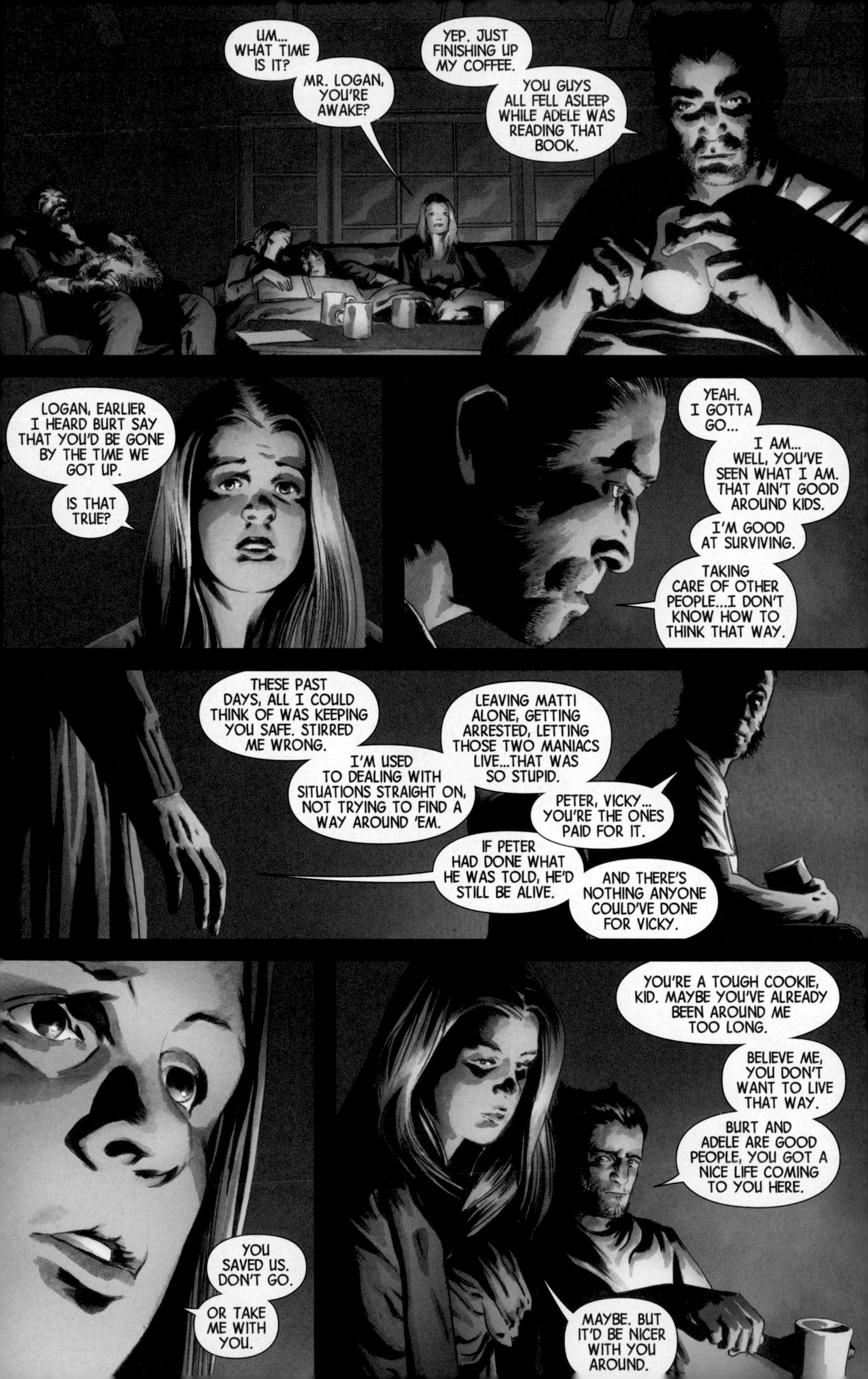
UM... WHAT TIME IS IT?
MR. LOGAN, YOU'RE AWAKE?
YEP. JUST FINISHING UP MY COFFEE.
YOU GUYS ALL FELL ASLEEP WHILE ADELE WAS READING THAT BOOK.
LOGAN, EARLIER I HEARD BURT SAY THAT YOU'D BE GONE BY THE TIME WE GOT UP.
IS THAT TRUE?
YEAH. I GOTTA GO...
I AM... WELL, YOU'VE SEEN WHAT I AM. THAT AIN'T GOOD AROUND KIDS.
I'M GOOD AT SURVIVING.
TAKING CARE OF OTHER PEOPLE...I DON'T KNOW HOW TO THINK THAT WAY.
THESE PAST DAYS, ALL I COULD THINK OF WAS KEEPING YOU SAFE. STIRRED ME WRONG.
I'M USED TO DEALING WITH SITUATIONS STRAIGHT ON, NOT TRYING TO FIND A WAY AROUND 'EM.
LEAVING MATTI ALONE, GETTING ARRESTED, LETTING THOSE TWO MANIACS LIVE...THAT WAS SO STUPID.
PETER, VICKY... YOU'RE THE ONES PAID FOR IT.
IF PETER HAD DONE WHAT HE WAS TOLD, HE'D STILL BE ALIVE.
AND THERE'S NOTHING ANYONE COULD'VE DONE FOR VICKY.
YOU'RE A TOUGH COOKIE, KID. MAYBE YOU'VE ALREADY BEEN AROUND ME TOO LONG.
BELIEVE ME, YOU DON'T WANT TO LIVE THAT WAY.
BURT AND ADELE ARE GOOD PEOPLE, YOU GOT A NICE LIFE COMING TO YOU HERE.
YOU SAVED US. DON'T GO.
OR TAKE ME WITH YOU.
MAYBE. BUT IT'D BE NICER WITH YOU AROUND.

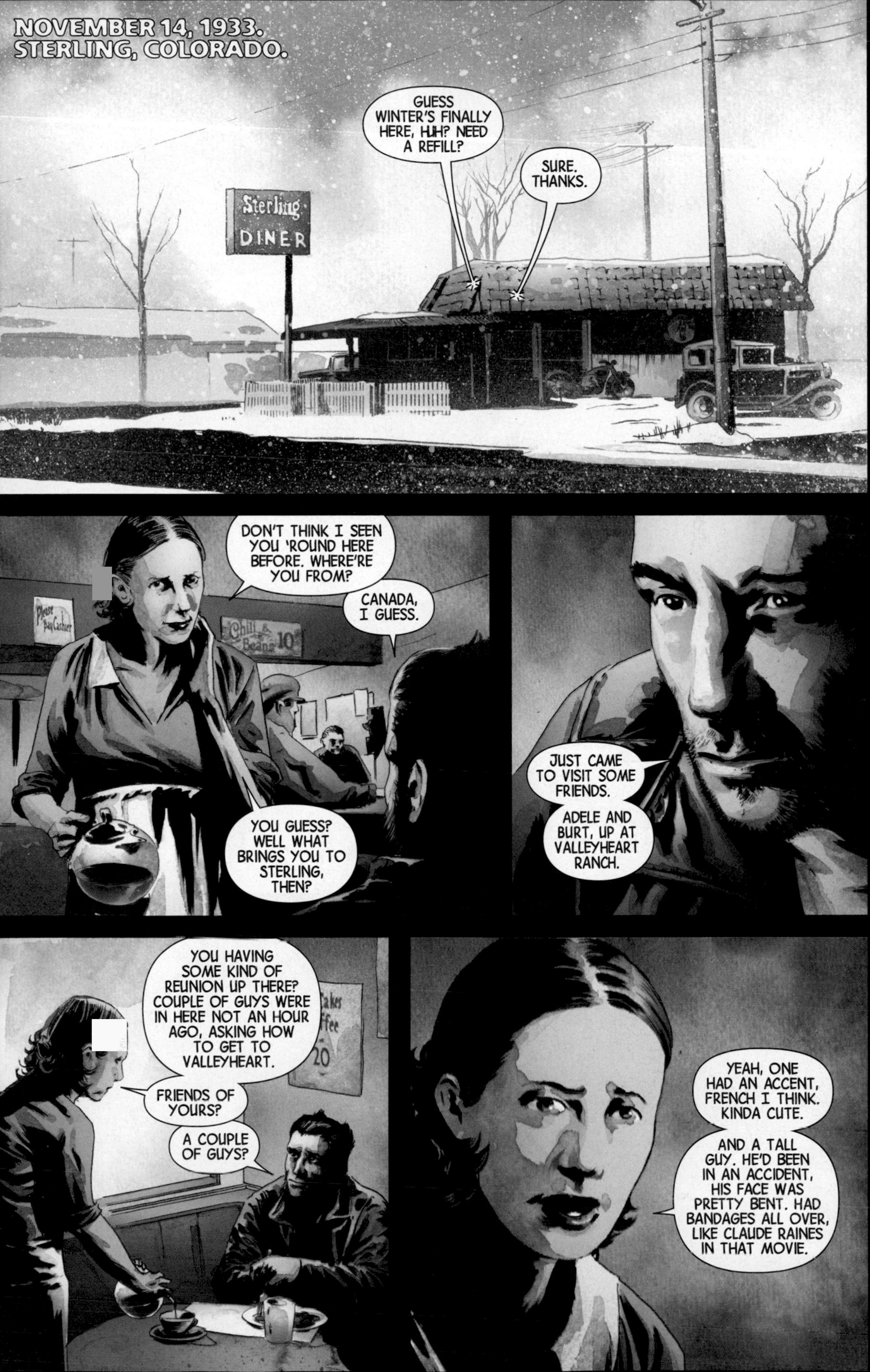
NOVEMBER 14, 1933. STERLING, COLORADO.
Sterling DINER
GUESS WINTER'S FINALLY HERE, HUH? NEED A REFILL?
SURE. THANKS.
Please Pay Cashier
Chili & Beans 10¢
DON'T THINK I SEEN YOU 'ROUND HERE BEFORE. WHERE'RE YOU FROM?
CANADA, I GUESS.
YOU GUESS? WELL WHAT BRINGS YOU TO STERLING, THEN?
JUST CAME TO VISIT SOME FRIENDS.
ADELE AND BURT, UP AT VALLEYHEART RANCH.
YOU HAVING SOME KIND OF REUNION UP THERE? COUPLE OF GUYS WERE IN HERE NOT AN HOUR AGO, ASKING HOW TO GET TO VALLEYHEART.
FRIENDS OF YOURS?
A COUPLE OF GUYS?
YEAH, ONE HAD AN ACCENT, FRENCH I THINK. KINDA CUTE.
AND A TALL GUY. HE'D BEEN IN AN ACCIDENT, HIS FACE WAS PRETTY BENT. HAD BANDAGES ALL OVER, LIKE CLAUDE RAINES IN THAT MOVIE.

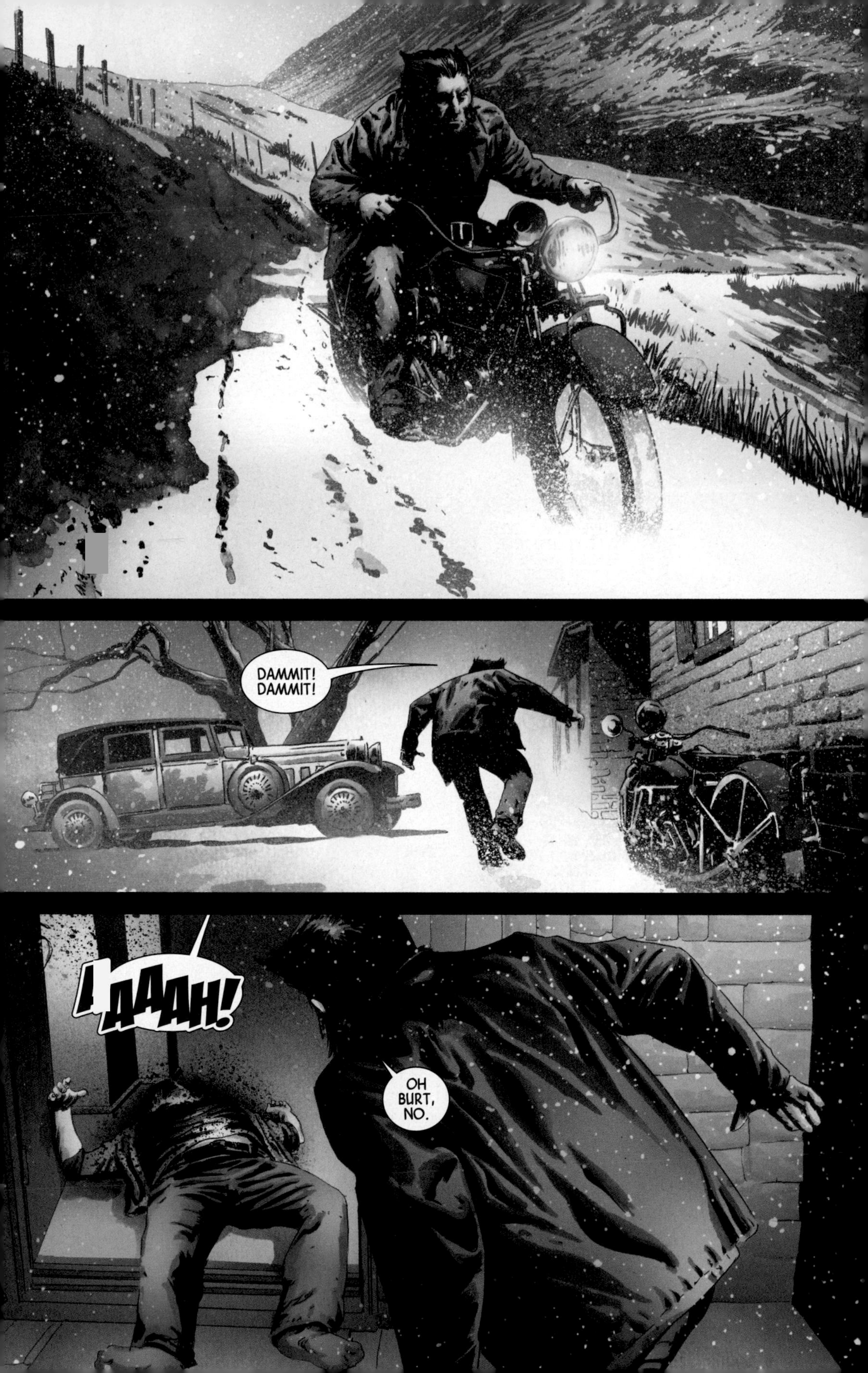
DAMMIT! DAMMIT!
AAAH!
OH BURT, NO.

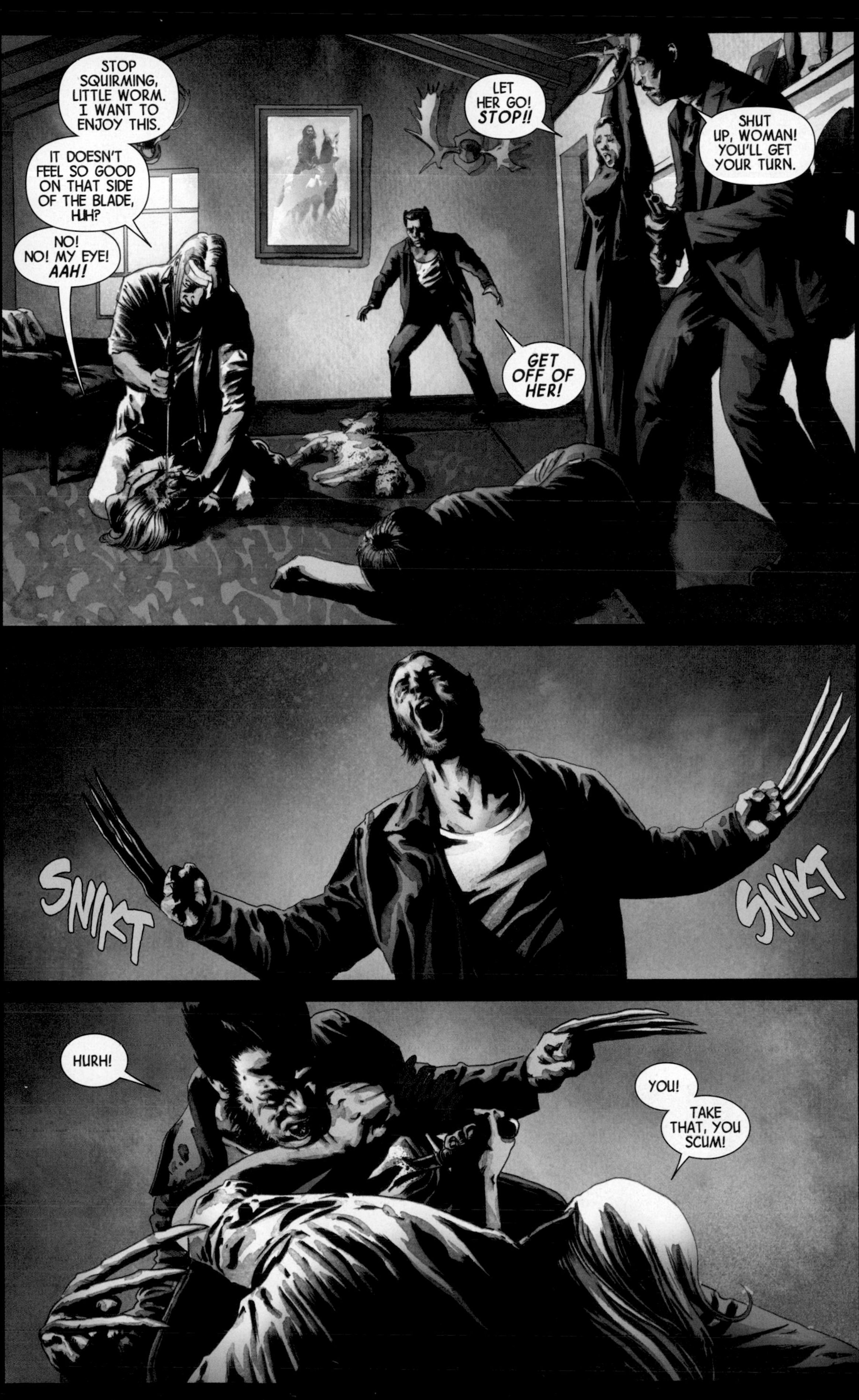

STOP SQUIRMING, LITTLE WORM. I WANT TO ENJOY THIS.
IT DOESN'T FEEL SO GOOD ON THAT SIDE OF THE BLADE, HUH?
NO! NO! MY EYE! AAH!
LET HER GO! STOP!!
SHUT UP, WOMAN! YOU'LL GET YOUR TURN.
GET OFF OF HER!
SNIKT
SNIKT
HURH!
YOU!
TAKE THAT, YOU SCUM!

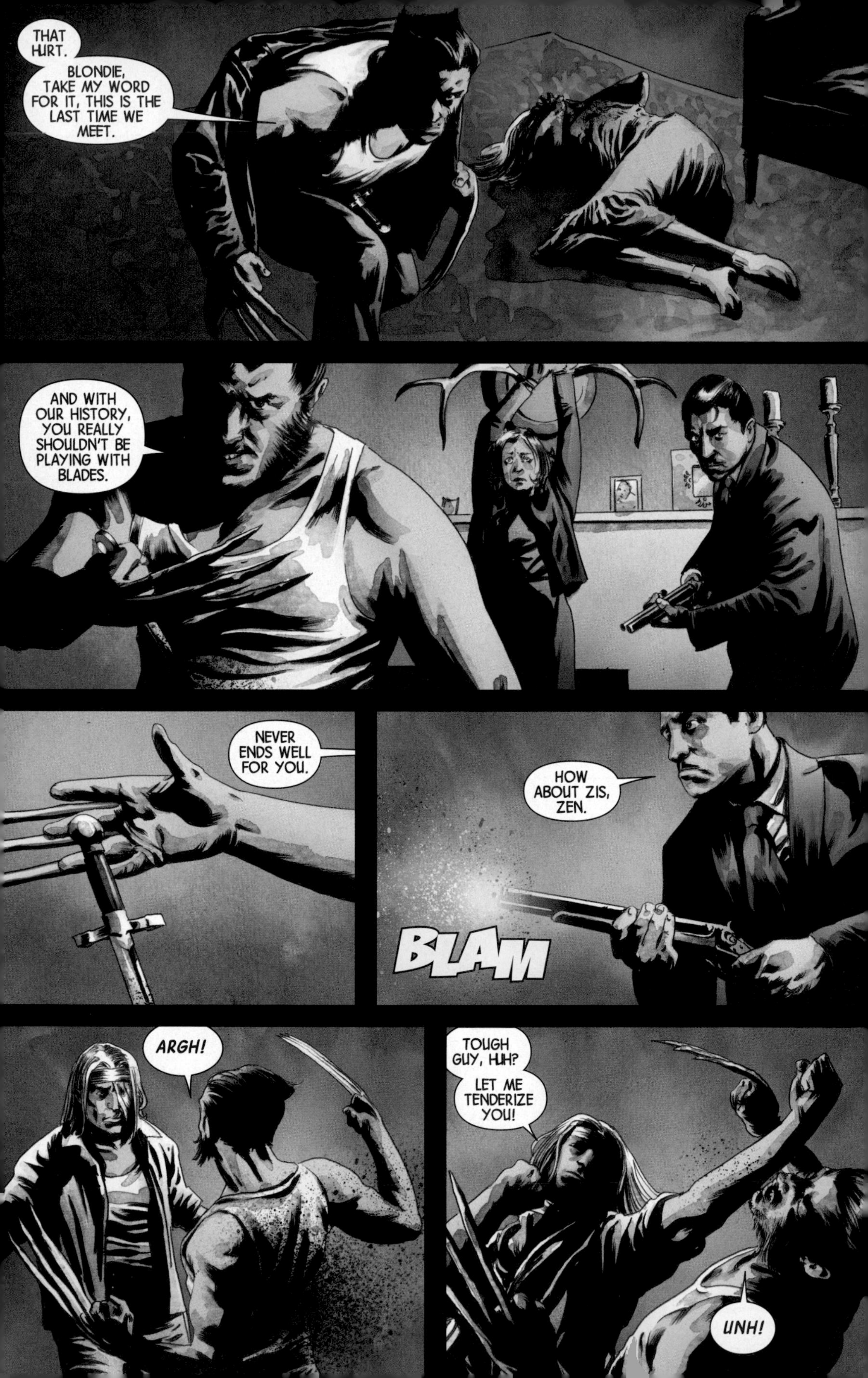
THAT HURT.
BLONDIE, TAKE MY WORD FOR IT, THIS IS THE LAST TIME WE MEET.
AND WITH OUR HISTORY, YOU REALLY SHOULDN'T BE PLAYING WITH BLADES.
NEVER ENDS WELL FOR YOU.
HOW ABOUT ZIS, ZEN.
BLAM
ARGH!
TOUGH GUY, HUH?
LET ME TENDERIZE YOU!
UNH!

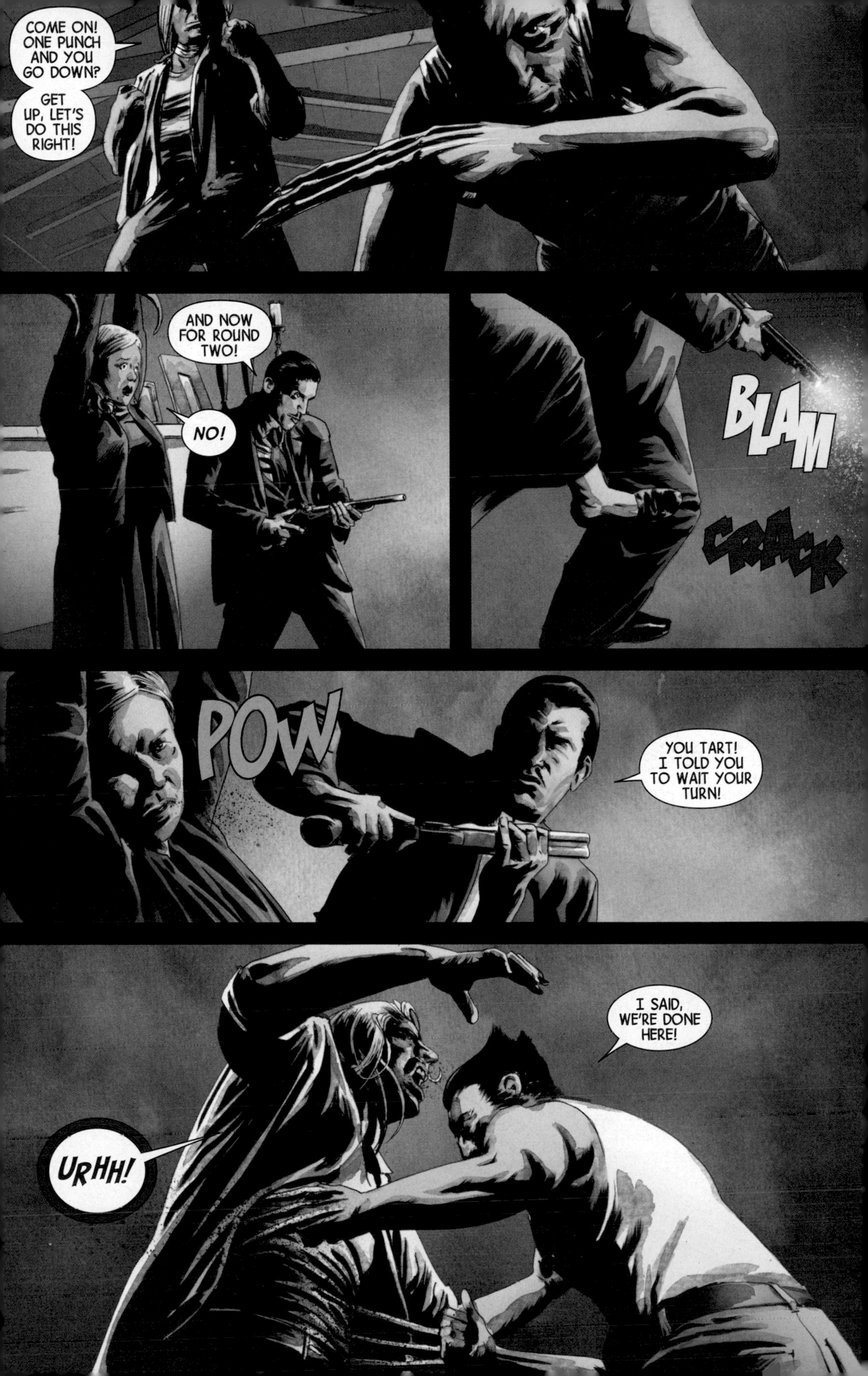
COME ON! ONE PUNCH AND YOU GO DOWN?
GET UP, LET'S DO THIS RIGHT!
AND NOW FOR ROUND TWO!
NO!
BLAM
CRACK
POW
YOU TART! I TOLD YOU TO WAIT YOUR TURN!
I SAID, WE'RE DONE HERE!
URHH!

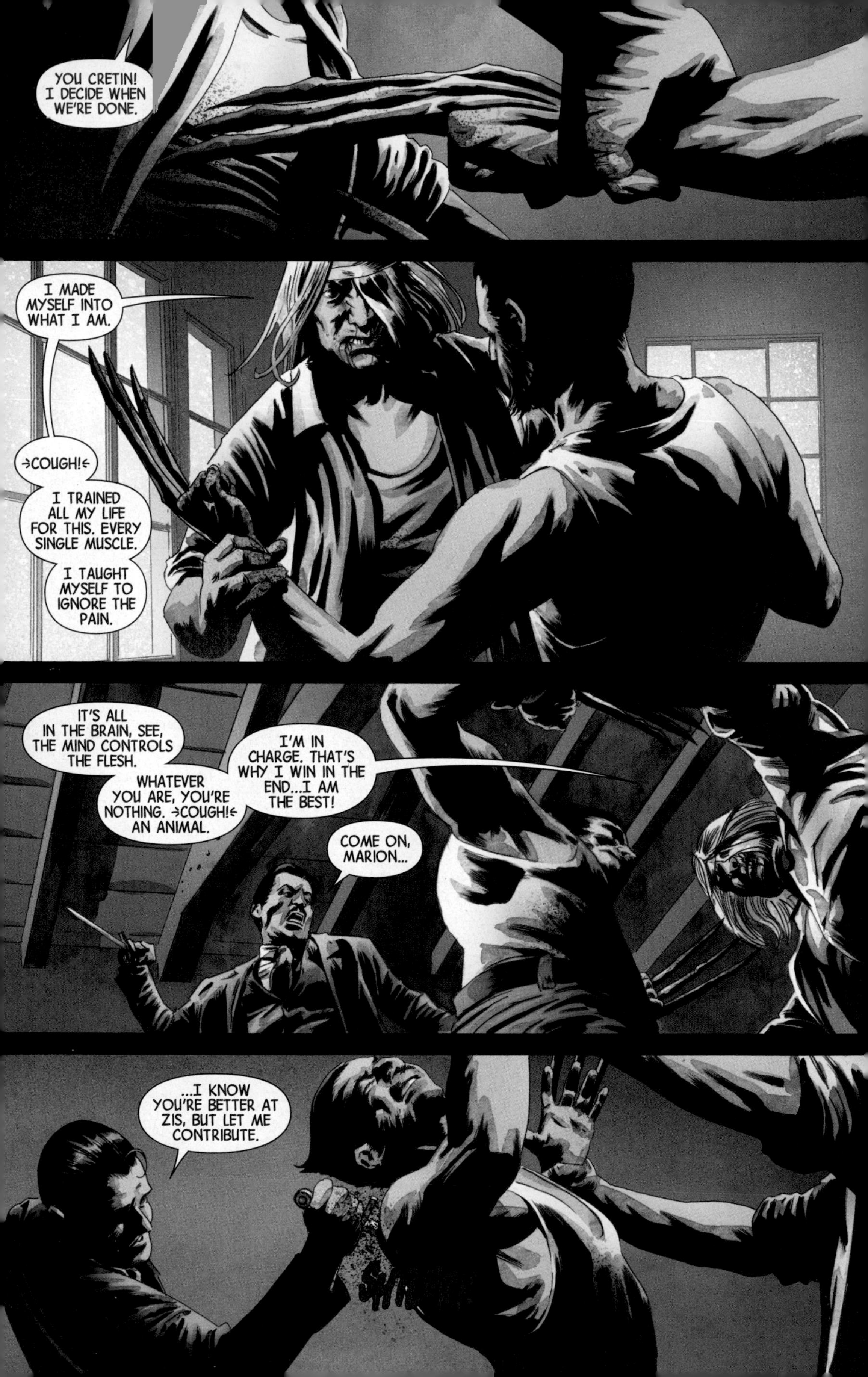
YOU CRETIN! I DECIDE WHEN WE'RE DONE.
I MADE MYSELF INTO WHAT I AM.
→COUGH!←
I TRAINED ALL MY LIFE FOR THIS. EVERY SINGLE MUSCLE.
I TAUGHT MYSELF TO IGNORE THE PAIN.
IT'S ALL IN THE BRAIN, SEE, THE MIND CONTROLS THE FLESH.
WHATEVER YOU ARE, YOU'RE NOTHING. →COUGH!← AN ANIMAL.
I'M IN CHARGE. THAT'S WHY I WIN IN THE END...I AM THE BEST!
COME ON, MARION...
...I KNOW YOU'RE BETTER AT ZIS, BUT LET ME CONTRIBUTE.

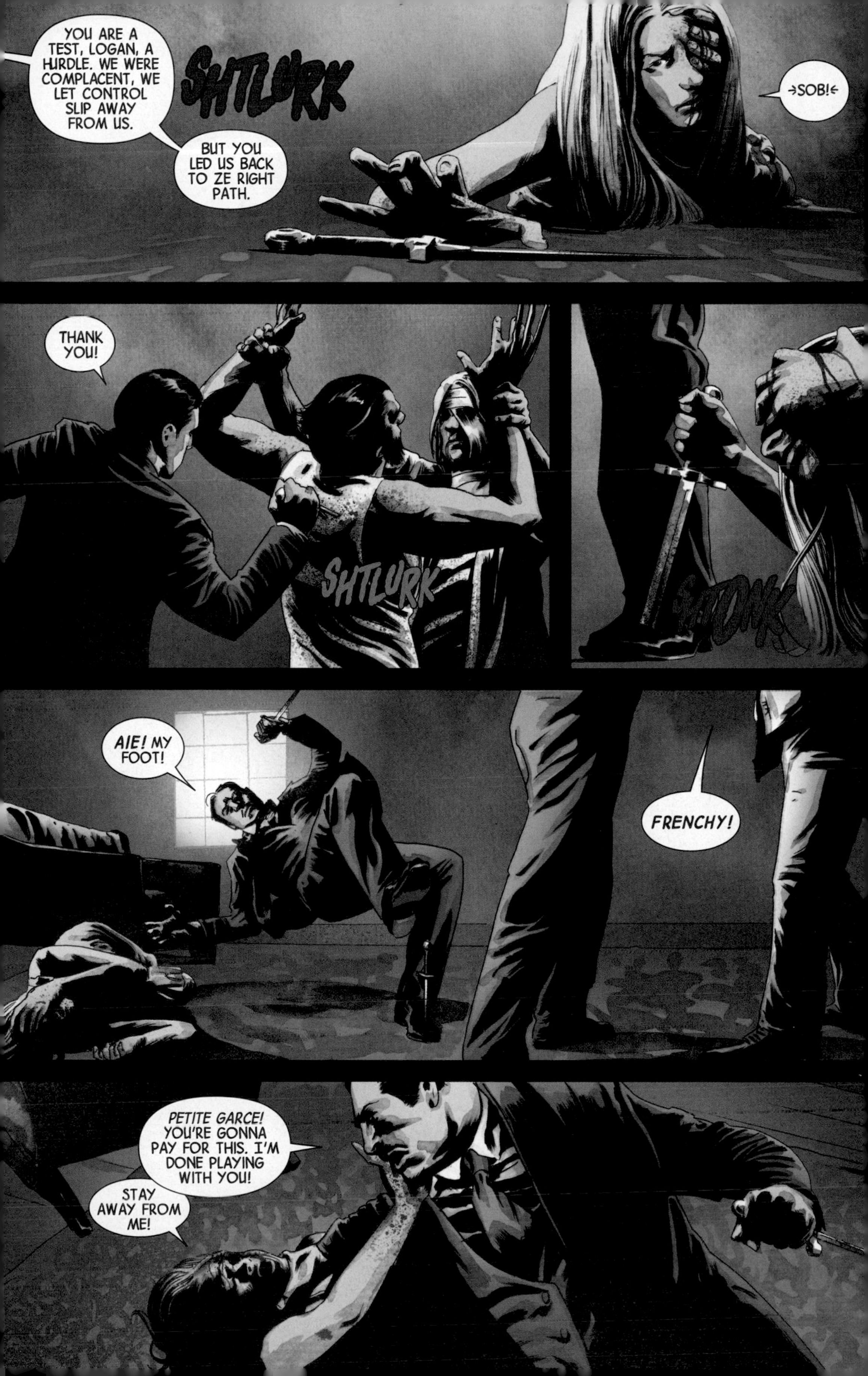
YOU ARE A TEST, LOGAN, A HURDLE. WE WERE COMPLACENT, WE LET CONTROL SLIP AWAY FROM US.
SHTLURK
BUT YOU LED US BACK TO ZE RIGHT PATH.
→SOB!←
THANK YOU!
SHTLURK
AIE! MY FOOT!
FRENCHY!
PETITE GARCE! YOU'RE GONNA PAY FOR THIS. I'M DONE PLAYING WITH YOU!
STAY AWAY FROM ME!

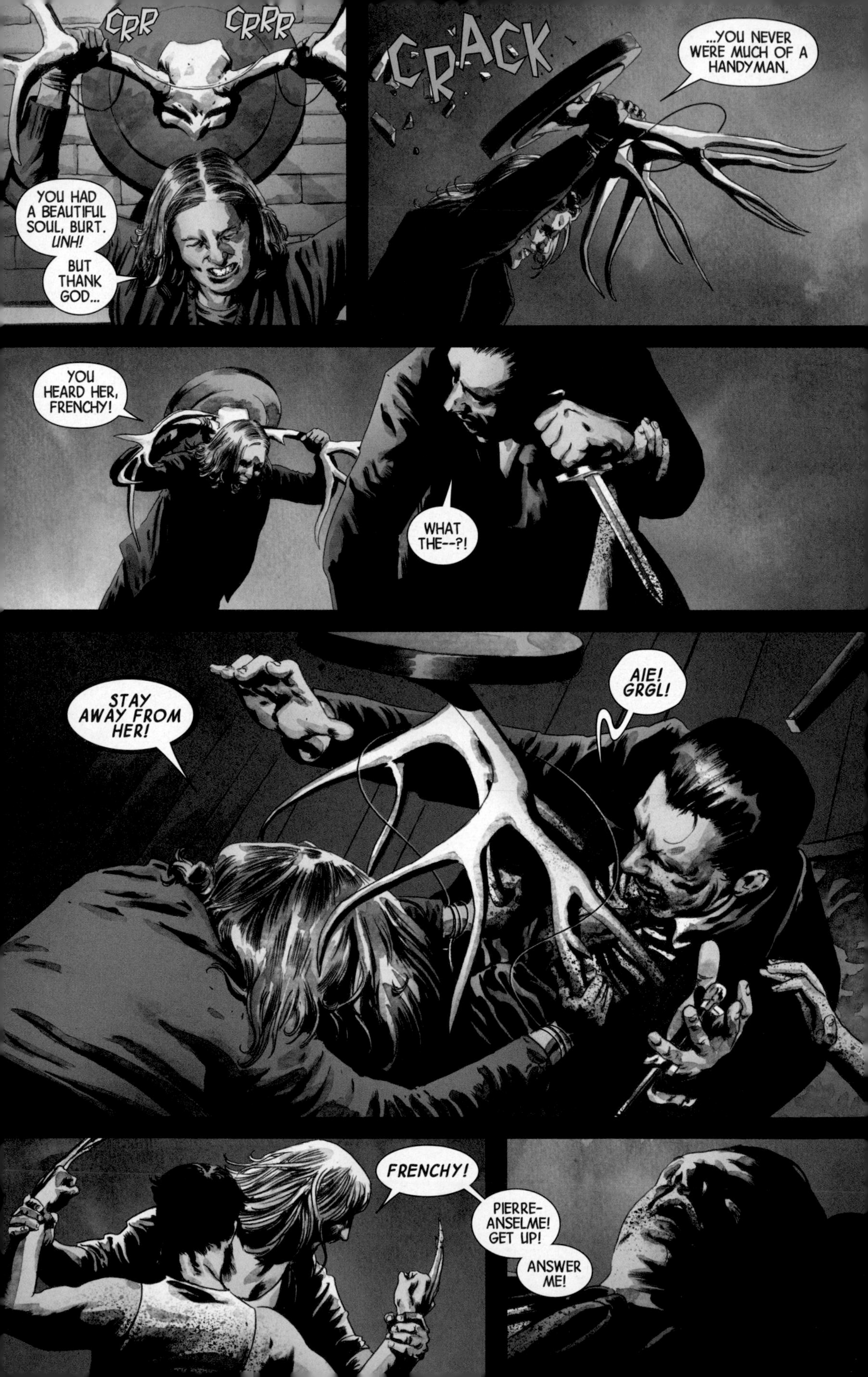
CRR
CRRR
YOU HAD A BEAUTIFUL SOUL, BURT. UNH!
BUT THANK GOD...
CRACK
...YOU NEVER WERE MUCH OF A HANDYMAN.
YOU HEARD HER, FRENCHY!
WHAT THE--?!
STAY AWAY FROM HER!
AIE! GRGL!
FRENCHY!
PIERRE-ANSELME! GET UP!
ANSWER ME!

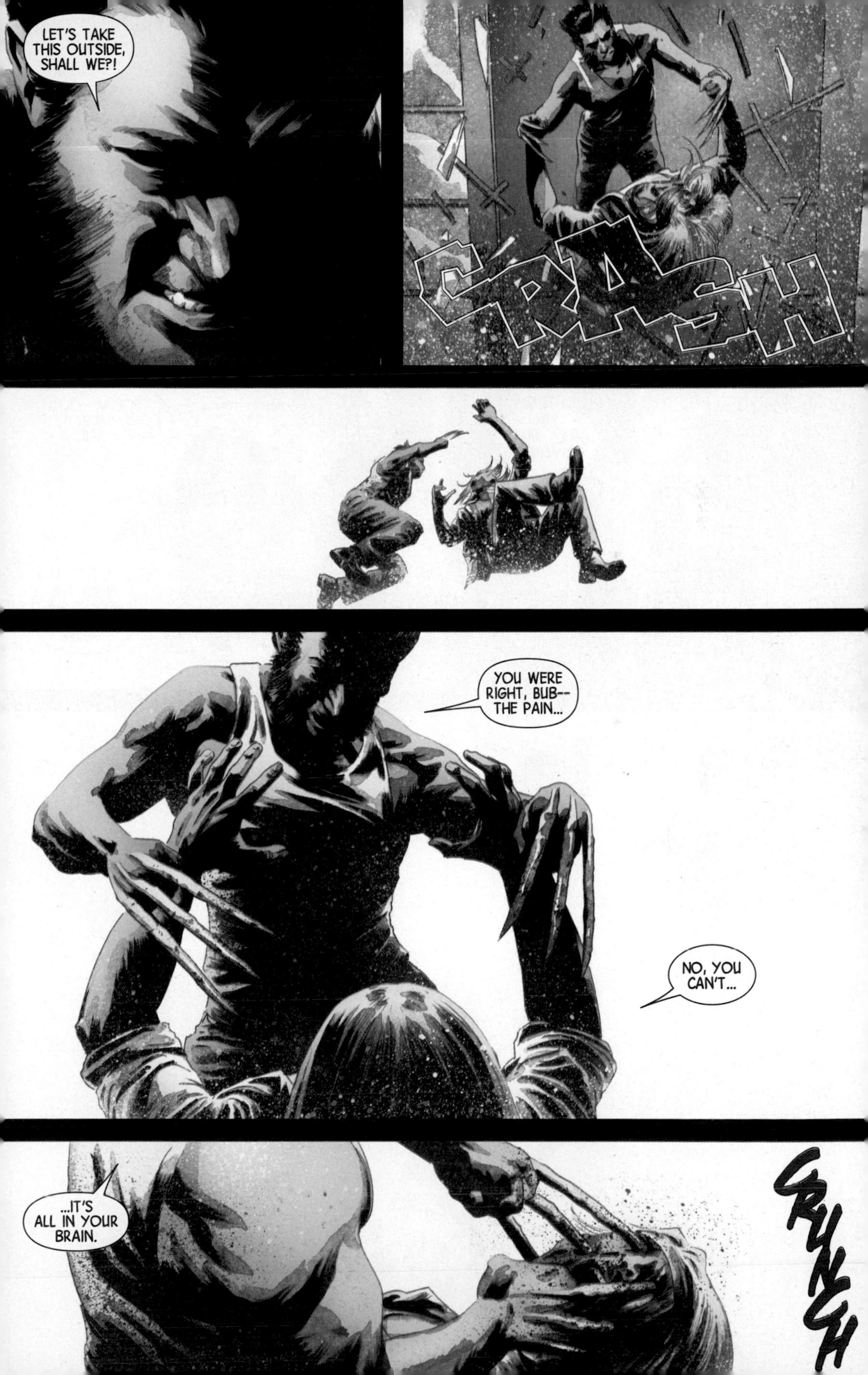
LET'S TAKE THIS OUTSIDE, SHALL WE?!
CRASH
YOU WERE RIGHT, BUB-- THE PAIN...
NO, YOU CAN'T...
...IT'S ALL IN YOUR BRAIN.
CRUNCH

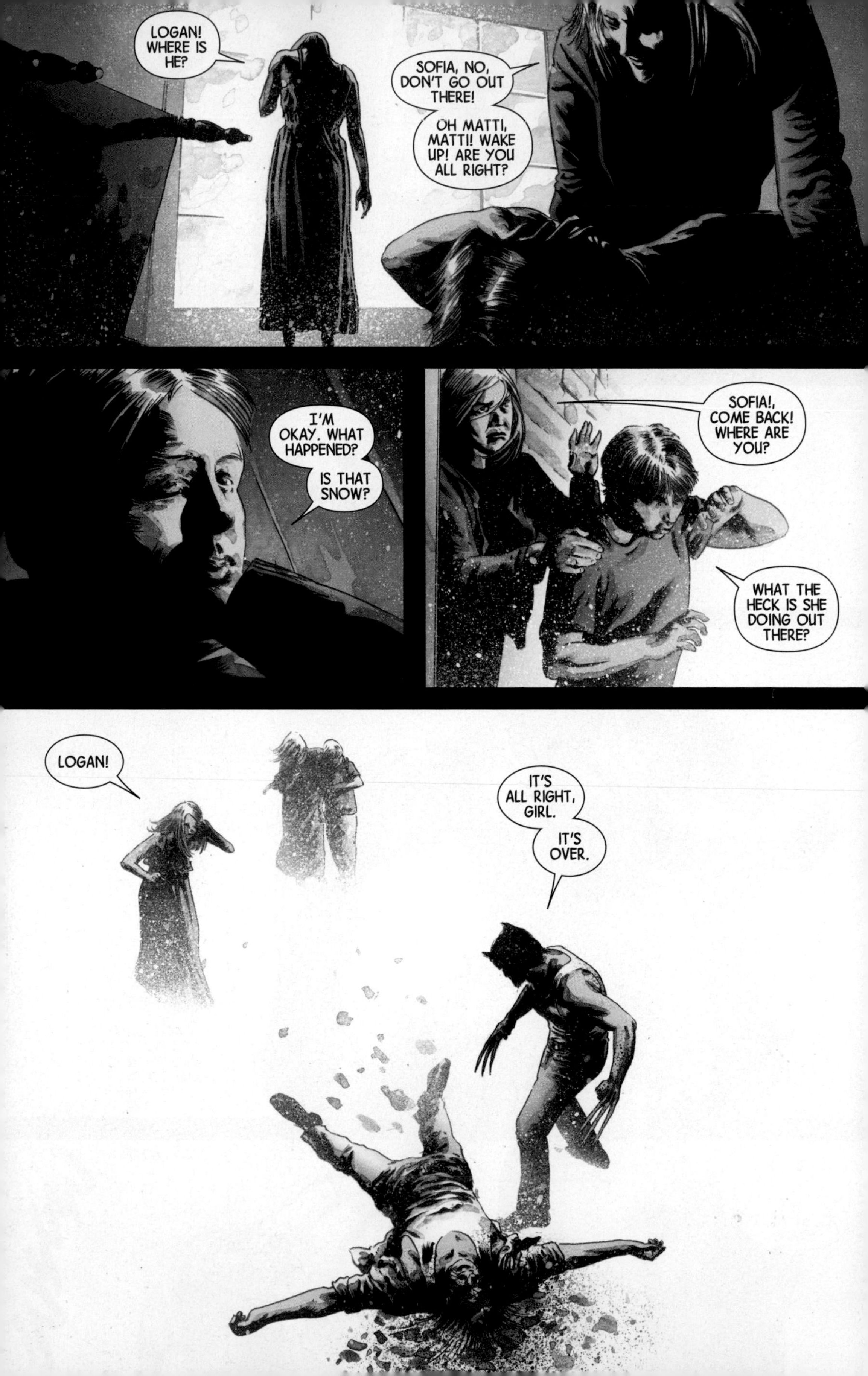
LOGAN! WHERE IS HE?
SOFIA, NO, DON'T GO OUT THERE!
OH MATTI, MATTI! WAKE UP! ARE YOU ALL RIGHT?
I'M OKAY. WHAT HAPPENED?
IS THAT SNOW?
SOFIA!, COME BACK! WHERE ARE YOU?
WHAT THE HECK IS SHE DOING OUT THERE?
LOGAN!
IT'S ALL RIGHT, GIRL.
IT'S OVER.

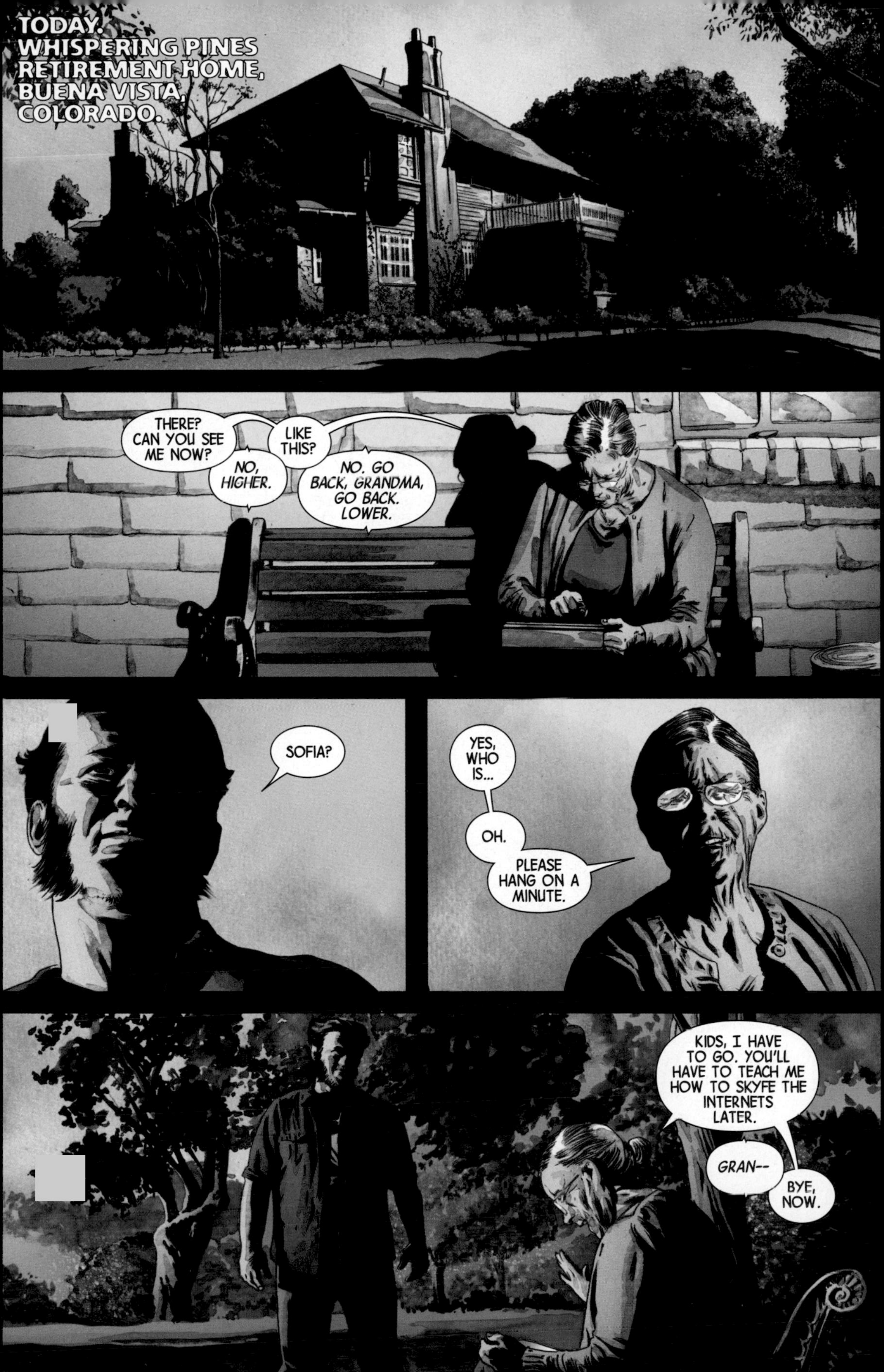
TODAY. WHISPERING PINES RETIREMENT HOME, BUENA VISTA, COLORADO.
THERE? CAN YOU SEE ME NOW?
NO, HIGHER.
LIKE THIS?
NO. GO BACK, GRANDMA, GO BACK. LOWER.
SOFIA?
YES, WHO IS...
OH.
PLEASE HANG ON A MINUTE.
KIDS, I HAVE TO GO. YOU'LL HAVE TO TEACH ME HOW TO SKYFE THE INTERNETS LATER.
GRAN--
BYE, NOW.

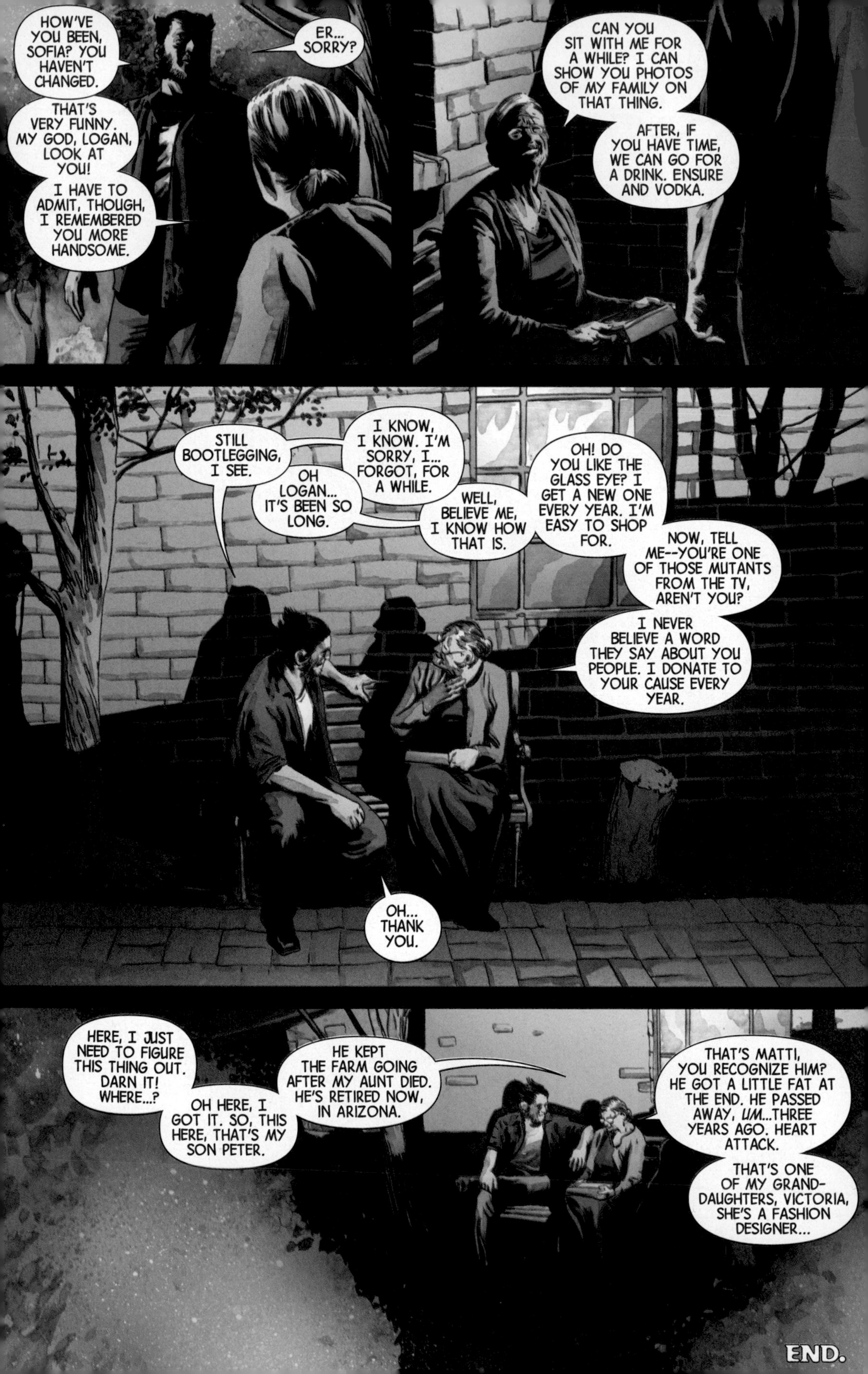
HOW'VE YOU BEEN, SOFIA? YOU HAVEN'T CHANGED.
ER... SORRY?
THAT'S VERY FUNNY. MY GOD, LOGAN, LOOK AT YOU!
I HAVE TO ADMIT, THOUGH, I REMEMBERED YOU MORE HANDSOME.
CAN YOU SIT WITH ME FOR A WHILE? I CAN SHOW YOU PHOTOS OF MY FAMILY ON THAT THING.
AFTER, IF YOU HAVE TIME, WE CAN GO FOR A DRINK. ENSURE AND VODKA.
STILL BOOTLEGGING, I SEE.
I KNOW, I KNOW. I'M SORRY, I... FORGOT, FOR A WHILE.
OH LOGAN... IT'S BEEN SO LONG.
WELL, BELIEVE ME, I KNOW HOW THAT IS.
OH! DO YOU LIKE THE GLASS EYE? I GET A NEW ONE EVERY YEAR. I'M EASY TO SHOP FOR.
NOW, TELL ME--YOU'RE ONE OF THOSE MUTANTS FROM THE TV, AREN'T YOU?
I NEVER BELIEVE A WORD THEY SAY ABOUT YOU PEOPLE. I DONATE TO YOUR CAUSE EVERY YEAR.
OH... THANK YOU.
HERE, I JUST NEED TO FIGURE THIS THING OUT. DARN IT! WHERE...?
OH HERE, I GOT IT. SO, THIS HERE, THAT'S MY SON PETER.
HE KEPT THE FARM GOING AFTER MY AUNT DIED. HE'S RETIRED NOW, IN ARIZONA.
THAT'S MATTI, YOU RECOGNIZE HIM? HE GOT A LITTLE FAT AT THE END. HE PASSED AWAY, UM...THREE YEARS AGO. HEART ATTACK.
THAT'S ONE OF MY GRAND-DAUGHTERS, VICTORIA, SHE'S A FASHION DESIGNER...
END.

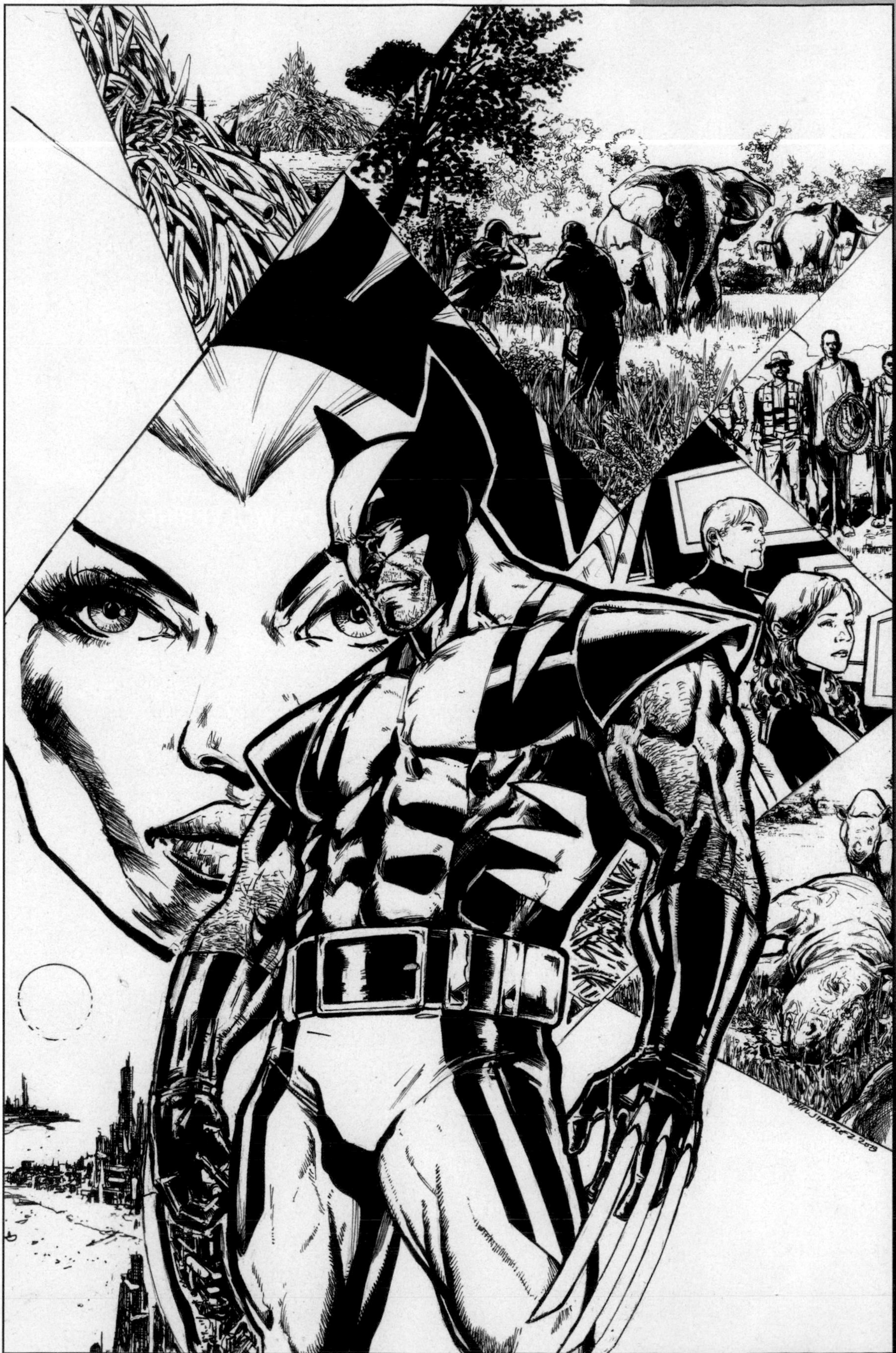
PHIL JIMENEZ 2013

INKED VARIANT BY PHIL JIMENEZ

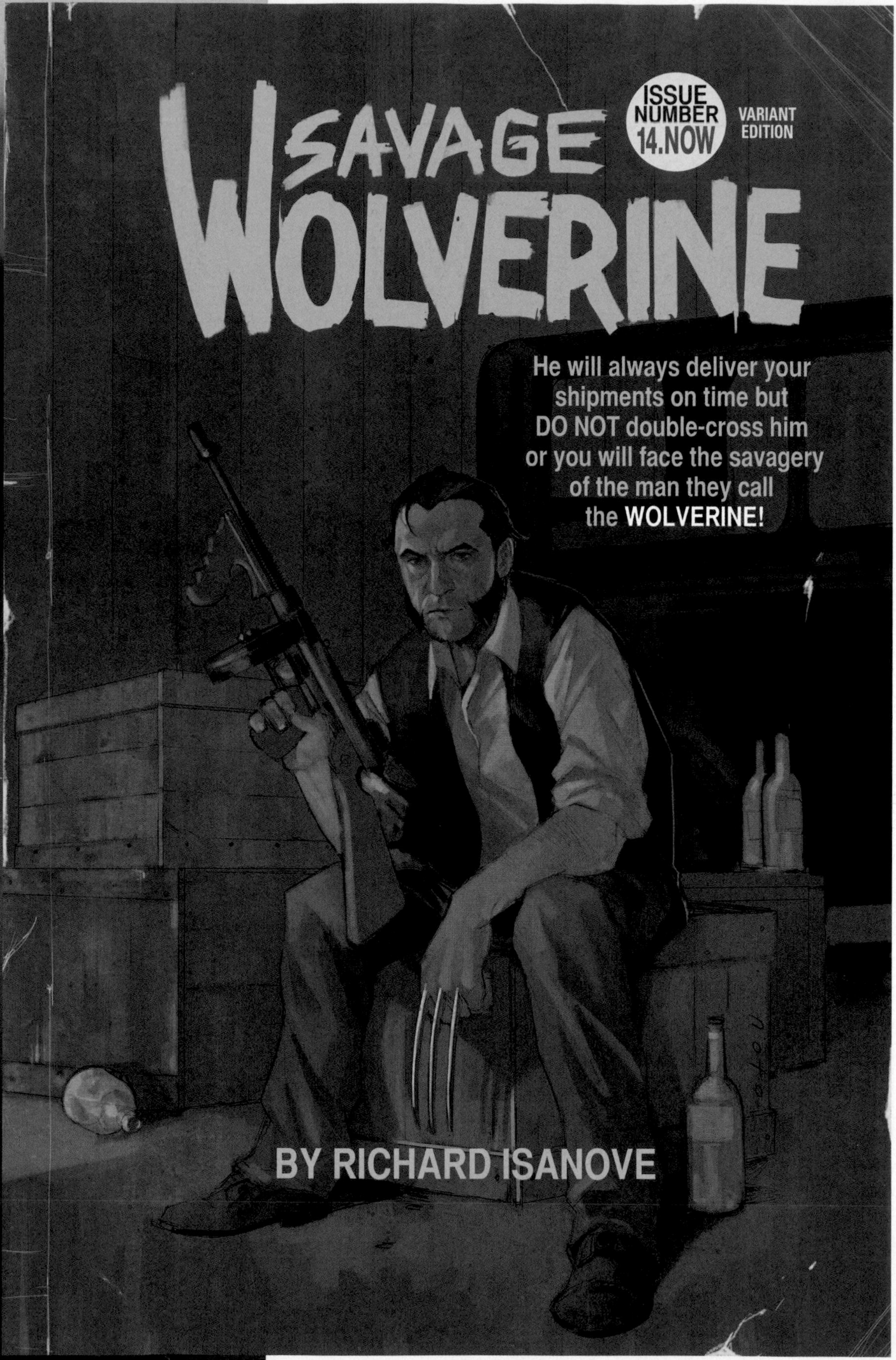




VARIANT BY PHIL NOTO

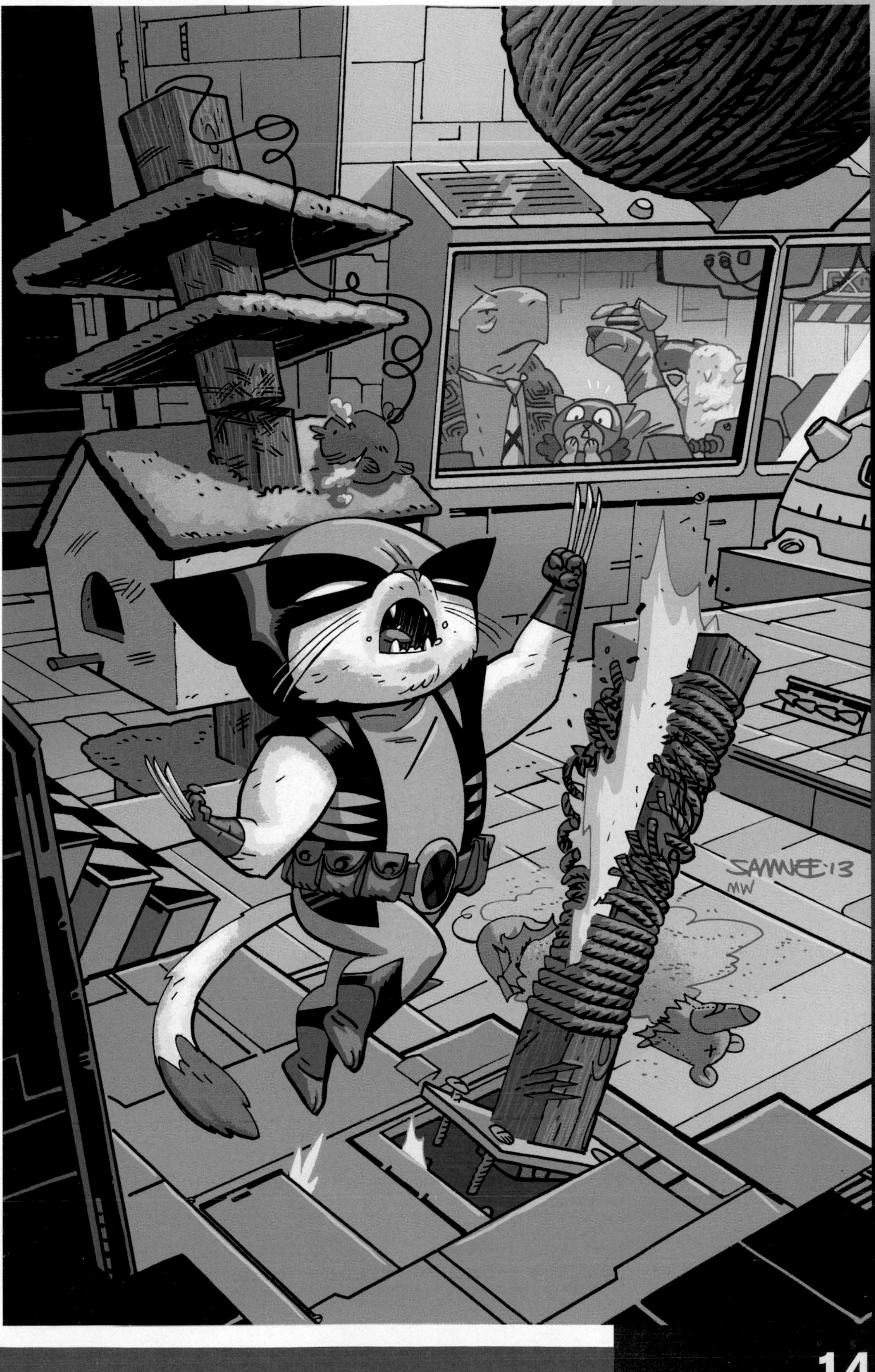
EXIT
SAMNEE '13
MW

ANIMAL VARIANT BY CHRIS SAMNEE & MATTHEW WILSON

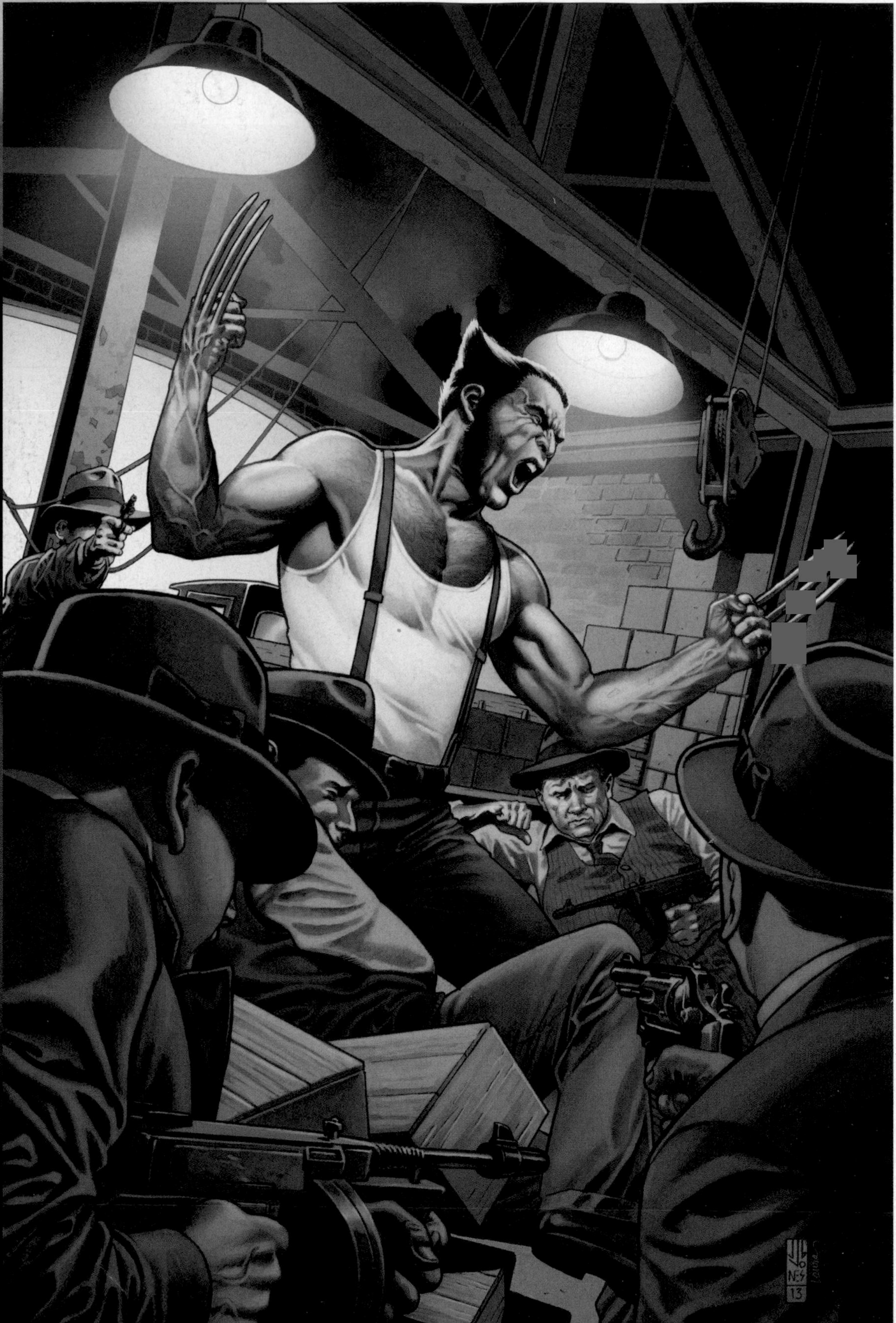

15

VARIANT BY J.G. JONES

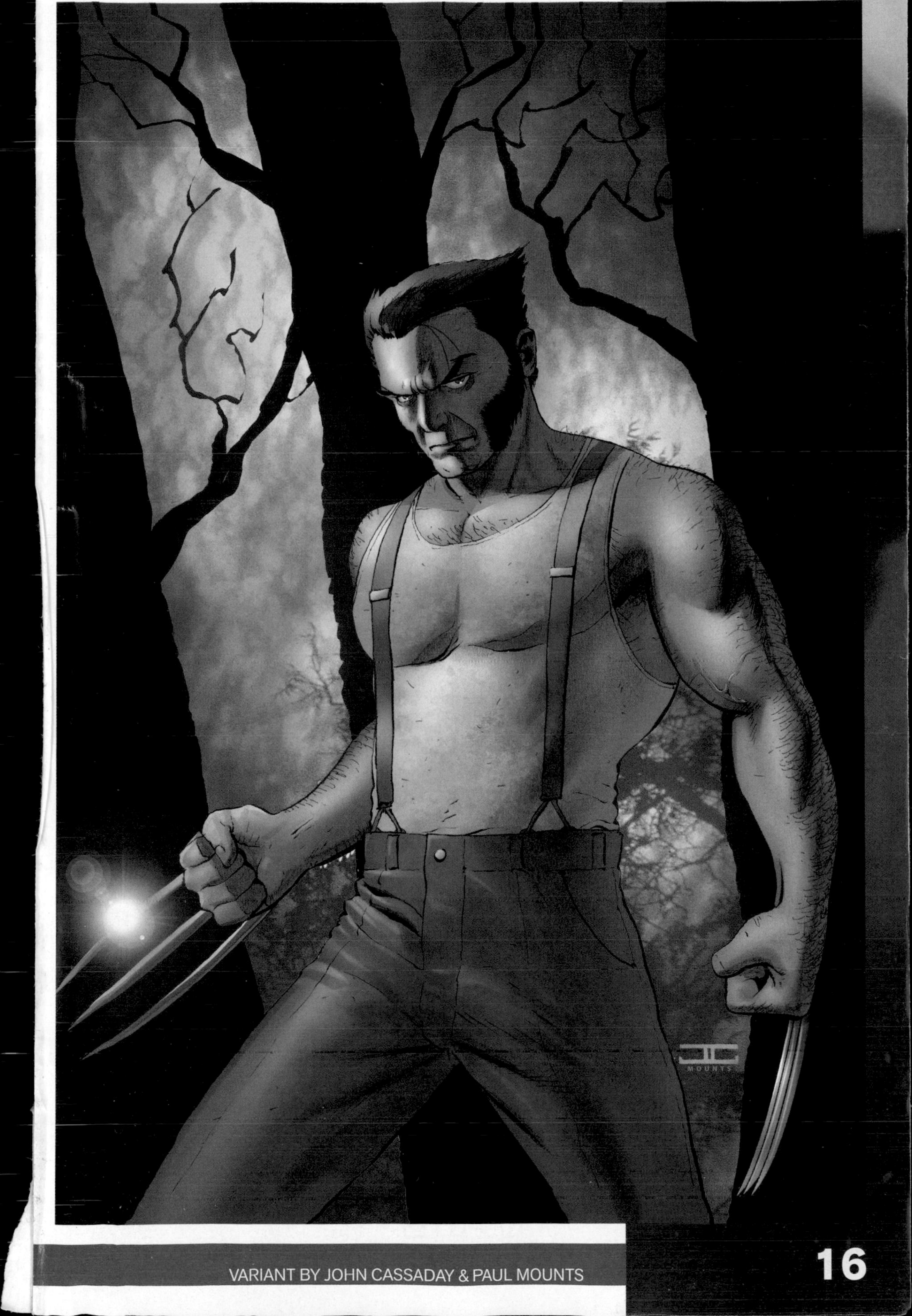
MOUNTS

VARIANT BY JOHN CASSADAY & PAUL MOUNTS